Civilizing Globalization

SUNY series in Radical Social and Political Theory
Roger S. Gottlieb, Editor

Civilizing Globalization

A Survival Guide

EDITED BY

Richard Sandbrook

STATE UNIVERSITY OF NEW YORK PRESS

Published by
State University of New York Press, Albany

© 2003 State University of New York

Cover photo: "Hungry World" by Zdenek Rada. Courtesy of Betty Sandbrook.

For information, address State University of New York Press,
90 State Street, Suite 700, Albany, N.Y., 12207

Production by Diane Ganeles
Marketing by Michael Campochiaro

Library of Congress Cataloging-in-Publication Data
Civilizing globalization : a survival guide / edited by Richard Sandbrook.
    p. cm.—(SUNY series in radical social and political theory)
  Includes bibliographical references and index.
  ISBN 0-7914-5667-6 (alk. paper)—ISBN 0-7914-5668-4 (pbk. : alk. paper)
  1. Globalization. I. Sandbrook, Richard.   II. Series.
JZ1318 .C58 2003
303.48'2—dc21   2002067031

10 9 8 7 6 5 4 3 2 1

Contents

Illustrations

Acknowledgments

I wish to acknowledge debts of gratitude to several people who contributed to the development of this book. Professor Louis Pauly, the director of the Centre for International Studies (CIS) at the University of Toronto, was a major supporter of this project. It originated as a series of panels on the theme "Reforming Globalization" in the CIS's Development Seminar in 2000–2001. Tina Lagoupoulos of the CIS worked tirelessly to make these popular panels a success. Robert W. Cox, professor emeritus of political science at Toronto's York University, provided a great deal of useful advice on contributors. Judith Barker of Wordwright Language Services did a remarkable job of editing many chapters. Karen Frecker proved assiduous in her checking of references and the preparation of the manuscript in the proper electronic form. I had a great deal of help; however, I alone remain responsible for the final product.

I would also like to thank two publishers for their kind permission to reproduce material that they hold under copyright. Princeton University Press has allowed James H. Mittelman in the book's conclusion to draw on material that he initially used in his book *The Globalization Syndrome: Transformation and Resistance* (2000). Routledge Publishers granted permission for Frank Cunningham to reproduce fig. 2.1 from p. 39 of *Global Democracy: Key Debates* by Barry Holden.

Envisioning a Civilized Globalization

Richard Sandbrook

First Seattle, then Washington, Prague, Zurich, Québec City, Genoa, Kananaskis—the list steadily lengthens. The staccato beat of hovering helicopters, waves of tear gas and pepper spray, fearsomely attired riot police, legions of mounted officers, high concrete and wire barricades—all these striking images provoke the conclusion that something of importance was at stake in the so-called antiglobalization protests. People around the world paused and took note.

The intense police reaction to each of the protests—against the World Trade Organization, the International Monetary Fund and the World Bank, the Free Trade Area of the Americas, the G8, and others—was accompanied by a media outcry against the dissenters. The media, whose ownership was consolidated in fewer and fewer corporate hands, treated the motley bands of protesters as a serious threat. Columnists variously dismissed protesters as "rebels without a cause," anarchists, misguided youths, and vested interests. Editorials responded with patient and condescending lectures on market economics, hinting that only an ignoramus could oppose global economic integration. The business sections of major newspapers expressed alarm that these demonstrations might divert decision-makers from the self-evidently beneficial route of further liberalizing global markets in goods, capital, skills, and finance.

Although some criticisms of global institutions were simplistic, protesters should not be dismissed as frivolous or ignorant. The demonstrators were a diverse group—including, according to my observations, people ranging in age from sixteen to eighty, religious groups of all denominations, and numerous union members and college students (though the composition varied according to locale). The protesters did not speak with a single voice; but what they agreed on was this: things were going terribly wrong in their world. Because the current pattern of globalization is heavily implicated in various problems, globalization must be radically altered. Although dissenters focused on a variety of trends, the consensus was that the current rules of international commerce favored corporate profits over environmental, health, labor, and cultural standards, and over issues of equity and poverty eradication. Yet corporate-dominated governments will resist the needed change in priorities, unless pushed by massive popular movements.

These criticisms are not outlandish, as many of the contributions to this book attest. *Civilizing Globalization* presents the following case:

- unfettered global markets harbor destructive tendencies;

- the solution is not to abandon markets but to tame them through regulation;

- such a program entails complementary transformations in global governance and resource flows; and

- humanizing globalization in this way depends upon the growing influence of a transnational and nonviolent protest movement.

Civilizing globalization, therefore, is a metaphor for harnessing global capitalism so that the economy serves society, and not vice versa.

However, this book does not provide a monolithic ideological viewpoint. An unusual feature of this volume is the diversity of its contributors: some are academics, some are activists, and some are both. Certain of the authors subscribe to a radical vision in which the role of markets is severely restricted. Others advocate more modest reforms of the global market economy and its governance. Astute readers will note the differences in viewpoint.

Destructive Tendencies

The globalization debate runs along well-worked grooves. On the one hand, neoliberals denounce their critics as failing to understand certain self-evident truths—that market liberalism is highly productive, raises living standards worldwide, and fosters innovation and individual initiative (see, e.g., Friedman 1999, 308; Micklewait and Wooldridge 2000). Free trade, according to theory, permits all countries to specialize and exploit their comparative advantages. The free movement of capital, again according to theory, leads to a more efficient allocation of resources around the globe, as capital flows to where it can most profitably be invested. Freely convertible currencies, in combination with open markets, should ensure the efficient allocation of goods and services on a global basis. And growth, while reducing poverty, will also solve its associated environmental problems by furnishing the resources and, ultimately, the demand for cleaner air and water.

On the other hand, the skeptics (such as the contributors in Part 1 below) contend that the free-market advocates exaggerate the economic gains and/or underestimate the social, health, cultural, and environmental costs. These alleged costs, or destructive tendencies, include the following:

- High and growing inequalities accompany market liberalization.[1] Although the North-South income gap has been narrowing for about a dozen countries of the South, it continues to grow for well over one hundred others. The UNDP's *Human Development Report 1997* famously estimated that the combined wealth of the world's three wealthiest families ($135 billion) was greater in the mid-1990s than the annual income of 600 million people living in the least-developed countries. Within countries, neoliberal policies have been associated with growing inequality and poverty, with the United States, New Zealand, Britain, and Latin America leading the way (see the chapters by economist Albert Berry, public-health analyst David Coburn, and political scientist Judith Teichman).

- Footloose global capital contributes to turbulence and periodic financial collapses (as, most dramatically, in Mexico in 1994 and East Asia and Russia in 1997–98) as it seeks short-term speculative gains (Judith Teichman and Albert Berry also address this tendency).

- The inequalities associated with neoliberal policies have a detrimental impact on health: the association between low socioeconomic status and relatively poor health obtains both within countries and across countries. (David Coburn explores this issue in chapter 2.)

- Free trade agreements often place a higher value on freer trade than on environmental and health protection in the deregulated global economy. (Michelle Swenarchuk explores this issue in chapter 6.) In addition, Third World countries are tempted to attract foreign investment by diluting or ignoring their own health and environmental standards.

- Cultural diversity is threatened as the media megacorporations, purveying a homogenizing mass culture, demand unrestricted access to foreign markets under the rubric of free trade in services. Longstanding national programs to nurture cultural activities may be vulnerable to challenge as constraints on trade (see Garry Neil's analysis in chapter 8). But nativist reactions to imported cultural norms and fashions also threaten individual freedom (as Anil

Mathew Varughese argues in chapter 4 in relation to the case of India).

- And democracy itself is diluted, even in the old democracies. Democracy shrivels when national governments, through international agreements, surrender their power to regulate in the public interest such areas as trade, financial flows, investment, and health and environmental standards, and when global financial markets effectively punish governments that deviate from conservative monetary, fiscal, and even social policies. (This tendency provokes Frank Cunningham in chapter 11 to discuss various approaches to bringing democracy to bear on vital decisions made outside nation-states.)

Such destructive tendencies, if they are real, demand a radical response.

Does this radical response entail reversing economic globalization? Surely not. What should we go back to? The danger, in light of the growing strength of the far right in the United States, Europe, and the Middle East, is a reversion to a defensive and quite possibly chauvinistic nationalism. Hence, we need to move forward to a more integrated world, not backwards. The old system of national states is weakening as many economic, social, political, and cultural activities escape national control. Many problems—terrorism and arms control, environmental pollution and climate change, human rights, drug trafficking, population migrations, mass poverty—demand global solutions. In any case, economic globalization, particularly international trade, does offer *potential* benefits that we should seek to realize: import of capital and intermediate goods at prices lower than domestic substitutes; the flow of ideas, technologies and institutional models; and access to foreign savings (Rodrik 1999). So how can we capture these potential benefits of global integration while building a peaceful, sustainable and prosperous world?

What Should Be Done

The problem, from the perspective of the editor and most of this book's authors, is not globalization per se; it is *neoliberal* or free-market globalization. And the solution is *not* to revert to protectionism; it is a regulated global capitalism in which markets are subordinated to social and ecological needs.

This position assumes that there is no realistic alternative to a largely market-based system. Although many critics of neoliberal globalization disagree, the real choice lies between more and less benign versions of capitalism. Socialism, at least in the sense of centrally planned economies, has been "voted out by history" (Isabel Hilton in *Guardian Weekly*, 4–10 May, 2000). Some protesters propose—as their placards proclaim—to "smash capitalism." But if the World Trade Organization, the International Monetary Fund, and the World Bank disappeared, then what? Critics who are skeptical of merely reforming global capitalism usually argue in favor of a very general alternative, involving, for example, "drastic redistribution and democratisation of resources and structures" (Went 2000, 123). But what, concretely, does this contention actually entail? The scenario remains murky, because "many more collective debates, analyses, experiments and experiences, by workers, young people, women, activists and scholars in and with social movements, are needed to determine exactly what this means concretely" (Went 2000, 123). As long as alternatives are framed this obscurely, a movement opens itself to the charge of left utopianism. Neoliberals can then claim that there is no realistic alternative to a lightly regulated global capitalism. Hence, our contributors, accepting the goal of "drastic redistribution and democratisation of resources and structures," identify concrete and largely incremental strategies and policies for its achievement.

The movement against neoliberal globalization, if it remains within the bounds of a market economy, may assume one of two forms. The division, in essence, lies between a soft and a hard regulatory, or social-democratic, approach. Both approaches rest on the view that it is wholly reasonable to develop global rules that protect society and nature, because nation-states have long imposed such rules. "Every society has restrictions, legal and moral, on what kinds of markets are allowed," observes economist Dani Rodrik (1997, 35). For instance, governments in industrial countries regulated labor markets to protect employees from exploitation: minimum wages, limits on hours of work, statutory holidays, health and safety standards, nondiscriminatory hiring, promotion, and pay rules, collective bargaining, and union rights. Where unequal bargaining power prevailed, a consensus emerged that governments could legitimately impose restrictions on free contracts to advance public (social and environmental) concerns. The neoliberal counterrevolution since the 1970s has attacked this consensus. The demand for "flexible" labor markets, for instance, involves a rolling back of the societal constraints on employers' prerogatives, justified in the name of global competitiveness. However, this ultraliberalism, being inherently destructive of society and nature, cannot endure.

How, then, can we ensure that markets assume the role of useful servants, rather than tyrannical masters?

One answer is the "Third Way," associated in particular with Tony Blair and former president Bill Clinton, and now popular throughout Europe and, via the World Bank, the developing world. The Third Way, promoted as a modernized social democracy, assumes that globalization in more or less its current form is broadly desirable, and in any event inexorable.[2] It, therefore, advocates minor reforms of global institutions and markets, together with national governments that see their role as *adjusting their populations and industries to the exigencies of global competitiveness as humanely as possible.* The Third Way's agenda includes principally the following (see e.g., Friedman 1999, 355):

- augmented transparency and accountability on the part of governments and financial markets;
- stricter banking regulations;
- some regulation of offshore tax havens;
- voluntary codes of conduct for transnational corporations concerning human and labor rights and environmental concerns;
- strong support for democratization in developing countries and the former communist countries;
- public investments in research and development activities, universal education, and training at the national level; and
- the maintenance of minimal safety-nets for those who lose out in competitive markets.

The alternative, within capitalism, is a "hard" social-democratic approach that aims *to adjust global markets to the needs of society*, rather than vice versa. This perspective demands more extensive changes than the Third-Wayists envisage in global governance, resource flows, and rules that set boundaries to the operation of market forces (see, e.g., Martin and Schumann 1997). Some readers will characterize this faith in regulation of capitalist firms as naïve, on the grounds that the regulated learn to evade rules or twist them to their own purposes. Loopholes are soon discovered, it is true. However, "flawed regulation that is reflexive in relation to its flaws . . . is better than no regulation at all" (Pieterse 2000, 6). The real world is a messy and unruly place: regulation must, therefore, be both flexible and responsive.

Civilizing Globalization explores the challenges that arise in a program to humanize globalization by regulating market forces, instituting redistributive mechanisms at the global level, and reforming and democratizing global governance. Part 2, "Adjusting Global Markets to Social Needs," asks: how can we subject global markets to social restrictions, without suffocating the "animal spirits" of entrepreneurship? This goal requires, first, a struggle to reassert the primacy of fundamental rights and protections over rules liberalizing foreign trade and investment. The chapters by Heather Gibb (5), Michelle Swenarchuk (6), and Garry Neil (8) consider, respectively, how core labor norms, health and environmental standards, and cultural diversity may be reinforced at the global level. Universally accepted conventions and declarations concerning human rights, economic, social, and cultural rights, labor and trade-union rights, and national laws and regulations to restrict harmful international trade—in toxic wastes, modified foods, and weapons—should not be overridden by rules designed to eliminate barriers to trade and investment.

Such a readjustment of priorities cannot succeed, however, without the cooperation of governments of the developing world, especially China, India, Brazil, and Indonesia. These governments justifiably suspect the motives of those from the industrial countries who champion environmental and labor standards. Are not these standards simply disguised protectionist devices to negate the poorer countries' comparative advantage in cheap and docile labor and a disposable environment? To overcome these suspicions, a quid pro quo is needed. Hence, the second ingredient in adjusting global markets to social needs: taxes and transfers designed to both discourage socially undesirable practices and generate revenues for redistribution on a North–South basis. Rodney White in chapter 7 explores the nature and feasibility of an international (and national) transfer scheme that rewards individuals, communities, and countries who are "carbon-frugal." The populous and less-industrialized countries of the South would be the major beneficiaries of such a scheme. Then Joy Kennedy in chapter 9 focuses on the nature and feasibility of a currency transaction tax (a "Tobin" tax) that, again, would both discourage a "bad" practice—destabilizing financial speculation—and redistribute at least $250 billion per year to the developing world. These transfers would ensure that all regions would receive a share of the benefits of global integration. If properly targeted, they would allow a rapid reduction in mass poverty.

Needless to say, such extensive restructuring of international regulatory regimes and North-South resource flows requires new forms of global governance. You can't have one without the others. Part 3, "Reforming Global Governance and Institutions," takes up this complex challenge.

- Robert O'Brien concisely dissects the process that will lead to a restructuring of global governance (chapter 10).

- Frank Cunningham explores the opportunities for enhancing democratic control over decisions made beyond national borders that nonetheless deeply affect people within particular nation-states (chapter 11).

- Jens Mortensen reflects on certain feasible reforms of the powerful World Trade Organization that would both enhance its accountability and transparency, and redirect its attention to assisting the least-developed countries (chapter 12).

- Cranford Pratt asks whether—and if so how,—aid institutions can be reformed so that they play a significant role in promoting an equitable and poverty-free international order (chapter 13).

- And Louis Pauly argues that, contrary to a widely held view, the national governments of industrial countries still possess the leeway to buffer their populations from harmful global trends—if they possess the political will to do so (chapter 14).

The Global Countermovement

But who will be the agent of civilizing globalization?

Civilizing Globalization assumes that globalization is largely a *"constructed system"* (Block 2000), and that it therefore can be reconstructed through human agency. We reject the popular image of globalization as an inexorable force, driven by technological change. If this image is accurate, individuals, communities, and nations must simply adapt to the exigencies of increasingly competitive global markets. But advances in information processing, the Internet, telecommunications, and transport merely *facilitate* global integration; they do not determine the particular rules governing that integration. Neoliberal globalization evolves from negotiated international agreements and the practices of key actors, especially transnational corporations. In principle, therefore, a less volatile, more egalitarian, more sustainable, more democratic, and less culturally homogenizing globalization can be won through further negotiated agreements.

Such an alternative globalization, however, will not be easy to attain. Its advocates confront a shift in the balance of power within nations that heavily favors capital. Consequently, governments are increasingly responsive to corporate viewpoints in policy design. Indeed, the main champion of neoliberal globalization—the United States—has a virtual veto power over international reform by virtue of its commanding position in the global economy.

Consider how globalization has both reflected and further augmented this power shift. First, the easier it has become for firms to move capital across borders, the more credible is their threat to depart, and the greater their leverage over national governments, their employees, and local communities. Fickle financial markets, where $1.5 trillion or more changes hands each day, hold particular clout with governments. President Bill Clinton's election chairman, James Carville, recognized this reality when he playfully observed: "I used to think if there was reincarnation I wanted to come back as the president or the pope or a .400 baseball hitter. But now I want to come back as the bond market. You can intimidate everybody" (quoted in Went 2000, 1).

Second, the more highly concentrated capital becomes, with mergers and takeovers justified by the requirements of international competitiveness, the greater the economic and political influence wielded by a small corporate elite. The largest transnational corporations boast annual sales that exceed the output of most developing countries. Royal Dutch/Shell, for example, posted sales in 1998 of $138 billion, a sum four times the annual income of Nigeria's 100 million people (Madeley 1999, 4). And the world's five hundred largest companies reportedly controlled about 70 percent of global trade, 80 percent of foreign direct investment, and 30 percent of world GDP in the early 1990s (Madeley 1999, 4).

Third, as organized labor declines in numbers and/or solidarity, the relative power of capital grows. Neoliberal governments, emulating Reagan and Thatcher, have perfected union-bashing as an art form. In the United States, organized labor now accounts for only about 16 percent of the labor force. Trade unions enrol a higher share of employees elsewhere in the industrial world, though not more than a quarter or third. In developing countries, co-optation of labor leaders and repressive labor legislation typically weaken labor.

Global protest has escalated as these three processes—the growing credibility of capital's exit option, the expansion of global cartels, and the decline of organized labor—feed a widespread perception that co-opted governments are unresponsive to their citizens. The protesters' significance is to identify dangerous social and environmental trends, and raise uncomfortable questions about their linkages to global economic processes from which many of us benefit. Neither the press nor mainstream political parties has effectively pressed such questions. Hence, it is left to the protesters to articulate, in their vivid way, the age-old yearning for a just, sustainable, and harmonious society.

Politics is therefore key to civilizing globalization. Governments are unlikely to venture beyond the Third Way unless prodded from below by a powerful protest movement. Part 4, "Building a Global Countermovement," and the book's conclusion explore this contention.

- Richard Falk in chapter 15 develops his notion of a popular "globalization-from-below" to counteract the existing neoliberal "globalization-from-above."

- Robert Weissman in the next chapter chronicles the ascent into global consciousness of transnational protest at the famous WTO meeting in Seattle in November 1999.

- Two vivid illustrations of globalization-from-below follow in chapters 17 and 18. The first, by aid worker Hans Edstrand, focuses on the invisible side of globalization-from-below: the human solidarity that underwrote a grassroots project of Honduran poor following the devastation of Hurricane Mitch. The second, by Rob Lambert and Eddie Webster, concerns the organization and activities of a transnational union movement (SIGTUR) involving unions in the Southern Hemisphere.

- James Mittelman, in the conclusion, reflects on resistance and alternative patterns of globalization, and in the process reviews many of the issues raised in the book.

Certain readers may regard this book's subtitle—*A Survival Guide*—as hyperbolic or alarmist. Yet global warming and climate change, "hot" money and the prospect of world financial collapse, and inequality, insecurity, and social disintegration constitute clear and present dangers. These dangers, as part 1 contends, are intimately related to global economic processes. If this is so, civilizing globalization is not only a moral imperative to create a more just world—though it surely is that. This goal is also a practical imperative, as its achievement will enhance the prospects of a liveable future in the North as well as the South. In the 1970s, a campaign for a "new international economic order" foundered because the North was unpersuaded that the rich countries shared "mutual interests" with the South in building a more egalitarian world (as the highly regarded Brandt Commission argued—Report of the Independent Commission on International Development Issues 1980). But today the issue of *survival,* raised in the Brandt Report, has more credibility. Although this book does not provide an integrated action plan to deal with this crisis, it at least points us down the right path and highlights the issues we'll debate in the years to come. As one hundred Nobel laureates observe in a statement marking the centenary of the Nobel Prize: "To survive in the world we have transformed, we must learn to think in a new way."

Notes

1. The relationship between globalization and inequality on an intranational and international basis is a controversial issue. Free traders are loath to admit that open markets augment income and asset inequality. There is, however, wide agreement that intranational inequality has increased since 1980, along with liberalization. For reviews of the evidence, see Cornia and Court 2001 and Berry and Serieux 2001. Whether the gap between the richest and poorest countries has widened depends on the analysts' assumptions and methodology. If fast-growing China, weighted for population, is included in the calculation, then the gap has remained constant. If China is excluded, the gap has grown. See Berry and Serieux 2001, and chapters 1 and 2 below.

2. Giddens (1998 and 2000) provides a cogent exposition of the Third Way.

References

Berry, Albert, and John Serieux. 2001. "Convergence, Divergence, or Confusion? Recent Trends in World Income Distribution, 1980-2000." Unpublished paper, University of Toronto, December.

Block, Fred. 2000. "Deconstructing Capitalism as a System." *Rethinking Marxism* 12 (3): 83–98.

Broad, Robin, and C. M. Landi. 1996. "Whither the North-South Gap?" *Third World Quarterly* 17 (1): 7–17.

Cornia, Giovanni Andrea, and Julius Court. 2001. "Inequality, Growth, and Poverty in an Era of Liberalization and Globalization." Policy Brief No. 4, World Institute for Development Economics Research, Helsinki.

Friedman, Thomas. 1999. *The Lexus and the Olive Tree: Understanding Globalization.* New York: Farrar, Straus and Giroux.

Giddens, Anthony. 1998. *The Third Way: The Renewal of Social Democracy.* Cambridge: Polity Press.

———. 2000. *The Third Way and Its Critics.* Cambridge: Polity Press.

Madeley, John. 1999. *Big Business, Poor Peoples: The Impact of Transnational Corporations on the World's Poor.* London: Zed Books.

Martin, Hans-Peter, and Harald Schumann. 1997. *The Global Trap: Globalization and the Assault on Democracy and Prosperity.* London: Zed Books.

Micklewait, John, and A. Wooldridge. 2000. *A Future Perfect: The Challenge and Hidden Promise of Globalization.* London: Heinemann.

Pieterse, Jan Nederveen. 2000. "Shaping Globalization." In *Global Futures: Shaping Globalization,* ed. J. N. Pieterse. London: Zed Books.

Report of the Independent Commission on International Development Issues under the Chairmanship of Willy Brandt. 1980. *North-South: A Program for Survival.* London: Pan Books.

Rodrik, Dani. 1997. *Has Globalization Gone Too Far?* Washington, D.C.: Institute for International Economics.

Rodrik, Dani. 1999. *The New Global Economy and Developing Countries: Making Openness Work.* Washington, D.C.: Overseas Development Council.

Soros, George. 1998. "Towards a Global Open Society." *Atlantic Monthly* 281 (1): 20–32.

Went, Robert. 2000. *Globalization: Neoliberal Challenge, Radical Responses.* London: Pluto.

PART 1

Globalization: Who Gains? Who Loses?

Core Issues

Does globalization do more good than harm? Do certain groups reap the gains while others bear the costs? These key issues arouse a passionate response from both supporters and critics of globalization.

Disputes arise in part, however, because people define this ambiguous term differently. Here, we use globalization as a convenient shorthand for the progressive integration of national economies into a global market economy, as measured by increasing flows of trade, investment, and skilled personnel across national boundaries. There are, of course, political, social, and cultural, in addition to economic, dimensions of global interdependence. Nonetheless, global market integration is sufficiently significant to warrant our attention.

Radical critics often prefer a more precise term, neoliberal globalization, to indicate that what they oppose is not necessarily this market integration, but rather a particular free-market vision of how this integration should proceed. For neoliberals, the ideal is a largely self-regulating global market economy. They envision a world in which companies, largely unconstrained by governmental regulations, invest where they want, buy and sell where they want, move their money where they want, and deal with their employees as they see fit. Radical critics do not uniformly reject markets, or even global markets. Anarchists, certain socialists, some environmentalists, and extreme right-wing populists do, from their sharply differing viewpoints, abominate global market capitalism, which they see as a malignant system. But many critics, including the diverse contributors to this book, can live with markets—provided markets are regulated to ensure the primacy of certain human and ecological values. They aim, therefore, to "civilize" globalization, that is, to neutralize the destructive and cruel tendencies of untrammeled markets.

Economist Albert Berry in chapter 1 advances this intellectual agenda. He provides both an extended definition of globalization and a careful assessment of the impact of increased economic interaction among countries since the 1970s. His conclusion is telling: "[T]he benefits of globalization, if they come quickly, are not very large, and, if large, do not come quickly." Not only are the

13

economic benefits meager, but the costs in terms of growing inequality, financial instability, and perhaps cultural homogenization are significant.

Extending Berry's discussion of costs, sociologist David Coburn then focuses on how free-market policies foster socioeconomic inequalities and negative health effects. He refers specifically to the experience of the industrial
countries in order to argue that it is not only developing countries that bear the
costs of neoliberal globalization.

Dealing with some of the same themes, political scientist Judith Teichman
provides a vivid study of Latin America (chapter 3). Many Latin Americans in
the 1980s welcomed the shift to market liberalization and the opening up of national economies to global market forces. State-led development was then associated in the popular mind with economic stagnation, inequality, and
repression. However, free markets have not reduced the numbers of poor people, while social inequalities have grown and incipient democratic institutions
have declined.

Finally, social researcher Anil Mathew Varughese builds his case about
globalization's cultural stresses by focusing on the controversy surrounding
Valentine's Day in India. Global integration and the advertising campaigns of
greeting card companies have stimulated an increasing observance of Valentine's Day by young Indians. This trend, in turn, has provoked a politically powerful fundamentalist Hindu group to undertake a campaign to humiliate couples
found celebrating this occasion. Globalization has, therefore, indirectly inspired an authoritarian and repressive reaction.

Part 1 provides the reader with ample reasons to embrace the goal of civilizing globalization.

CHAPTER 1

Who Gains and Who Loses?
An Economic Perspective

Albert Berry

Few subjects have created such heated debates as globalization. Its proponents sing its praises, while its many-hued critics are just as certain of its evils.

Both sides have drawn their lines in the sand. Authorities such as the
Chicago school of economists, a much wider group of international trade spe-
cialists, and the *Economist* see globalization as the road to higher incomes and
the end of poverty, and the vehicle whereby a country can take maximum advantage of new technologies in a fast-changing world. However, its critics
blame globalization for a wide range of disasters. These include: the economic
problems of Africa; the stagnation and instability of many Latin American
countries; increasing pollution; the presence and spread of mad cow and hoof-
and-mouth disease; the demise of the family farm; and the increasing domination of American ideas of the good society, of faceless bankers and the CEOs of
other multinational companies, and of the capitalist class as a whole. They
argue that globalization represents the best instrument yet devised for wealthy
industrial countries to control and exploit poor ones.

Certainly, forcing the world into a straitjacket in which competition at the
individual, group, and national levels is required for success has sounded the
death knell of the quiet, stable life that many might have preferred. Government
has become ever more remote for most of the world's people; power is in the
hands of the United States or the multinationals, especially the bankers. Perhaps even worse, there is no real governance of these processes at all. Rather,
the world careens out of control as technological change proceeds without social management in directions whose ultimate impacts are understood by
and/or controlled by no one.

While the alleged benefits are deemed large, the alleged damage is viewed
as even more dramatic. Few categorize globalization as a matter of secondary
importance. Rather systematically, proponents sneer at the unsophisticated

15

ideas of most critics, such as the protesters in the Seattle meetings of the World Trade Organization. Many critics harbor an abiding suspicion of globalization's supporters that sometimes appears to be based more on intuition than reasoned argument, more on conspiracy theories than on more prosaic ones, and heavily on the vague feeling that much is wrong with the world. If, as both sides agree, globalization is a dominant force in the world, then surely, many people conclude, it must be to blame for a lot.

It is striking how ill-conceived is the bulk of the debate around globalization, given the significance of the topic. Generally, though, its proponents are guiltier than its opponents, since the former more often claim the high ground in terms of support from economic theory and empirical analysis. My perception is that, on a scale from zero to ten, the proponents' arguments score between two and five. Most of the critics' concrete arguments are even less developed; however, where they may warrant more respect is in the validity of their rather vague suspicion that the other side is not to be trusted and should not be given the benefit of the doubt.

Consider for a moment a few of the more frequently mooted points before turning to a more systematic look at the economic gains and costs of globalization.

- *Myth or fact: Globalization is inevitable.* More myth than fact: it is not preordained, for example, that trade ratios (i.e., a measure of countries' integration into the international economy) will continue to rise.

- *Myth or fact: The potential benefits from globalization are large relative to those of most other contemporary economic processes.* Myth: few have argued seriously that the benefits would be as great as those from the information revolution, or from large increases in human capital in the developing world.

- *Myth or fact: A high level of integration into world markets makes it impossible to develop and sustain a strong social support system.* Myth: the Scandinavian countries are among the most internationally oriented, yet they are also leaders in social programs.

- *Myth or fact: Free flows of capital are necessary to obtain the bulk of the benefits from foreign investment.* Myth: most of the "hot money," which causes instability and in extreme cases collapse (Mexico in 1995, East Asia more recently), brings questionable benefits to the receiving country.

- *Myth or fact: Trade never helps poorer countries.* Myth: no serious student doubts that countries such as Taiwan and Korea have benefited greatly from their access to international markets.

- *Myth or fact: Both benefits and costs from increasing economic integration can be fairly accurately estimated using existing economic models.* Myth: the possible "error of estimate" appears to be large. If anyone does know how to predict with accuracy benefits and costs, the rest of us fail to recognize that happy person; a high level of confidence in one's predictive capacity tends to imply incompetence or dishonesty—or both.

To begin, globalization must be defined. For present purposes, I define it as increased economic interaction among countries, which takes several forms. First, trading ratios increase (i.e., a higher share of output is traded internationally than before). Next, there is a more substantial flow of investments across borders, both of foreign direct investment (the resources that enter the host country go directly into a business that is managed by the foreign investor) and of portfolio investment (where funds cross a border to be invested in stocks, bonds, or other financial assets in the receiving country). Many believe that technology flows across borders also rise. Since measurement is less straightforward in this area, it is more difficult to be sure. Finally, there could be increased labor migration across borders, but this has not, in fact, been a major component of recent developments, if indeed it has happened at all. Some observers consider faster information flows across countries—the international manifestation of the "information revolution"—to be an aspect of globalization. Certainly the rapidity and low cost of this flow does have the effect of bringing the world closer to the so-called global village. This essay, however, does not attempt to deal with the matter of who gains and loses from this particular revolution, except inasmuch as it helps to explain the increases in trade and investment flows.

Part of "globalization" as defined above has occurred as a result of policy changes (reduction of tariffs, elimination of impediments to capital movements), and part as a consequence of falling costs of conducting trade, especially information costs.

Economic theory provides only hints on the likely impact of globalization. Under some rather restrictive assumptions (perfect competition, perfect information on the part of all economic agents, benefits from an additional dollar of income the same for everyone in a given country, and the like), theory tells us that each country that engages in trade will benefit from it. This proposition, of course, implies that the world as a whole will benefit. Each country can be thought to have a net benefit that is the difference between the gross benefits to its winners and the gross losses of its losers. At one level of analysis, the winners are expected to be the factors of production (land, labor, capital, and technology) that are heavily engaged in the industries in which a country is relatively competitive. When barriers to trade (whether policy-based or related to transportation and other costs of trade) fall, those industries will be expected to expand as they now sell to foreign markets, as well as the domestic ones they previously supplied. The losers will be the factors of production deeply engaged in industries with the opposite characteristics; they now shrink, as the domestic market is at least partially captured by cheaper imports from other countries. When capital mobility is increased by a reduction of barriers to its movement, the returns to capitalists in the source countries are expected to rise; those of the capitalists in the recipient countries may fall as a result of increased competition from "international capital."

When one allows for the many complications found in the real world, the straightforward predictions of the very simple models of trade and investment become muddier and more ambiguous. For example, when the prevalence of imperfectly competitive international markets is taken into account, it becomes much harder to predict exactly how they will work and who the gainers and losers will be. Another example: the bigger markets that come with globalization tend to wipe out local versions of some products; is this bad (loss of variety) or good (the now-dominant brand is a better buy)?

Since the hints provided by economic theory must be confirmed in the real-world record before being taken too seriously, one must closely heed that record. As very little can be unequivocally drawn from this body of knowledge, divergent views inevitably reflect differences in how people read that (same) record. My own judgments on the economic benefits of globalization follow.

First, the net effect of globalization on world economic growth has been small, as reflected in the fact that world growth has not been higher in the last quarter-century than in the previous one. In fact, it decelerated from about 4.7 percent per year over 1950 to 1975 to about 3.1 percent over 1975 to 1999.[1] This comparison is a much too simple to be viewed as a test of that effect (it would only tell the story if other determinants of world growth had remained unchanged over this period). Yet, it does suggest that globalization is probably not one of the major determinants of world economic growth, in either a positive or a negative direction. This perspective may seem surprising, given the hype that surrounds the phenomenon, but it is consistent with many attempts to measure *(ex post)* or to predict *(ex ante)* the impacts of freer trade. Thus, in the context of Canada-U.S. free trade, most predictions were that the impact would be quite small when measured in GDP terms. This conclusion partly reflects the fact that most of the gains that could come from trade between these two countries were already being reaped before the accord of 1988.

Although based on a misreading of economic theory, the idea is widespread that in a competitive international setting countries must attempt, by every possible means, to keep costs low, including low wages, high levels of efficiency in resource utilization, and so on. This view contradicts the most basic tenet of international trade theory, and one of the components that is not open to question—the theory of comparative advantage. That theory explains why countries are able to sell at least some products internationally, no matter how low their productivity levels. They are able to export those items in which their productivity is relatively high, vis-à-vis what it is in other products. The exchange rate between that country's currency and those of its trading partners moves to a level such that the balance of payments is kept in equilibrium. A country that has high levels of productivity in all sectors of the economy—for example, the United States—enjoys a high level of income as a result, but no general tendency for its balance of payments to be in surplus. Just witness the huge balance of payments deficit currently run by the United States.

Because most business people and many policy-makers misunderstand this aspect of international competition, freer trade has sparked the fear that all countries will be forced to control wages, reduce spending on social services such as health and education, and the like. The fear has turned out to be justified, but not primarily because the world economy systematically works in the way these groups believe it does. Rather, in accepting its validity, they make the fears come true. In some respects, though, the fear of a "race to the bottom" in terms of social services, for example, does have validity. The market-friendly package of policy reforms currently on sale at the international financial institutions and in other places includes macro-economic prudence—that is, the avoidance of public sector deficits that could give rise to high rates of inflation. The limitation on governments spending more than they take in, together with the fact that freer trade removes one of the easiest taxes to administer, that on imports, makes it difficult to collect enough public revenues to achieve a desirable level of public spending. Optimists claim that reducing government corruption and inefficiency would more than compensate for the loss of tariff revenues; whether they are right remains to be seen.

Second, increasing trade and migration (in only some high-skill categories) contributes to increasing intracountry inequalities in both the North and in many countries of the South. The last two decades have seen many cases of increasing inequality and few of the opposite trend. In the North, the suspected causes have been labor-saving technological change (usually the prime one) and increased imports of labor-intensive goods (e.g., garments) from low-wage countries. As for the South, though our simplest theory suggests that the rapid growth of trade should work in favor of higher wages and thus improve income distribution, the more common result seems to have been the opposite. Several mechanisms have been suggested to explain such a result (see Berry, Horton and Mazumdar 1997). One relates to the fact that large firms (especially multinationals) systematically control a higher share of international trade and sales than of domestic trade and sales. These large firms are significantly more capital-intensive in their technologies than are smaller firms producing comparable items. Thus, globalization would be expected to increase the role of large firms in all countries, which in turn would be expected, ceteris paribus, to lower the demand for labor and, thereby, to worsen income inequalities. Undeniably, export booms can produce large wage gains and contribute to falling inequality, as they appear to have done in several East Asian countries. But it is unlikely that the experience of those countries could be generalized; they pushed an export-oriented industrial policy when their wages were very low, and achieved such high export-to-GDP ratios that these simply could not be replicated by all the large developing countries taken together. East Asian countries were generally successful in linking smaller producers to exports (through subcontracting and other devices), such that the negative impact of trade on inequality through its impact on firm size was absent, or nearly so, in those countries.

Migration also appears to affect wage structures. Sometimes it raises the earnings of relatively unskilled workers, as in the case of the flow to the Middle Eastern oil countries, which not only greatly increased the incomes of the migrants but also increased wages in some of the countries of origin (e.g., Pakistan). But episodes in which unskilled wage rates have been greatly affected by such migration appear to have been few. The relative loss to some Southern countries of higher-skilled workers (doctors, nurses, computer workers) is much bigger and appears to have pulled up the earnings of the nonmigrants in those categories, which tends to increase income inequality in those countries. In the case of doctors, for example, an additional effect is likely the lowering of the poor's welfare, since access to medical care depends on an ample supply of local medical personnel.

The overall impact of globalization on this income distribution front would seem to be negative in most cases, both in the developed countries and in the developing ones. It has probably been one contributing factor to the general trend towards increasing inequality over the last couple of decades.

Third, one factor in the relatively slow growth of many developing countries during the globalization phase has been the instability of international capital flows—that is, the hot money problem that led to the 1990s crises in Mexico and East Asia. Not only has growth been slowed by these events, but there is also an "uncertainty" cost associated with the fact that the threat of such crises renders the economic future less predictable. It remains to be seen whether, and when, improvements to domestic financial systems and to the international financial structure will together leave countries significantly less vulnerable to such episodes. One way to look at this cost of capital instability is as the other side of the coin from the benefits of international investment. Attempts to quantify such benefits have been less frequent than on the trade side. My guess is that they are also of quite modest proportions when one looks at the Third World as a whole. The benefits are likely to be modest for two reasons. First, the arrival of foreign capital sometimes simply discourages domestic savings without greatly affecting the available pool of capital. Second, through what one might call macroeconomic malfunctioning, its arrival sometimes discourages real investment, which is its raison d'être, by leading to an overvalued exchange rate. In particular, the benefits of speculative capital flows are likely to be less than for other types of capital, because they are less likely to lead to real investment, and more likely than other types to create macroeconomic instability.

Fourth, certain observers feel that one of the most significant benefits accruing to Southern countries from globalization is enhanced access to technological improvements. As with each of the other effects considered, one should be cautious about accepting this view. Had such improvements become more widely available as a result of globalization, we should have seen an acceleration of growth in the South. This simplest proof of the benefits is not yet unequivocally evident, just as it is not evident for the benefits of increased trade or of increased investment flows.[2] In the case of technology, optimists may have been overly confident for two reasons. First, we know that certain advanced-country technology is inappropriate for developing countries, since it involves capital-labor ratios that imply too little job creation or too much job destruction when the advanced technology replaces a previous one. Thus, only part of the developed countries' technology arsenal is really of potential benefit to most developing countries. In addition, much technology transfer occurs without the very reduced barriers to trade, international investment, and so on, that we now have. The benefit from globalization is only the additional technological flow resulting from tariff reduction and the like, and this gain may be small. In the judgment of authors such as Wood (2000), the movement of skilled labor is the main channel for technology spillover, and the multinational corporation less so. How globalization has affected such skills migration is unclear. In the extreme, globalization may decrease the net benefits from technology borrowed from the North; the preglobalization flow may have been about the right size and composition, whereas that flow now includes a lot of inappropriate technology. This line of thought is, of course, speculation, since it is very hard to sort out these issues in the historical record. But in the absence of serious analysis, it is as defensible a view as the opposite.

One sector in which both good and bad technology flows is health-medicine. The important discoveries, most of which are created in the industrial countries, are transferred to the developing nations. How much what we call globalization accelerates this flow is unclear; probably the faster flow of information, rather than increase in trade, has accelerated the transfer. Falling barriers to trade and investment have also, however, increased the presence of foreign investment in, as well as ideas about, the health care system, including the costly focus on curative rather than preventive health care that characterizes Western medicine in general and the American system in particular. However, successful "selling" of this system in developing countries may have a negative effect on the efficiency with which they use health-directed resources.

Fifth, globalization will substantially benefit certain developing countries, while harming others or benefiting them very little. The winners are likely to fall into several groups sharing certain characteristics. One group will likely be the high-income developing countries that are already competitive in many tradable goods markets, able to adopt and use effectively relatively modern technologies, and strong enough to influence the terms and conditions under which they trade and receive foreign investment. Those at the other end of these spectra are more likely to be losers. Another group of likely winners (not mutually exclusive with the previous one) includes countries like Vietnam and Bangladesh with very low wages and reliable workforces, which can become major exporters of unskilled labor-intensive items such as garments. The benefits of this trade will accrue, sooner or later, to the workers. A third group encompasses those countries with relatively low wages (by international standards) for skilled workers, which can export the output of such workers. India's computer software-related exports are a well-known example. Finally, physical proximity or, more generally, easy access to large markets will give certain countries an advantage.

The balance between winning countries and losers is hard to guess. Since 1980, the population of the poor countries as a whole has seen strikingly high income increases, but this phenomenon is due almost entirely to the very strong performance in China and the relatively successful one in India. When these two countries are excluded, growth has been weak in the rest of the Third World, especially Sub-Saharan Africa.

Sixth, few economists question the idea that a high level of international trade can benefit developing countries, as judged by our standard criteria (GDP growth, employment, income distribution). Among economists, the debate runs more to the question of whether the trade should be close to free at all times. When it is, trade policy cannot be the centrepiece of an industrial policy built around the idea of providing protection to industries until they can build up their efficiency to become competitive without protection. This "infant-industry" approach, used by virtually all countries but most successfully by the East Asians and perhaps by Latin American countries like Brazil and Mexico, is explicitly removed from the policy tool kit under free trade. Dyed-in-the-wool free traders either deny the relevance of the infant-industry approach from an economic point of view, or argue that developing-country governments are generally unable to implement it effectively even if the idea, in theory, has merit. The intransigence of some international financial institutions and Northern governments in this regard leads many developing-country economists to the view that they have been pushed towards free trade simply because that is the strategy most beneficial to the multinational corporations and, perhaps, to the North in general. It seems extreme to argue that the relatively subtle use of the infant-industry model in such East Asian countries as Taiwan and Korea slowed their growth when that growth has been the fastest in the world since the late 1960s. Those countries have been noted not only for providing tariff and other protection/support to certain industries but also for exerting pressure on those industries to raise their productivity and their international competitiveness. Although many economists not opposed in principle to some degree of support saw Brazil's protection as excessive, the fact that between 1945 and 1980 this was the fastest growing country in the world bespeaks caution before condemning its economic strategies on the grounds of simple theory. In all these cases of very fast growth, the national rate of investment was high, based mainly (as in virtually all countries) on national savings. It is arguable that more market-friendly policies simply leave economic agents under too much uncertainly; thus, they invest less than they would under a more controlled, more predictable system. Perhaps the more market-oriented systems do lead to a better allocation of resources at a given point in time. However, they produce less growth, because they do not induce such a rapid buildup of capital. At present, this proposition cannot be either demonstrated or contradicted; of all the key variables in an economic system, the rate of investment is the one that is least well understood in developing, as in developed, countries.

Seventh, the level of GDP, determined by its rate of growth over time, even when complemented by information on income distribution, gives a narrow perspective on the ways economic performance affects human welfare. Even employing this narrow perspective, one would form an uncertain conclusion about globalization's overall impact on the Third World. It is not obvious that this process has contributed to significantly faster growth, but it is clearly a suspect as a contributor to increasing inequality within countries. A broader perspective would take account of impacts on culture, on the sense of a country's citizenry that they control their own destiny, and on the environment. With global warming now beyond debate, and with a variety of other forms of environmental damage of increasing concern, it becomes important to evaluate globalization against this yardstick, as well. Does it aggravate or alleviate these environmental threats? Here, too, theory provides hints; on balance, however, it is difficult to draw any interesting judgments. Certainly, the opportunity to export wood or other products has contributed greatly to deforestation in some countries. But it is not clear that the shift from fairly high to higher trade flows under globalization accounts for this difference.

Eighth, one of the more apparent costs of globalization, emphasized in the recent antiglobalization protests, is the feeling that governance of the global system is beyond the direct or indirect control of ordinary people; increasingly, it lies in the hands of powerful corporate and, especially, financial interests (Pauly 1997). Although some people may not feel affected by this change, others clearly do. How much weight should be attributed to this "loss" of control? Will globalization increase the decision-making power of cities even as it reduces that of countries, as some have argued? Will the net effect be positive or negative in this sense of maintaining control over one's destiny? These are complex questions to which many citizens seek answers.

Ninth, globalization increases the cultural presence of the North, and most particularly of the United States, in the developing countries, as well as in other developed ones. Like most of the effects of globalization, this one is probably a mixed blessing. If the impact is to erode local cultures and replace them with an alien one or with a perhaps not very coherent mixture, this arguably lessens the cultural richness of the world. When beautiful old buildings are swept aside and replaced with McDonald's, do we give globalization a positive credit, or hold it responsible for a cultural loss? That many thoughtful people adopt the latter stance seems entirely understandable. The intrusiveness of American culture, coupled with the high level of confidence of its salespeople that it is the best the world has to offer and their high-powered sales techniques is a lethal combination. Given our inability to measure the gains from globalization with any precision and the likelihood that they are in any case modest, it is possible that these cultural losses will ultimately greatly outweigh any gains. They will have been borne for naught.

In sum, economic theory tells us virtually nothing about the likely benefits of shifting from a situation of substantial trade and capital movement to near-free movement of goods and funds. The empirical record to date suggests that the benefits of globalization, if they come quickly, are not very large (since we have not seen a discrete increase in growth, etc.); if large, do not come quickly. It also raises the serious possibility that this wave of globalization is contributing to increasing inequality, not only within countries but also between the North and the many Southern countries that have done badly over the last couple of decades.[3] Put another way, globalization may tend to increase inequality among countries of the South. With little evidence of major economic benefits after a couple of decades of globalization, prudent citizens may wonder why. They may also note that, if there are noneconomic costs (or economic ones not picked up in the simplistic indicators we typically use), these would not have to be substantial to outweigh the probably small benefits of the process.

Notes

1. Calculated on the basis of World Bank data from selected issues of the *World Development Report* and of *World Tables*. Results are mildly sensitive to how national figures are converted to a common measure of value and to statistical errors. But there is no dispute over the fact that growth slowed between the third and the fourth quarters of the twentieth century. Maddison (1986, 32), on the basis of thirty-two countries (those of the OECD and fifteen developing nations, including those with the largest

populations—China, India, Indonesia, and Brazil) estimated average annual growth of 5.1 percent over 1950 to 1973 and 3.4 percent over 1973 to 1987. Our figures indicate a decade-by-decade deceleration, from 3.8 percent over the 1970s to 3.2 percent over the 1980s to 2.5 percent over the 1990s. These patterns clearly reflect such important phenomena as the crash of the formerly planned economies in the early 1990s.

2. Over 1950 to 1977 the growth of developing countries, excluding the Soviet bloc, averaged about 5.5 percent (World Bank 1980, 372) and over 1973 to 1998 it averaged about 3.85 percent (World Bank 1999: 194).

3. See Berry, Horton, and Mazumdar (1997).

References

Berry, A., S. Horton, and D. Mazumdar. 1997. "Globalization, Adjustment, Inequality and Poverty." In *Human Development Papers 1997: Poverty and Human Development*. New York: United Nations Development Programme.

Helliwell, J. 2000. "Linkages between National Capital Markets: Does Globalization Expose Policy Gaps?" Paper presented at conference, Critical Issues in Financial Reform: Latin American/Caribbean and Canadian Perspectives, June, University of Toronto.

Maddison, Angus. 1986. *The World Economy in the Twentieth Century*. Paris: OECD Development Centre.

Pauly, L. 1997. *Who Elected the Bankers? Surveillance and Control in the World Economy*. Ithaca: Cornell University Press.

Wood, A. 2000. "When and Why Does Globalization Increase Rather than Reduce Labor Market Inequalities in Developing Countries?" Paper presented at Annual Forum of the Trade and Industrial Policy Secretariat, 18–20 September, Johannesburg.

World Bank. 1980. *World Tables*. 2d ed. Washington, D.C.: World Bank.

———. 1999. *Global Development Prospects and the Developing Countries*. Washington, D.C.: World Bank.

CHAPTER 2

Globalization, Neoliberalism, and Health

David Coburn

Everywhere the rich live longer, healthier lives than do the poor. This reality is starkly evident at both the global and the national levels. Economic globalization has magnified these health inequalities to levels unseen in decades. But the major culprit is not globalization per se; rather, it is a very specific form of economic globalization—neoliberalism, otherwise known as free-enterprise or New Right economics.

This chapter examines the health consequences of the global spread of neoliberalism in the developed, industrial countries. It demonstrates, first, that neoliberalism increases within-nation inequalities, and that these inequalities are intimately related to increasing health disparities between the rich and the poor. Secondly, it shows that those industrial countries with neoliberal policies and higher income inequality tend to report poorer average national health status than do other nations.

Globalization and Neoliberalism

Globalization refers to those interactions that indicate humankind belongs to a single world, ecologically, socially, politically, and economically. Currently, influential corporations, international agencies, and key national governments (especially the United States and the United Kingdom) have adopted a very narrow view of global integration. This perspective assumes that there is really only one aspect of globalization and one way to globalize—societies must adjust to markets or economies rather than the reverse. This blinkered view renders dialogue about key issues difficult: what type of globalization? what type and degree of integration and interdependence? Global, economic, and social relationships are desirable in one form or another, but not on terms set by multinational corporations.

A major criticism of economic globalization is that it vitiates democratic processes. Corporations are now geographically mobile. Business has freed itself from national controls. Jurisdictions compete with one another to attract capital. National financial accounts are at the mercy of currency traders and bond-rating agencies. Corporate power has been vastly increased; it is entrenched in international free-trade treaties at the expense of the autonomy and power of states, workers, and citizens.

This is not to argue that global economic integration makes particular policies or outcomes inevitable. National business classes lobby for global neoliberalism to enhance their own power both nationally and internationally. Thus, globalization is as much a political project as an economic inevitability. Markets are constructed by groups with specific (self-) interests; they do not simply emerge. The neoliberal project has also been driven by the policies of a dominant international power, the United States. It is thus a mistake to sever international from national political and social development.

Global processes are significant for two reasons. First, their *material* effects are important: international economic, political, and social forces directly and indirectly shape national economic, political, and social policies. Of course, countries react differently to international economic pressures, depending upon the given nation's status in the international division of labor, extant national institutions and political cultures, and divergent class structures. Second, assertions about the inevitability of neoliberal globalization are used *ideologically* to defend national neoliberal politics and policies and to reinforce a one-sided emphasis on the necessity for corporate power. Arguments that "we have no choice" and that particular kinds of economic processes are isomorphic with, or are necessary and sufficient for, increased human well-being need therefore to be challenged.

Neoliberalism is a doctrine that shapes global integration. Though composed of a complex combination of characteristics, the basic assumptions of neoliberalism, the philosophy of the New Right, are these:

- markets are the best and most efficient allocators of resources in production and distribution;

- societies are composed of autonomous individuals (producers and consumers) motivated chiefly or entirely by material or economic considerations;

- competition is the major market vehicle for innovations.

Neoliberalism is distinguished from neoconservatism by the fact that the latter contains a social component supportive of traditional family values and particular religious traditions—not only a free-enterprise economic doctrine.

The essence of neoliberalism, its pure form, is an adherence to the virtues of a free-market economy, and, by extension, a market-oriented society. The

New Right is not particularly concerned about inequality. It regards income or wealth disparities as either a virtue (reflecting unequal contributions to the public welfare) or as inevitable or necessary. If the market, including the market for labor, is the best or most efficient allocator of goods and resources, neoliberals are inclined to accept the social consequences of markets. Political parties that espouse neoliberal principles have been the mainspring behind attacks on the Keynesian welfare state, whose functions included not only the correction of economic boom and bust within the marketplace, but also the amelioration of market-produced inequalities (Kenworthy 1999; Navarro 1999a). The welfare state, in the neoliberal view, interferes with the normal functioning of economies. (For a discussion and empirical rebuttal of neoliberal views of the welfare state, see Kenworthy 1999.)

Welfare State Regimes

Esping-Andersen's description of regime types facilitates understanding of why nations have responded somewhat differently to common global pressures. Esping-Andersen (1990, 1999) argued insightfully that there were groups of welfare states with quite different configurations of welfare provision, not simply different levels of welfare state expenditure. A country might, for example, spend funds either on job training to prevent unemployment or on unemployment insurance simply to support the unemployed— with different consequences. Welfare state regimes can be roughly aligned according to the degree to which they decommodify citizens' relationships to the market. Decommodification refers to the degree to which citizens have a public alternative to complete dependence on the labor market (working for money), in order to earn a socially acceptable standard of living (O'-Connor and Olsen 1998). Esping-Andersen notes three major empirical types of welfare state:

- the social democratic welfare state, showing the greatest decommodification and emphasis on citizenship rights;

- the liberal welfare state, which is the most market-dependent and emphasizes means and income testing;

- an intermediate group, the corporatist welfare state, which is characterized by class and status-based insurance schemes and a heavy reliance on the family to provide support.

These countries might be viewed as strong, weak, and intermediate welfare states, respectively.

30   *David Coburn*

The major examples of the social-democratic welfare states are the Scandinavian countries. The liberal welfare states include the Anglo-American nations, particularly the United Kingdom and the United States (with the United Kingdom earlier being on the verge of a social-democratic welfare state). The corporatist/familistic states include such countries as Germany, Austria, France, and Italy. It is noteworthy that these groups of countries represent different approaches to both market and state welfare provision based on differing class structures and class coalitions—that is, they constitute distinct sociopolitical regimes and not only welfare state ones (O'Connor and Olsen 1998; Navarro 1999a).

Neoliberal Globalization, Social Inequality, and Health Disparities

International economic neoliberalism leads to the predominance of business, the rise of market-dominated policies on the national level, and pressures on the welfare state (see Esping-Andersen 1990, 1999; Navarro 1999b; Ross and Trachte 1990). The rise of neoliberalism and inequality following the 1970s is historically tied to a reduction in state entitlements such as unemployment insurance and welfare. Neoliberal welfare policies highlighted means testing regarding various income support measures, that is, a reduction of the benefits obtained simply by being a citizen (as opposed to being assessed as needy). The power of labor unions or other organizations opposing the strict application of market mechanisms was undermined. State functions and reductions in state expenditures in some critical areas such as welfare, housing, unemployment policies, education, and health were restructured. In addition, neoliberalism is clearly linked to greater individualism, that is, the decline of collective feelings of solidarity. Some argue that lowered social cohesion or social fragmentation is a major precursor of poorer health (Kawichi, Kennedy, and Wilkinson 1999). Not surprisingly, the World Bank and the International Monetary Fund, early purveyors of neoliberal economic policies, have recently taken an intense interest in such matters as social capital, social cohesion, and poverty.

What then are the findings concerning the relationship between neoliberalism and social and health inequalities? Although a vast literature addresses this question, space permits only illustrative examples drawn mainly from the more neoliberal nations, especially the United States, the United Kingdom, and Canada.

Income and Wealth Inequalities

In the last three or four decades of the twentieth century, neoliberal globalization augmented wealth and income inequality on a worldwide basis. The wealth ratio between the richest and the poorest fifth of countries increased from 30–1 in 1960 to 60–1 in 1990 to 76–1 in 1997. Disparities are startling. The net worth of the 358 richest people in the world is equal to the combined income of the poorest 45 percent of the world's population—2.3 billion people (Korzeniewicz and Moran 1997; Navarro 1999b).

Among the developed nations, the most recent evidence from the United States, Britain, Australia, Canada, and the OECD in general, indicates that inequality has been exacerbated under neoliberalism. Within the developed OECD nations, data from the exemplary Luxembourg Income Studies, demonstrate rising income inequality between 1979 and 1995 for fourteen of seventeen OECD countries (Gottschalk and Smeeding 1999, fig. 4). Comparatively, not only the United States and the United Kingdom but also Canada and Australia exhibit much greater inequality than do such countries as Switzerland, Germany, or the Netherlands, which, in turn, record higher inequality than do the Scandinavian countries (Gottschalk and Smeeding 1999; Kenworthy 1999; Korpi and Palme 1998).

Beginning with the Reagan and Thatcher regimes, the United States and the United Kingdom demonstrate particularly high, and ever-increasing, rates of inequality. Prior to neoliberal regimes, income inequality in the United States and the United Kingdom was relatively low and had been declining since the Second World War—the welfare state, such as it was in those two nations, actually performed true to form. Inequality rose to unprecedented heights from about 1968 in the United States and 1977/78 in the United Kingdom, a rise that continued into the 1990s (Gottschalk and Smeeding 1999, fig. 6). The lowest 60 percent of households in the United States actually experienced a *decrease* in after-tax income between 1977 and 1999. During the same period, the top 5 percent of household incomes grew by 56 percent while the top 1 percent mushroomed by 93 percent (Bernstein, Mishel, and Brocht 2001, 7). In fact, the United States, despite being the richest nation, suffered in the early 1990s from one of the highest rates of *absolute* poverty amongst the developed nations— out of fifteen countries only Italy, Ireland, Australia, and the United Kingdom had higher rates (Kenworthy 1999, 1125).

Canada similarly faced startling contradictions. While the government of its largest province, Ontario, cut welfare by 22 percent in 1995 and further in 1998, top managers earned ever-increasing salaries and other rewards such as stock options. Of note was the CEO of Nortel, a communications company, who received over U.S.$100 million in salary and stock options in 2000, despite the fact that Nortel stock lost over 90 percent of its value in the recession of 2000–2001. After 1981, when restructuring became more prevalent, incomes (in constant dollars) actually fell for the bottom 60 percent of Canadian families with children under eighteen, both before and after taxes (Yalnizyan 1998). Over the period 1984 to 1999, the top 20 percent of family units in Canada increased their median net worth by 39 percent, while the lowest 20 percent suffered a decline in median net worth of $600 (Statistics Canada 2001). For many Canadians, extended hours of work were not rewarded with higher pay, better working conditions, enhanced community facilities, or improved well-being. In fact, just the reverse was the case (Raphael 1999, 2001; Statistics Canada 2001; Teeple 1995; Yalnizyan 1998).

Health Differences within the Developed Nations

Increasing socioeconomic status (SES) differences have been closely linked with health differences within nations—the higher a group's SES or income, the higher its health status. All nations exhibit this gradient, albeit to a greater or lesser degree. These relationships cannot be explained away by reverse causation, i.e., that sicker people have lower incomes. The sick are more likely to be downwardly mobile, but this phenomenon accounts for only a minor part of SES health differences. SES differences in health are substantial. In a comparison of U.S. metropolitan areas the health differences between high and low SES areas were equivalent to "the combined loss of life from lung cancer, diabetes, motor vehicle crashes, HIV infections, suicide and homicide" (Lynch et al. 1998). Mortality would be reduced by 139.8 deaths per 100,000 if the SES differences noted were eliminated. In the United States, people in the very poorest households were four to five times more likely to die in the next ten years than were those in the richest (Kaplan 2000). In Britain, in 1996, the differences in longevity between the highest SES group and the lowest (of five groups) were 9.5 years for men and 6.4 years for women. In Canada there are similar, but perhaps less extreme, health differences between those high and low in income (Humphries and Doorslaer 2000). SES differences in health appear however health is measured—whether by morbidity, self-assessed health, infant mortality rates, potential years of life lost, disability-free years, age-standardized mortality, or longevity.

Despite expanding economies, health inequalities have proliferated. A commentator in the *British Medical Journal* noted: "The inequalities in health between social classes are now the greatest yet recorded in British history" (Yamey 1999; see also Dorling 1997). Another British study reports: "The ratio of deaths due to all causes between social classes 1 (high) and V (low) widened from 2.1:1 in 1970–72 . . . to 3.3 in 1991–93" (Blane and Drever 1998). For the first time in decades in 1992 some sex/age groups (males aged twenty-five to forty) actually began to exhibit increasing mortality rates per 100,000 as compared to a decade earlier (*Economist*, 11 January 1997). One recent study reported that simply reducing current wealth inequalities in Britain to their 1983 level would save 7,500 deaths among people younger than sixty-five (Mitchell, Shaw, and Dorling 2000; see also Dorling 1997).

Health Differences among the Developed Nations

GNP/capita cannot explain differences in health status among nations. Many nations with high GNP/capita show lower average health status than those with lower GNP/capita (Kawachi, Kennedy, and Wilkinson 1999; Wilkinson 1996). In fact, the closest correlate of average health status amongst the developed nations is *income inequality,* i.e., the distribution of income, rather than national wealth. The relationship between income inequality and health also holds true for regions within countries. For instance, within the United States, those states recording higher inequality also have lower average state health status, even controlling for average state product per capita (Kawachi, Kennedy, and Wilkinson 1999; but also see Deaton 2000).

There is considerable controversy regarding explanations of the link between income inequality and intercountry/region health inequalities (Coburn 2000; Deaton 2000; Muntaner and Lynch 1999; Lynch et al. 2000; Kawachi, Kennedy, and Wilkinson 1999). Some analysts argue that income inequality hierarchies create psychological stress and lower social cohesion, which in turn produce health problems. Others feel that income inequality is really a proxy for general inequalities in access to material resources. That is, countries exhibiting higher inequality have weaker social infrastructures, poorer housing, transportation, schooling, and provisions for the poor and/or simply have greater percentages of their populations exposed to the health risks associated with lower SES than do the more equal nations (Lynch et al. 2000, 2001). The issue here, however, is not the precise mechanism producing poor health. Rather, the main point is that neoliberal globalization produces income inequalities and/or impoverished social conditions, which in turn contribute to lower population health (Coburn 2000). Since most of the research has been carried out on income inequality, that factor is used here as an indicator for what may turn out to be a number of inequality-related social conditions.

Significantly, the more social-democratic Scandinavian nations record lower social inequalities and/or a lesser relationship between social inequalities and health status than do the nations with a neoliberal regime. Differences amongst nations are so great that the *lowest* social class in social-democratic Sweden in the mid-1980s showed better infant mortality rates than did the *highest* SES group in Great Britain, a group much higher in absolute income (Wilkinson 1996, fig. 5.7). In 1993–94, every one of five social classes in Sweden revealed better health than did their corresponding classes in the United Kingdom (Whitehead et al. 1997).

The United States is a striking outlier in respect to national health status. Whereas the United States is the highest-ranked nation in the world in GNP/capita, it displays a dismal inequality and health record. As noted, the United States is high even in absolute poverty and not only relative poverty.

And that country ranks well below other, much poorer nations regarding health status. For example, in 1999 the United States ranked twenty-third in the world and the United Kingdom twentieth in longevity, one measure of health. These two countries thus ranked below, for example, Italy, Greece, Spain, and Ireland. Using another measure of health, Potential Years of Life Lost (PYLL), which measures the average number of years death occurs before age sixty, amongst twenty-one developed nations the United States ranks twentieth, just above Portugal. Regarding the probability of dying before age five, the United States ranks twenty-third in the world regarding males and thirty-third regarding females. The corresponding ranks for the United Kingdom are fifteenth for males (tied with six other countries) and fourteenth for females (tied with ten other countries).

Canada shows lower income inequality than does the United States (Ross et al. 2000), though higher inequality than many European countries. Concomitantly, Canada can boast of higher longevity rates, lower infant mortality rates, better rates of PYLL and lower SES or income-related health differences than the United States or the United Kingdom. In fact, in 1996 the infant mortality rates in the poorest neighborhoods in Canada were better than the national rate of infant mortality in the United States. Yet the rates in the richest Canadian neighborhoods were not much better than the national average rates in Sweden (Statistics Canada 2000). There is speculation that Canada's remaining social support programs, from medicare to education and social infrastructure, generally mediate or reduce the effect of income inequality on health in Canada more so than in the United States. There are fears, however, that recent state cutbacks (for example in the proportion of the unemployed receiving employment insurance), will soon begin to worsen health. Moreover, positive comparisons of Canadian data with the worst-case developed nation, the United States, is hardly reassuring.

Conclusions

When such conservative bastions as the *Economist* (5 November 1994), the World Bank, and the IMF express concern about burgeoning inequality, growing poverty, and increasing social disintegration and exclusion, alarm bells ring. Neoliberal globalization has led in the developed world to increasing within-nation and internation social and health inequalities. That neoliberalism rather than some type of inevitable globalization is the major issue is seen by the success of some sociopolitical regimes in combining good economic performance with lower rates of inequality and better overall health and well-being.

The dominance of an economistic viewpoint regarding globalization has led to mistaking means for ends. Too often, we hear of "well-functioning" economies without concomitant improvements in the lives of citizens. The assumption of a direct relationship between economic growth and human well-being is unwarranted. Studies in both Canada and the United States indicate that since the 1970s, a time of increasing neoliberal globalization, there has been a widening divergence between generally rising GNPs and flat or worsening measures of citizen well-being (Brink and Zeesman 1997).

An important issue is the explanation underlying general global trends, as well as national differences in inequalities. In the early postwar phase, states had attained a relative autonomy from dominant business classes because of a more equal balance of class power between capital and labor and because of the divisions within capital. Ross and Trachte (1990) indicate that global capitalism has replaced this previous nationally based monopoly phase. The increasing globalization of financial and industrial capital in the 1970s gave business greater political power. The state is now more directly shaped and constrained by business interests. The consequence is the dominance of class-based market doctrines and policies and, as indicated, higher inequality, health inequalities, and poorer health status than would have been the case under a different international regime.

Yet, the social-democratic nations have weathered the global neoliberal crisis better than have the more laissez-faire Anglo-American liberal regimes. Different national regime-types reflect variations in working-class strength as compared to the strength of capital, and the political loyalties of the large middle class. Countries with a stronger, more organized working-class movement, in which the working class is politically engaged and in which unions are stronger, are more likely to show greater social equalities, fewer health inequalities, and generally higher health status and social well-being than do those with weaker working-class movements. The social welfare literature is almost unanimous. It assigns a key role to labor and the working class in the production of stronger welfare state regimes. Interestingly enough, labor union membership also positively correlates with national and regional health measures (Gustafsson and Johansson 1999; Lynch et al. 2001; O'Connor and Olsen 1998).

Viewing global economic and political processes as joined to national events and processes helps to clarify what it is about globalization that many find objectionable. Neither globalization nor "internationalization" is the problem; rather, the problem resides in the specific neoliberal form of economic globalization in which markets dominate societies. Such an extreme doctrine is now creating its own resistance, for example, successful opposition to the Multilateral Agreement on Investment and to the unfettered functioning of the WTO. There are signs, for example, in the World Bank's increasing concern with "social capital," that even some supporters of global neoliberalism are beginning to recognize its detrimental human effects. The increasing international resistance to corporate global rule, shown by successful opposition to the MAI, and the increasing sensitivity (however inadequate) of the WTO, World Bank, and IMF to poverty and social factors indicates that inequality and corporate domination are not necessary conditions produced by extrahuman forces but are subject to modification. There *are* alternatives.

Understanding global and regional forces and their effects will provide support for those seeking change in a more positive direction and help reclaim the concept of globalization from those who have appropriated it for their own narrow purposes.

References

Bernstein, J., L. Mishel, and C. Brocht. 2000. "Anyway You Cut It: Income Inequality on the Rise Regardless of How It's Measured." Briefing Paper No. 99, Economic Policy Institute. Available from: <http://epinet.org>.

Blane, D., and F. Drever. 1998. "Inequality among Men in Standardized Years of Potential Life Lost, 1970–93." *British Medical Journal* 317 (25 July): 255–60.

Brink, S., and A. Zeesman. 1997. "Measuring Social Well-Being: An Index of Social Health for Canada." Applied Research Branch, Strategic Policy, Human Resources Development Canada, R-97-9E.

Coburn, D. 2000. "Income Inequality, Social Cohesion, and the Health Status of Populations: The Role of Neoliberalism." *Social Science and Medicine* 51:135–46.

———. 2001. "Health, Health Care, and Neoliberalism." In *The Political Economy of Health and Health Care in Canada*, ed. P. Armstrong, H. Armstrong, and D. Coburn. Toronto: Oxford University Press.

Deaton, A. 2000. "Health, Inequality, and Economic Development." Paper prepared for Working Group 1 of the WHO Commission on Macroeconomics and Health, Research Program in Development Studies and Center for Health and Well-being, Princeton University, May.

Dorling, D. 1997. *Death in Britain: How Local Mortality Rates Have Changed: 1950s to 1990s.* Joseph Rowntree Foundation. Available from: <http://www.jrf.org.uk>.

Esping-Andersen, G. 1990. *The Three Worlds of Welfare Capitalism.* Princeton: Princeton University Press.

———. 1999. *Social Foundations of Postindustrial Economies.* Oxford: Oxford University Press.

Gottschalk, P., and T. M. Smeeding. 1999. "Empirical Evidence of Income Inequality in Industrialized Countries." Luxembourg Income Study Working Paper no. 154, Maxwell School of Public Affairs, Syracuse University.

Gustafsson, B., and M. Johansson. 1999. "In Search of Smoking Guns: What Makes Income Inequality Vary over Time in Different Countries?" *American Sociological Review* 64:585–605.

Humphries, K. H., and Eddy van Doorslaer. 2000. "Income-Related Health Inequality in Canada." *Social Science and Medicine* 50:663–71.

Kaplan, G. A. 2000. "Economic Policy Is Health Policy." Paper presented at the Income Inequality, Socioeconomic Status, and Health Conference, April, Washington, D.C.

Kawachi, I., B. Kennedy, and R. G. Wilkinson, eds. 1999. *The Society and Population Health Reader: Income Inequality and Health.* New York: The New Press.

Kenworthy, L. 1999. "Do Social-Welfare Policies Reduce Poverty? A Cross-National Assessment." *Social Forces* 77 (3): 1119–39.

Korpi, W., and J. Palme. 1998. "The Paradox of Redistribution and Strategies of Equality: Welfare State Institutions, Inequality, and Poverty in the Western Countries." Working Paper no. 174, Luxembourg Income Study. Available from: <http://lisweb .ceps.lu/publications/wpapers.htm>.

Korzeniewicz, R. P., and T. P. Moran. 1997. "World-Economic Trends in the Distribution of Income, 1965–1992." *American Journal of Sociology* 102 (4): 1000–1039.

Lynch, J., George Davey Smith, M. Hillemeier, M. Shaw, T. Raghunathan, and G. Kaplan. 2001. "Income Inequality, the Psychosocial Environment, and Health: Comparisons of Wealthy Nations." *Lancet* 358 (21 July): 194–200.

Lynch, J. W., G. Davey-Smith, G. A. Kaplan, and J. S. House. 2000. "Income Inequality and Mortality: Importance to Health of Individual Income, Psychosocial Environment, or Material Conditions." *British Medical Journal* 320 (29 April): 1200–1204.

Lynch, J. W., G. A. Kaplan, E. R. Pamuk, R. D. Cohen, K. E. Heck, J. L. Balfour, and I. H. Yen. 1998. "Income Inequality and Mortality in Metropolitan Areas of the United States." *American Journal of Public Health* 88 (7): 1074–80.

Mitchell, R., M. Shaw, and D. Dorling. 2000. *Inequalities in Life and Death: What If Britain Were More Equal?* Bristol: Policy Press.

Muntaner, C., and J. Lynch. 1999. "Income Inequality, Social Cohesion, and Class Relations: A Critique of Wilkinson's Neo-Durkheimian Research Program." *International Journal of Health Services* 29 (1): 59–81.

Navarro, V. 1999a. "The Political Economy of the Welfare State in Developed Capitalist Countries." *International Journal of Health Services* 29 (1): 1–50.

———. 1999b. "Health and Equity in the World in the Era of Globalization." *International Journal of Health Services* 29 (2): 1–50.

O'Connor, J. S., and G. M. Olsen, eds. 1998. *Power Resources Theory and the Welfare State: A Critical Approach.* Toronto: University of Toronto Press.

Raphael, D. 1999. "Health Effects of Economic Inequality." *Canadian Review of Social Policy* 44:25–40.

———. 2001. "From Increasing Poverty to Societal Disintegration: How Economic Inequality Affects the Health of Individuals and Communities." In *Unhealthy Times: Political Economy Perspectives on Health and Care in Canada,* ed. P. Armstrong, H. Armstrong, and D. Coburn. Toronto: Oxford University Press.

Ross, N. A., M. C. Wolfson, J. R. Dunn, J.-M. Berthelot, G. A. Kaplan, and J. W. Lynch. 2000. "Relations between Income Inequality and Mortality in Canada and in the United States." *British Medical Journal* 320 (1 April): 898–902.

Ross, R. J. S., and K. C. Trachte. 1990. *Global Capitalism: The New Leviathan.* Albany: State University of New York.

Statistics Canada. 2000. "Health Reports: How Healthy Are Canadians?" *Daily,* 31 March. Statistics Canada Cat. no. 11-001E.

Statistics Canada. 2001. "The Assets and Debts of Canadians." Catalog no.: 13-595-XIE. Available from: <www.statcan.ca>.

Teeple, G. 1995. *Globalization and the Decline of Social Reform.* Toronto: Garamond Press.

Whitehead, M., M. Evandrou, B. Haglund, and F. Diderichsen. 1997. "As the Health Divide Widens in Sweden and Britain, What's Happening to Access to Care?" *British Medical Journal* 315 (18 October): 1006–9.

Wilkinson, R. G. 1996. *Unhealthy Societies: The Afflictions of Inequality.* London: Routledge.

Yalnizyan, A. 1998. *The Growing Gap: A Report on Growing Inequality between the Rich and Poor in Canada.* Toronto: The Centre for Social Justice.

Yamey, G. 1999. "Study Shows Growing Inequalities in Health in Britain." *British Medical Journal* 319 (4 December): 1453.

CHAPTER 3

Latin America:
Inequality, Poverty, and Questionable Democracies

Judith Teichman

Globalization, a process that has been underway since the mid-1970s, is commonly understood as the elimination of economic borders and the increase in international exchange, particularly in terms of trade and investment flows. For the countries of Latin America, as well as for other less-developed countries, the era of globalization has involved a variety of additional ingredients—international pressures and domestic policy reforms that have patterned a distribution of benefits and losses with profound implications for democratic politics.

Initially, the prospect of policy reforms that would substantially reduce the role of the state in the economy was greeted with optimism. The nature and direction of state intervention in Latin America had long been blamed, not only for economic failures but also for the social inequalities that characterized most countries. Such reforms were seen as strengthening the prospects for democracy by reducing the economic power of the state and the opportunities for corruption. However, these expectations have not been fulfilled. By the early twenty-first century, the policy reforms that were to help Latin America establish its place in the new global order have not only contributed to the worsening of social inequalities but also have eroded fragile procedural democracies.

The Experience of Structural Adjustment

International and domestic factors have interacted to produce the social and political difficulties Latin American countries now face. If the onset of globalization dates from the world energy crisis of 1973–74, this crisis also arises from the recycling of petroleum dollars through the Euromarket and heavy lending to the largest Latin American countries, leading to the debt crisis of the early 1980s. The effects of the 1982 debt crisis lingered in Latin

America through the decade. Indeed, in the years following the international debt crisis, most Latin American countries have enjoyed only fleeting spurts of growth, punctuated by economic crises of varying intensity and duration. While the eighties were coined the Lost Decade, the nineties were also characterized by economic difficulties. The 1995 Mexican peso crisis, which rocked the other economies of the region, was followed by further economic troubles generated by the 1997 Asian and 1998 Brazilian financial crises.

The debt crisis and its attendant endless negotiations and renegotiations with multilateral lending institutions (the IMF and the World Bank) and the commercial banking community spawned a multitude of policy recommendations. These policy prescriptions initially focused on the standard economic stabilization formula geared to rectify balance of payments difficulties; that is, policies reducing the public deficit, restricting credit, instituting devaluation, and holding down wage increases. By the mid-1980s, more extensive economic policy changes, in the form of market-liberalizing reform programs, were pressed on governments. These programs—known as structural adjustment—entailed a variety of measures: trade liberalization (the reduction of tariffs and the elimination of quota restrictions), the privatization of public companies, deregulation, particularly the deregulation of foreign investment regimes, and labor "flexibilization," a euphemism for reduction in the cost of labor.[1] Both the IMF and the World Bank developed policy-based instruments to encourage Latin American governments to reduce the role of the state in the economy. Meanwhile, initiatives by two former U.S. secretaries of the treasury, James Baker and Nicolas Brady, encouraged market liberalizing measures; they offered additional loans (the Baker Plan, 1985) and, later, debt relief (the Brady Plan, 1989). Hence, by the late 1980s, most countries of the region had embarked on market-liberalizing reforms.[2]

During the debt negotiations from the early eighties to the early nineties, the World Bank negotiators and the IMF largely ignored the social implications of reform policies. The positions of these institutions reflected, for the most part, the American concern to ensure debt repayments, as well as the overwhelming desire to promote the stability of the private international banking sector (Kapur, Lewis, and Webb1997, 607). The late 1980s, however, marked the beginning of an altered attitude; both the World Bank and the IMF began to express concern for poverty alleviation. The social programs supported by the World Bank, however, have been and remain narrowly targeted programs. They operate on the assumption that, over the long term, the market will provide the answer to poverty.

The transfer of the new free-market international policy culture to Latin American policy elites has been an integral component of the policy reform process. Much of the literature on policy conditionality—the stipulations attached to structural adjustment loans by the World Bank and the IMF—documents the failure of conditionality per se to induce policy change (Killick 1995, 121). Rather, a process described by multilateral officials as *policy dialogue* was established; its explicit purpose was to create ownership of new policy directions by domestic policy elites (Kahler 1992, 123). In this way, multilateral institutions have played a key role in strengthening the more radical market reformers, and in helping them expand their power within the state (Teichman 2001, 56–61). In general, Latin American radical reformers shared the disregard of the multilaterals for the social implications of their policy choices, were obsessively concerned with certain macroeconomic indicators (public deficits, inflation), and had little regard for democratic processes when these threatened their policy reforms. Furthermore, Latin American policy reformers were willing to use coercive methods to implement their reforms, and demonstrated a tendency to cronyism and favoritism in their allocative decisions. Market reforms, moreover, have handed the private sectors inordinate economic and political power. This development has rendered it difficult to effectively address the social deficit, even when the difficult reforms of trade liberalization, privatization of major public enterprises, and deregulation have been largely completed.

Winners and Losers in the Process of Market Reform

In those Latin American countries in which market-liberalizing reforms have been carried out with the greatest enthusiasm, the process has produced a concentration in wealth and assets reminiscent of the nineteenth century. Probably the most notorious example of the concentration of assets stemming from privatization is the first phase of Chilean market reform (1975–81). The top three conglomerates (Cruzat-Larraín, the Mortgage Bank of Chile, and the Edwards Group) purchased public companies at bargain-basement prices. They acquired control of 53 percent of the country's banking sector, as well as seventy-one of the country's largest firms engaged in such activities as forestry, financial services, export agriculture, and mining (Silva 1995, 98). With the military's second privatization phase, the country's biggest companies, in partnership with foreign companies, gained ownership of privatized public enterprises (Délano and Traslaviña 1989, 126). Although Chile returned to civilian rule in 1990, it remains a country dominated economically by very large and powerful conglomerates.

The reform processes in Mexico, then a one-party dominant regime, and in Argentina, where reforms were carried out in the context of a competitive party democracy, similarly increased the clout of the few conglomerates able to acquire public companies and take advantage of export incentives. In both cases, a small number of conglomerates profited from tax breaks designed to stimulate exports. And in both countries—albeit in Argentina more so than in

Mexico—privatization benefited cronies close to the presidents in power during the height of the reform programs. Former Mexican president Carlos Salinas's close friend, Carlos Slim, procured a monopoly on the country's telecommunications industry. With the privatization of the state copper companies in Mexico, one man, Jorge Larrea, obtained control of over 90 percent of copper production (Teichman 1995, 153). In Argentina, a few domestic companies, such as the Pérez Companc Group, Compañia del Plata, and Techint, were part of consortia otherwise composed of multinational banks and foreign companies that purchased public companies (Schvarzer 1995, 142). In fact, in Argentina, the owners of these conglomerates were directly involved in the formulation of tenders (Teichman 2001, 124). Without mechanisms of accountability, the Argentine privatization process became one in which kickbacks and commissions were rewards for rigging bids and selling privileged information (Saba and Manzetti 1997, 355). The Mexico peso crisis of 1995 repeated the experience of the Chilean financial collapse of the early 1980s; both were characterized by reckless borrowing and lending on the part of privileged conglomerates (Teichman 2001, 148). And in both Mexico and Chile, when economic disaster struck, governments bailed out failing banks and passed the cost on to taxpayers by converting the bailouts into public debt.

Indeed, the commitment of Latin American policy elites to free markets is highly selective. On the one hand, they have been willing to proffer export subsidies and oversee policies fostering monopolies or near monopolies that favor powerful domestic business interests. In Mexico, conglomerate executives, in the banking and telecommunications sectors, had little difficulty persuading policy elites that their economic activities should be protected from foreign capital. Thus, the entry of foreign capital into these sectors was restricted (Teichman 2001, 146). But while protecting and promoting the interests of their private sector allies, reforming governments in Latin America have had no compunction against intervening directly and decisively to create so-called free labor markets by repressing the unions.[3] Labor repression in the market reform process was by no means confined to the highly authoritarian military regime in Chile. In Mexico, labor resistance to actions such as public enterprise restructuring and the consequent layoffs, privatization, and various forms of deregulation was met with state manipulations of the labor code. This jockeying allowed the government to end strikes and force workers back to work. In addition, more direct tactics such as the use of the police and the military and the arrest of labor leaders were also employed (LaBotz 1992). In Argentina, a 1990 law prohibiting strikes in essential services—legislation that was imposed by presidential decree when it was blocked in the House—became instrumental in handling workers in public companies subject to privatization, such as electricity, gas, water, and health. A group of anti-Menemist striking telephone workers saw their leaders fired, their organization forcefully dissolved, and their facilities taken over by police (Erro 1993, 212). Through such methods, in both Mexico and Argentina (although more so in the case of the former) considerable de facto labor flexibility was achieved, without formal changes in labor codes.

With market-liberalizing reforms, the owners and executives of the big domestic conglomerates acquired unprecedented political power. This development can be largely explained by the circumstances these reforms created, as they concentrated assets and, hence, economic power. As the state divested itself of public companies, the conglomerates became ever more important economic actors. Not only were they the owners of the country's largest private enterprises, but given the enormous weight placed on achieving export markets, they now assumed center stage; they were virtually the only enterprises capable of participating in the new model.[4] Once the initially difficult phase of trade liberalization was achieved, the owners and executives of the big conglomerates became permanent fixtures, accompanying top government officials when important trade agreements loomed.[5] Because of their close ties with political leaders, these powerful businessmen gained preponderant influence over public policy, often cemented by under-the-table business deals in which political leaders received kickbacks, or businessmen fronted business deals of politicians.[6]

Meanwhile, market-liberalizing reforms, within the context of globalization, have not brought Latin America into the developed world, with perhaps the exception of Chile. Here, there was a steady growth rate of over 7.5 percent for over a decade, until the Asian crisis of 1997 (American Chamber of Commerce of Chile 2000). An increase in social spending was instrumental in reducing poverty: between 1990 and 1994, Chile's proportion of poor was reduced from 40 to 28 percent (CEPAL). But Chile is unusual by Latin American standards. Not only did it experience steady economic growth from the mid-1980s until recently, but it also carried out politically difficult economic policy reforms much earlier than other countries. In addition, a broad layer of small, medium, and large private firms pursue export expansion, its human development indicators are comparable to those of developed countries, and corruption is low. Furthermore, Chile's antipoverty drive rejected the World Bank's recommendation of a highly targeted approach to poverty reduction. Moreover, Chile's status in the new global order has clearly done little to reduce the extent of inequality.[7] Furthermore, economic growth rates declined in 1998 (4 percent) and 1999 (1 percent), while unemployment, the major political issue, was stalled at 10.5 percent, up from 6 percent in 1997 (American Chamber of Commerce of Chile 2000; *Latin Focus* 2000). Growing public criticism of the government's poor performance in the areas of employment and poverty reduction suggests that, despite Chile's relative success, much work remains.[8]

In Latin America generally, poverty has deepened. Between 1980 and 1990, the proportion of the population living in poverty rose from 41 to 46 percent. The proportion living in extreme poverty increased from 14 to 22 percent in the same period (Wilkie 1999, 431). By 1995, unemployment in Argentina reached a record high of 18.5 percent, while real wages stagnated or declined after 1989 (ILO 1999). Inequality and poverty have increased in Mexico, especially following the 1995 peso crisis. Between 1989 and 1996, the proportion of the Mexican population living in poverty varied only slightly between 42 and 43 percent, while those living in extreme poverty increased from 12 to 16 percent. By the end of the decade, some 43 million people were living in poverty and 18 million in extreme poverty (CEPAL). Rural dwellers in the south have been most clearly excluded from the benefits of globalization in Mexico. Between 1989 and 1994, when extreme and moderate poverty fell in the urban areas, rural poverty did not improve; indeed, it rose in the mining and agricultural sectors. Southern Mexico has been completely excluded from the new market model. Between 1989 and 1994, poverty in the southeast of Mexico rose; in the states of Chiapas, Guerrero, and Oaxaca, it was five times higher than in northeast Mexico and forty times higher than in the federal district (Lustig 1998, 204). These states host large indigenous populations, and they are precisely the areas where guerrilla groups, particularly the EZLN (the Zapatista Liberation Army), are active.

Proponents of market reforms have frequently suggested that market-liberalizing reform is politically difficult because it involves tough measures that hurt relatively privileged groups with political power. These groups include unionized workers, the bureaucrats of the public companies slated for privatization, and private entrepreneurs benefiting from state protection and contracts (Williamson 1994, 13; Hausman 1994, 115). It is now clear that structural adjustment programs have involved measures—the reduction and elimination of subsidies on basic consumer products, layoffs, and changes in labor practices—that have exacerbated unemployment, underemployment, and poverty, thereby hurting many of the most vulnerable and least politically powerful members of society. Other measures integral to market-reform packages have provided disproportionate benefits to the already powerful.

Globalization and Questionable Democracies

Alongside the dramatic reduction in the traditional role of the state in Latin America, the 1980s also witnessed a concerted move toward political liberalization and democratization, as countries shed military rule and established a variety of formal democratic practices. Recent work notes impressive progress in the formal procedural requisites for liberal democracy (Agüero 1998). Indeed, some observers believe that the democratizing regimes of Latin America are more firmly rooted and more durable than ever, as a growing number of them prove capable of surviving economic crises and transferring power through elections (such as Remmer 1996). However, as the threat of military intervention has dissipated, praise for procedural advances in democracy has been tempered by mounting concerns about obstacles that appear to diminish the quality of Latin American democracy. Latin American democracies have been described as "delegative democracies" (O'Donnell 1994), "hybrid" (Conaghan, Malloy, and Abugattas 1990, 26) and "fragile"(Hakim and Lowenthal 1993). These characterizations signify that, while such regimes have electoral processes, they also have features seen as antithetical to the spread and consolidation of democracy.

Market reforms have not necessarily advanced the process of democratic consolidation. Indeed, the very process of pushing through the reforms, combined with the concentration of economic power that accrued afterwards, has undermined democratic deliberative mechanisms. Presidential candidates such as Alberto Fujimori in Peru and Carlos Menem in Argentina, who had campaigned on antimarket reform platforms or vague agendas, surprised their supporters when they enthusiastically adopted such programs upon assuming power. In Bolivia, Peru, and Argentina, presidential decrees squelched opposition to market-reform measures from resistant congresses (Conaghan and Malloy 1994, 145–48; Teichman 1997). Labor opposition was greeted with stiff, often brutal, resistance. Political leaders strove to insulate the domestic architects of market-reform policies—often technocrats with graduate degrees from American universities—from the opposition of so-called populist pressures. Mexican president Carlos Salinas reduced to three the number of cabinet ministers with access to the economic policy-making process (Teichman 1995, 148). And President Menem ensured that Argentinian policy reform would be tightly controlled by his economy minister, Domingo Cavallo, as well as his small and tightly knit technocratic team (Teichman 1997).

Moreover, the dismantling of the state through market-liberalizing reforms failed to reduce the importance of certain forms of rent-seeking and clientelistic relationships. Most notably, the granting of monopolies for extended periods (in the case of telecommunications in Mexico, for example), or the provision of export subsidies to companies already exporting or in a position to do so, was effectively a continuation of state-supported private sector profit-making. Furthermore, traditional clientelistic methods of political co-optation and control were adapted to deal with societal opponents of market reform, particularly labor. Patronage was distributed selectively to trade unions and key leaders. In Mexico the government-installed leader of the state petroleum workers union, for example, was permitted to establish his own contracting company; it then cashed in on the state petroleum company's move to make greater use of outside contractors. President Carlos Menem employed explicitly clientelistic methods in channeling funds toward the *Obras Sociales* (social

Funds) of trade unions that supported his market reforms. Then, he selectively allocated wage increases, in accordance with which labor unions had supported his reform programs (Grassi, Hintz, and Neufeld 1994, 153–54).

But perhaps the most innovative adaptation of clientelism to the exigencies of the new era—that is, to neoliberalism and globalization—can be discerned in the allocation of resources to combat extreme poverty. Indeed, neoliberal policy-makers, despite the numerous economic crises of recent years, have not questioned the viability of the neoliberal model; rather, they have relied on poverty alleviation programs as a necessary complement to the widely accepted neoliberal formula. In reaction to the belief that state spending in social areas had been highly inefficient (for example, in social security systems), the objective became to target poverty groups—most often, people living in extreme poverty.

Social Investment Funds (SIFs) constitute the mechanism by which the World Bank has sought to stimulate such targeted social programs. First established in 1985 to mitigate the devastating impact of harsh stabilization in Bolivia, they have been implemented in nearly every Latin American country that has carried out structural adjustment (ECLAC 1997, 108). The SIFs have been designed to be administered by institutions independent of the state bureaucracy and responsible only to the president; this arrangement has rendered them pliant tools of political patronage (Stahl 1996, 33). In most countries, such poverty alleviation programs have also involved contributions by other lending agencies (such as the Interamerican Development Bank) and from home governments. Spending in these programs tends to focus on short-term measures such as emergency employment and aid programs. Hence, such initiatives are unlikely to create productive, long-term employment.

The most extensively documented case of the political use of targeted poverty alleviation programs is that of PRONASOL, Mexico's Solidarity Program, a program introduced by a market reformer, President Carlos Salinas, in 1989. PRONASOL and similar programs played an important role in the PRI's surprise victories in the 1991 mid-term elections, as well as in the federal election of 1994. Salinas's successor in the Mexican presidency, Ernesto Zedillo, employed an even more targeted program. PROGRESA handed over money to women in extreme poverty, provided that their children attend health clinics and school regularly. The manipulation of this program in rural areas to secure votes for the PRI was widely documented during the months leading up to the 2000 federal election (Global Exchange 2000, 10). In Peru, the Social Investment Fund was secured just in time for the upcoming referendum in 1993 on Fujimori's new constitution; this constitution contained antidemocratic features such as provisions allowing the president to dissolve Congress at will, veto laws, and promulgate laws by decree. Alberto Fujimori, like Carlos Salinas, appeared on television handing over checks to poor communities for schools and other facilities, a tactic that reinforced a personalistic conception of poverty alleviation (Burt 1996, 34).

Latin American publics are weary of both the social cost of neoliberal reform and the corrupt manner in which it has been instituted. Most notably, in the fall of 2000, as public support for former Peruvian president Alberto Fujimori plummeted in the face of political scandal, he lost control of Congress, announced a new election, and was subsequently forced from power by the Peruvian legislature. With government corruption, poverty, and unemployment as the key electoral issues in the Argentine 1999 federal election, the Radical Party defeated the Peronists, installing Fernando de la Rúa in office. In Mexico's 2000 election, the PRI was defeated by the Alianza por Cambio coalition led by PAN (Popular Action) party leader Vicente Fox. Various negative factors were major election issues; they included disgust with the government's economic management and with government corruption, and growing disillusionment with an economic model that had failed to bring promised prosperity. Although Vicente Fox and his right-wing PAN party applaud the market as the panacea to poverty, he was forced to address the poverty issue during the election campaign and, increasingly, in the interim between his election in July 2000 and his assumption of office in December.

In Chile, a very close electoral win returned the Christian Democratic/Socialist alliance known as Concertación to power in 2000/01. Concertación had been seriously challenged by a right-wing coalition led by the charismatic leader Joaquín Lavín. From the mid-1990s, the rank and file of the socialist parties belonging to Concertación had been growing impatient with the alliance leadership's commitment to the neoliberal model. Both the socialist parties and the communist parties boasted electoral gains in 1996 municipal elections, and in the 1997 midterm congressional elections. At the same time, more poor and working-class voters grew deeply disillusioned with the failure of the Concertación, in power for a decade, to improve significantly their social situation.[9] Instead, they were attracted by the charismatic and populist appeal of Lavín, who promised them jobs, education, and a reduction in crime (Winn 2000, 8, 9–10).

Although these recent electoral upsets are, in many ways, encouraging signs of a basic public faith in the efficacy of democratic institutions, public expectations may not be met. Argentine president Fernando de la Rúa, pursuing further adjustments under IMF auspices, confronted increasing political unrest, including widespread strike activity. The newly elected Mexican president, Vicente Fox, pledged to strengthen democratic processes in Mexico, offering a number of good-faith measures such as the withdrawal of troops from Chiapas and executive support for an earlier agreement ending that conflict. However, he has excessively raised Mexican public expectations, promising everything from the reduction of poverty to a doubling of foreign investment and an economic growth rate of more than 4 percent. His failure to deliver on his most important promises could engender public disillusionment with the democratic process. Fox is particularly vulnerable on the poverty issue, especially in Mexico's southern states, given his assumption that the market will ultimately be the best solution for Mexico's massive poverty.

The freeing of markets in Latin America has not only fallen short on providing growth and sustained prosperity but has also bequeathed a legacy of negative features that will be an enormous challenge to alter. Structural adjustment/market-reform policies strengthened big conglomerates and, oftentimes, created domestic monopolies in essential services that have proved difficult, sometimes impossible, to regulate in the public interest.[10] At the same time, neoliberal reform has reduced the ability of other social groups, especially organized labor, to oppose or to influence government policy choices. Although social movements and NGOs have proliferated during the neoliberal era, these groups remain highly fragmented (Oxhorn 1998, 212). Thus, their ability to contribute to the consolidation of democracy by effectively criticizing the political leadership and holding it accountable is weak.

Despite formal democratic procedures, political power remains concentrated in the hands of powerful executives and private-sector interests. Macroeconomic policy and social policy lie largely in the hands of closed networks of senior-level government officials and the officials of multilateral lending institutions, especially the World Bank and the IMF (Teichman 2001). Executives generally have wide discretionary power, with recourse to presidential decree powers, should legislatures prove recalcitrant. As congressmen enjoy very little access to research and technical support, they find it difficult to challenge government initiatives and hold powerful presidents accountable. At the same time, powerful private-sector interests are demanding further reductions in the legal protection for labor. They bitterly oppose tax reform, which is necessary to increase government revenues and hence facilitate social programs without instigating budget deficits (Teichman 2001, 216).

Conclusions

Born out of the energy crisis of the 1970s, globalization and the international debt crisis propelled Latin American countries into well-intentioned market-liberalizing policy reforms. These policies were intended not only to improve economic efficiency and productivity but also to benefit the countries of the region as members of the new global order. It was assumed that the magic of the marketplace would disperse benefits widely within Latin American societies. Observers believed these reforms would contribute to democratization by diffusing economic power and reducing the power of vested interests that had benefited from state intervention. But, in fact, market-liberalizing reforms were themselves carried out in a highly authoritarian fashion. The process augmented the authority of already powerful economic elites within Latin America, while proving quite compatible with the perpetuation of targeted clientelism. Concentrated political and economic power ensured that the costs and benefits of economic change would be distributed unequally; solutions to these inequities will not be easy to achieve. What had, in Latin America, always been an unequal power structure—social, economic, and political—became even more so.

International actors have played a key role in these developments. Latin American technocrats and big-business conglomerates have enthusiastically endorsed the free-market policy culture of the international economic community. They have become the interlocutors between the domestic and the international economies. At the same time, officials of multilateral lending institutions worked assiduously to support and promote the power of the most radical Latin American free marketers. They helped to tip the balance of power in the direction of Latin America's particular brand of "savage capitalism," thereby exacerbating globalization's devastating social impact in the region. In short, global forces have strengthened the technocratic and business groups bent upon dismantling the ability of the state to provide a modicum of social protection. Given the extent of social inequality and the political arrangements that underpin it, even steady economic growth is unlikely to adequately rectify the region's glaring social problems. Recently, the institutions of electoral democracy have registered public dissatisfaction with issues related to the market-reform experience and, by extension, to concern over the social and political consequences stemming from globalization.

Let us hope that Latin America's fragile procedural democracies are equal to the task of reforming the worst aspects of the free-market model in the region— for if they are not, the sacrifices of the last two decades will have been in vain.

Notes

1. Labor flexibility involves practices that dilute established labor codes: for example, policies allowing employers greater discretion in laying off employees, reducing obligations for severance pay, and easing restrictions on the hiring and remuneration of temporary workers so as to enable a company to reduce payroll expenses. The objective of labor flexibilization is to increase international competitiveness.

2. The earliest market-reform programs were carried out in Chile and Mexico. Chile's initial reform phase occurred between 1975 and 1981, while a second stage occurred between 1985 and 1989. Both took place under military rule. Mexico's reform process began in 1985. The most radical and most rapid reform occurred in Argentina between 1989 and 1994. On the other end of the spectrum, reform has been blocked in Venezuela after an initial attempt in the late 1989s, while market reform in Brazil has

also lagged, stalled by a recalcitrant congress and a concern to avoid some of the mistakes of the early reform experiences.

3. The standard argument is that labor rights in Latin America have been overly generous, have produced gains unrelated to productivity, and have fomented corruption and inefficiencies. While this argument has considerable validity, it neglects the inefficient and corrupt practices of the private sector that have been and are at least equally responsible for the misallocation of resources.

4. The exception was Chile, especially after the return of civilian rule in 1989. Small and medium firms, grouped together in their own cooperative export association, have been able to obtain export markets.

5. In Mexico, Argentina, and Chile under the civilian Concertación government, business participated closely in the negotiation of trade agreements.

6. It has been charged, for example, that businessman Cabal Peniche was a front man for former Mexican president Miguel de la Madrid in the purchase of public companies (Teichman 1995, 156) and that Menem loyalists, Jorge Triaca and Maria Julia Alsogaray, appointed to head up public companies to be privatized, enriched themselves in the process of carrying out their public duties and were later charged (*Latin American Weekly Report*, 1 March 1990, 11).

7. The Gini coefficient, an inequality index that increases as the distribution of income becomes more skewed, was 56.3 in 1997 for Chile, compared with 54 in 1983 and 50 in 1975 (World Bank 1997, 215; Edwards and Cox Edwards 1987, 167).

8. According to a public opinion survey carried out by the Centro de Estudios Públicos (*El Mercurio*, http://www.emol.com/noticias/detalle/detalle_diario.asp)

9. Chile's labor code remains one of the most flexible in the world.

10. This is because powerful private interests with direct and personal ties to political leaderships succeeded in capturing regulatory boards (Teichman 2001, 124, 155).

References

Agüero, Felipe. 1998. "Conflicting Assessments of Democratization: Exploring the Fault Lines." In *Fault Lines of Democracy in Post-Transition Latin America*, ed. Felipe Agüero and Jeffery Stark. Coral Cables, Fla.: North South Center, University of Miami.

American Chamber of Commerce of Chile. 2000. Available from: <http://amcham-chile.cl/usa-chile/chiledat.htm>.

Burt, Jo-Marie. 1996. "Local NGOs in Peru Devise an Alternative Anti-Poverty Program." *NACLA Report on the Americas* 6 (May–June): 34–35.

CEPAL. *America Latina: Magnitud de la pobreza y indigencia.* Cuadro 16. Available from: <www.eclac.cl/español/estadisticas>.

Conaghan, Catherine, James A. Malloy, and Luis A. Abugattas. 1990. "Business and the Boys: The Politics of Neoliberalism in the Central Andes." *Latin American Research Review* 25 (2): 3–30.

Conaghan, Catherine M., and James M. Malloy. 1994. *Unsettling Statecraft: Democracy and Neoliberalism in the Central Andes*. Pittsburgh, Pa.: University of Pittsburgh Press.

Délano, Manuel, and Hugo Traslaviña. 1989. *La herencia de los Chicago Boys*. Santiago: Las Ediciones del Ornitorrinco.

ECLAC (United Nations Economic Commission for Latin America and the Caribbean). 1997. *The Equity Gap: Latin America, the Caribbean, and the Social Summit*. Santiago: United Nations.

Edwards, Sebastian, and Alejandra Cox Edwards. 1987. *Monetarism and Liberalization: The Chilean Experiment*. Cambridge: Ballinger Publishing Co.

Erro, David G. 1993. *Resolving the Argentine Paradox: Politics and Development, 1966–1992*. Boulder, Colo.: Lynne Rienner.

Global Exchange/Alianza Civica International Delegation. 2000. *Pre-electoral Conditions in Mexico, 2000*. San Francisco: Global Exchange.

Grassi, Estella, Susana Hintz, and María Rosa Neufeld. 1994. *Politicas sociales, crisis, y ajuste estructural*. Buenos Aires: Espacio Editorial.

Hakim, Peter, and Abraham Lowenthal. 1993. "Latin America's Fragile Democracies." In *The Global Resurgency of Democracy*, ed. Larry Diamond and Marc P. Plattner. Baltimore: Johns Hopkins University Press.

Hausman, Ricardo. 1994. "Sustaining Reform: What Role for Social Policy?" In *Redefining the State in Latin America*, ed. Colin I. Bradford. Paris: Organization for Economic Cooperation and Development.

ILO (International Labour Office), Oficina Regional para America Latina. 1999. *Panorama Laboral '99*. Anexo Estadistica. Available from: <www.ilolim.org.pe/>.

Kahler, Miles. 1992. "External Influence, Conditionality, and the Politics of Adjustment." In *The Politics of Economic Adjustment*, ed. Stephan Haggard and Robert R. Kaufman. Princeton: Princeton University Press.

Kapur, Devash, John P. Lewis, and Richard Webb. 1997. *The World Bank: The First Half Century*. Vol. 1. Washington, D.C.: Brookings Institution Press.

Killick, Tony. 1995. *IMF Programmes in Developing Countries*. London: Routledge.

LaBotz, Dan. 1992. *Mask of Democracy: Labor Suppression in Mexico Today*. Boston: South End Press.

Latin American Weekly Report. 1 March 1990.

Latin Focus. 2000. Available from: <http://www.latin-focus.com/economic/Chile.htm>.

Lustig, Nora. 1998. *Mexico: The Remaking of an Economy.* 2d ed. Washington, D.C.: Brookings Institution Press.

El Mercurio. Available from: <http://www.emol.com/noticias/detalle/detalle_diario.asp>.

O'Donnell, Guillermo. 1994. "Delegative Democracy." *Journal of Democracy* 5 (1): 55–69.

Oxhorn, Philip. 1998. "Is the Century of Corporatism Over? Neoliberalism and the Rise of Neopluralism." In *What Kind of Democracy? What Kind of Market?* ed. Philip Oxhorn and Graciela Ducatenzeiler. University Park: Pennsylvania State University Press.

Remmer, Karen. 1996. "The Sustainability of Political Democracy: Lessons from South America." *Comparative Political Studies* 29 (December): 689–718.

Saba, Roberto Pablo, and Luigi Manzetti. 1997. "Privatization in Argentina: The Implications for Corruption." *Crime, Law, and Social Change* 25:253–369.

Schvarzer, Jorge. 1995. *Grandes grupos-económicos en la argentina: Formas de propriedad y lógicas de expansión.* Buenos Aires: Fundación Fredrick Ebert.

Silva, Eduardo. 1995. "The Political Economy of Chile's Regime Transition: Radical to Pragmatic Neoliberal Policies." In *The Struggle for Democracy in Chile,* ed. Paul Drake and Iván Jaskic. Rev. ed. Lincoln: University of Nebraska Press.

Stahl, Karen. 1996. "Anti-Poverty Programs: Making Structural Adjustment More Palatable." *NACLA Report on the Americas* 6 (May–June): 69–73.

Teichman, Judith A. 1995. *Privatization and Political Change in Mexico.* Pittsburgh, Pa.: University of Pittsburgh Press.

———. 1997. "Mexico and Argentina: Economic Reform and Technocratic Decision Making." *Studies in Comparative International Development* 32 (Spring): 31–55.

———. 2001. *The Politics of Freeing Markets in Latin America: Chile, Argentina, and Mexico.* Chapel Hill: University of North Carolina Press.

Wilkie, James W., ed. 1999. *Statistical Abstract of Latin America.* Vol. 35. Los Angeles: UCLA Latin American Center Publications.

Williamson, John. 1994. "In Search of a Manual for Technopolis." In *The Political Economy of Policy Reform,* ed. John Williamson. Washington, D.C.: Institute for International Economics.

Winn, Peter. 2000. "Lagos Defeats the Right—By a Thread." *NACLA Report on the Americas* 33 (March/April): 5–10.

World Bank. 1997. *World Development Report, 1997.* Washington, D.C.: The World Bank.

CHAPTER 4

Globalization versus Cultural Authenticity?
Valentine's Day and Hindu Values

Anil Mathew Varughese

Yet another earthquake rocked Indian soil on Valentine's Day, one that registered high on the cultural seismograph of this diverse country. All across Northern India—in Delhi, Mumbai, Kanpur, Pune, Varanasi, and Jabalpur—the impact was palpable. The seismic activity began when Shiv Sena, a Bombay-based Hindu nationalist political party, unleashed a campaign against Valentine's Day and its attendant festivities. Several mass organizations of the Sangh Parivar,[1] of which the ruling BJP is a principal constituent, joined the fray.

The chief of Shiv Sena, Bal Thackeray, exhorted the people, through an article in the party mouthpiece *Saamna*, to shun the Western-inspired Valentine's Day and its public admission of love as it was "alien to Indian culture" (*Hindustan Times,* 12 February 2001). He also forewarned fellow Indians that cultural squads would be dispatched to halt celebrations.

In a country where arranged marriages are still the norm, though waning rapidly in the urban areas, Valentine's Day is a relatively recent phenomenon. Major greeting card companies, and more recently Internet companies, have created much hype around the festivities to woo urban youth who are increasingly eager to escape their restrictive cultural heritage. Yet only a tiny minority of the Indian population in the urban centers can afford to celebrate this lover's day; the excitement and pomp are a distant dream for the rest.[2]

For those lovers who did not heed the self-proclaimed guardians of culture, the festival of love turned out to be a bitter affair. Shops were ransacked, Valentine cards and decorations set ablaze, restaurants vandalized, markets forcibly closed, and cinemas and amusement parks warned against organizing "uncultured functions." Couples were taunted and humiliated, and soundly thrashed for offering any resistance. Belligerent young male lovers were treated to a humiliating public haircut, and their partners were insulted and frightened away. In Delhi alone, twenty-five squads of protesters, comprising fifty members each, disrupted the celebrations. They were instructed not only to obstruct the celebrations but also to "punish the participating couples."

Although civilizing globalization includes preserving cultural diversity from the homogenizing impact of the Western advertising, entertainment, and information industries, it does not imply transforming indigenous cultures or religions into penal colonies. Cultures or civilizations are dynamic bodies of values and practices that benefit from contact with other cultures. Governments should therefore preserve cultural diversity by establishing their legal right to subsidize local cultural expressions and even to impose restrictions on cheap cultural imports. But they should not send in their police or thugs to intimidate those who deviate from a narrow interpretation of traditional values.

Yet people are subjected to just such harassment in the world's biggest democracy, which constitutionally guarantees freedom of expression. Ironically, Alexis de Tocqueville (1994), who cautioned the world against the potential of democracy to be ruled by the tyranny of the majority, would be appalled by India's tyranny of the minority. The Hindu right, clearly a minority, defines what it means to be Indian, culturally authentic, and patriotic. Their definition of "authentic" (mis)appropriates the mantle of nationalism. They take for granted an enormous overlap in personnel, assumptions, and symbols between Indian nationalism and Hindu majoritarianism. This conflating of "Indianness" and "Hindu-ness," and the resulting xenophobic rhetoric toward the religious minorities, has shredded the secular fabric of India.

A spate of recent events has focused unprecedented public attention on this dogmatism. Recently, the sets of Indo-Canadian filmmaker Deepa Mehta's new film, *Water*, were destroyed by the same self-appointed "cultural police," allegedly for anti-Hindu content. They decried her earlier film, *Fire*, again on charges of cultural apostasy. More recently, these groups have demanded a ban on two Bollywood[3] movies. One of these films, *Zubeida*, shows a Hindu king taking a second wife; the other, *Mohabbatein*, a current box office hit, depicts Amitabh Bachchan, one of the India's greatest actors, wearing shoes while doing *puja*, the Hindu worship. The chief minister of Uttar Pradesh has banned all beauty contests in his state, while others have denounced New Year's parties, birthday cakes, honeymoons, and candles, seemingly for perpetuating anti-Indian values. Some have suggested that St. Nicholas (Santa Claus) is as Western as St. Valentine and deserves the same treatment. The latest in this melodrama is the BJP-led national government's attempt to appoint a panel of "nipple police" to watch for any flicker of bosom in the French fashion channel FTV that may undermine the cultural values of Indian youth (*Hindustan Times*, 14 February 2001).

These self-appointed nationalists restrain their militantly intolerant, majoritarian discourse within the permissible limits of democratic practice largely to cater to the exigencies of coalition politics. However, their skin-deep commitment to democracy and freedom and their underlying authoritarian agenda surfaces when radical elements express their frustrations over working within the constitutional and democratic framework. The Indian constitution envisages four situations in which an individual's right to freedom of expression can be overridden: libel, threats to national security, threats to morality, and threats to public order. The last two are often invoked in protests over cultural content. In the interest of protecting a citizen's right to choose, one would expect the state to advise dissenters to avoid what offends them. On the contrary, the Indian state has lately played a regressive role by banning the whole product, book or film, citing the potential for public disorder. In other words, public intolerance is often presented as in the national interest and is promoted by the state, either by unwanted intervention or by its conspicuous absence in enforcing the law.

As a result, the cultural nationalists stand ready to engineer a riot over petty issues, permanently defacing India's finely woven multicultural tapestry. Everything from books to paintings to pageants to clothes to food is objectionable, to one group or the other. One can imagine a future in which all foreign entertainment will be banned in India.

Why does the well-educated Indian middle class give credence to these histrionics? How does one account for their support of political parties with such obscurantist ideas?[4] There must be a stronger explanation than the simple one—that a lie repeated often enough begins to sound like a truth.

At a deeper level, there seems to be a striking dichotomy in the behavior of the Indian masses. On one hand, India is a world leader in software production and skilled computer personnel. The information technology boom has revolutionized the lives of the middle class in terms of lifestyle and social mobility. Coca Cola, McDonald's, Pizza Hut, and Kentucky Fried Chicken outlets have penetrated the interiors of the country. Cable television introduces the Western dream to even the remotest villages, and India's cities are crammed with foreign cars and the markets are brimming with foreign products. When Bill Gates and Bill Clinton came visiting, the politicians, not to speak of the masses, treated them like gods on earth. On the other hand, a substantial share of the population obstinately hangs on to a traditional culture that manifests a feudal mentality over women and lower castes, and is filled with religious superstition. What is the explanation behind this seemingly conflicting behavior?

I believe this contradiction is not peculiar to Indians, but common to many peoples in the contemporary world—in Iran, Egypt, Algeria, erstwhile Yugoslavia, Japan, and many other countries. The "Western" style of life associated with globalization uprooted people from their secure sites of consciousness. The staggering influx of foreign capital into India inevitably brought with it "social" capital—a set of collective norms and values—that promoted and reinforced consumerism rather than community. A creeping "McWorld"[5] challenged traditional values and ways of life, reshaping everyday experiences of personal and collective well-being. It altered the construction of meaning in daily life.

The average Indian clearly embraced the new economic opportunities that globalization presented, but s/he resented its social costs. The rightist parties exploited this growing uneasiness or social dislocation of the Indian middle class in order to hawk their political project—in the name of national culture and nationalism. Caught up in the vortex of tradition and modernity, robbed of their locus of identity, many people readily swallowed the premade cultural pill marketed by the Sangh Parivar and its cohorts. Whereas pursuing cultural fault lines was a political strategy for right-wingers to promote their regressive vision of culture and nation, it served as an antidote for the masses that felt alienated from their familiar surroundings. The opening up of India's economy to the global market offered fertile grounds for the Hindu right to pursue their program. They incited protests against fast-food outlets, popular Western entertainment, and anything and everything that was even distantly Western, all in the name of safeguarding the culture of the Indian people.

Their critique of the West and Western values has proceeded from an ambivalent denunciation of modernity and modern life. While they incessantly indict modern ways of life for all the social evils of contemporary India, they ride piggyback on the apparent benefits of modernity, especially technological advances in transport and communications. They use the Internet and the latest modes of communication to spread their gospel and attract material and moral support from all over the world. They also invoke the very modern discourse that they denounce to portray Muslims as traditional, uncivilized, patriarchal, lustful, and premodern. Thus, for them, the contamination of Indian culture is marked not only by the hybridization of Indian values by Westerners but also by its decay and "plebianization" (Hansen 1999) through the "encroachment" of Muslims and untouchables in the public domain.

Their crusade for *swadeshi* and *sanskriti*[6] is, therefore, marked by a vehement opposition to any sort of cultural or social change that may disturb the status quo. Their opposition to modern social life is understandable: modernity entails individualism that accords larger personal autonomy for everyone including women, and organizes society on the basis of achievement rather than ascription. It releases women from the shackles of patriarchy, and the lower castes from the oppressive caste system. This situation is evidently inimical to the vision of the religious right. They contest all such breaking free, and what enables it, as antithetical to Indian culture. Their notion of culture and Indianness is a fiction that is frozen in time and space, one that negates the unique variation from place to place and person to person. They stand guilty of the same charge that they hurl against the West—of imposing a homogenized version of culture from above.

The Hindu chauvinists are determined to steer the construction of culture in a certain direction. They promise to recreate the strong, glorious Bharat[7] of the past against the impending Western hegemony. This undertaking feeds the desire of the Indian middle class, which comprises some of the world's most intelligent and best-educated people, to be respected as the "civilizational other," or equal, of the West. Political defiance of the West and nuclear adventures are mere tools in this jingoistic project. This promise to elevate the average Indian from a sense of powerlessness to one of global recognition is what makes their campaigns alluring.

Does the alternative, in fact, necessitate bowing to the indiscriminately homogenizing pressures from the West? Certainly not. Globalization's potential to imperiously obliterate local cultures needs to be tamed. Globalization should not and does not mean losing the cultural diversity of the world. There is strong evidence of penetration of a Western capitalist monoculture into much of the developing world; at the same time, there is also an indication that globalization has given voice to many forgotten, marginalized cultures in an increasingly pluralist world. Apparently, the relationship between globalization and culture is a dialectical one that involves paradoxical interdependence. There is a tension between homogeneity and heterogeneity that is integral to this relationship. The local shapes the global and, in turn, is molded by the global. Globalization destroys the securities of the local and makes it vulnerable; but it also opens up the world to the notion that people are entitled to their distinctiveness and particularity.

If globalization trivializes and commodifies local cultures, cultural puritans essentialize cultures. Americanization is certainly not the answer to modern life's cultural disjunctures, but neither is Talibanization. The dangers are clear. While globalization is capable of annihilating local cultures, xenophobic responses threaten to transform the contested realm of culture into an ossified code to which all must pay obeisance.

In a world of ever increasing interconnections and interdependency, history tells us that cultures cannot be isolated for the sake of cultural purity and authenticity. When capital, goods, people, ideas, knowledge, images, and diseases flow across national boundaries, no culture can survive if it attempts to be exclusive. Cultures must engage in a dialogue—with themselves and with the others—to remain vital.

People cannot be required to respect a culture that traps them in a concentration camp. Indian civilization has absorbed many foreign influences without losing its uniqueness—and that is precisely why India is renowned as a tolerant society. It would be tragic if xenophobes are permitted to destroy a civilization that has endured centuries of conquest. Their paranoia certainly helps to deflect the masses' attention from more pressing issues of poverty and unemployment.

Ironically, what goes around comes around. Just as India's culture cops were busy inveighing against Western values, a band of Muslim clerics in Malaysia demanded a ban on Indian movies in Malaysia—apparently for "polluting the youth with immoral values" (*Hindustan Times,* 15 February 2001).

Notes

1. Sangh Parivar or Sangh is a collective name for the numerous political, cultural, and social organizations that consider Rashtriya Swyamsevak Sangh (RSS) as their ideological parent. Prominent among them are the Bharatiya Janata Party (BJP), Vishwa Hindu Parishad (VHP), and Bajrang Dal.

2. Although Valentine's Day is celebrated in North America as an occasion for expression of love toward friends, family, colleagues, and teachers, in India it has acquired an exclusively romantic connotation. Only couples or aspiring couples commemorate the day.

3. Bollywood is the popular name by which the Mumbai-based Indian film industry is known.

4. The Bharatiya Janata Party, the political arm of Sangh Parivar, founded in 1980, won two seats in the lower house of the Indian parliament in the general elections in 1984. They went on to become the single largest party in Parliament by the 1996 elections. They have retained this position in the subsequent elections in 1998 and 1999 and remain the biggest party in the current ruling coalition.

5. A term used by Barber (1995) to refer to the global trend towards homogenization of cultures.

6. *Swadeshi* means indigenous or native and *sanskriti* means culture. The Sangh Parivar use the term *swadeshi* to refer to a kind of economic nationalism, roused and directed against the specter of globalization. They mix *swadeshi* and *sanskriti* in interesting ways in their political rhetoric.

7. Bharat is another name for India. Taken from ancient history, the term is often used by the cultural nationalists to evoke the cultural oneness of the nation, from the Himalayas to the seas. They also use the name Hindustan, emphasizing "Hindutva" or "Hindu-ness" as the common thread uniting the people inhabiting the territory. The name India is considered a remnant of colonial rule.

References

Barber, Benjamin R. 1995. *Jihad vs. McWorld*. New York: Times Books.

Hansen, Thomas Blom. 1999. *The Saffron Wave: Democracy and Hindu Nationalism in Modern India*. Princeton: Princeton University Press.

Tocqueville, Alexis de. 1994. *Democracy in America*. Edited by J.P. Mayer. London: Fontana Press.

PART 2

Adjusting Global Markets to Social Needs

Core Issues

How can we capture the potential benefits of closer economic integration while safeguarding such values as equity, environmental sustainability, cultural diversity, financial stability, and democratic decision-making? This key question animates a great deal of today's debate.

Those who subscribe to a "Third Way" on the model of Tony Blair's Labour Party provide one answer. They see the role of government as humanely adjusting citizens, communities, and national firms to the exigencies of competition within an inexorably advancing global market economy. Governments are therefore assigned rather narrow socioeconomic responsibilities: to ensure high-quality education and training, orchestrate the necessary physical infrastructure, promote technological innovation, maintain macroeconomic stability, and ensure a minimal social safety net. This approach is congruent with the efficiency criteria of global capital.

Critics on the left reject the Third Way as neoliberalism with a human face, urging a more radical approach to globalization. International socialist groups and anarchists want to abolish global capitalism altogether, though it is unclear what feasible economic system would take its place. Others, including many of the contributors to this volume, advocate what might be termed a social-democratic approach to globalization. This vision essentially holds that core features of the nationally bounded welfare state be extended to the global realm. Regulation of global market forces could be achieved in various ways—from enforceable social, environmental, and cultural charters to a more incremental approach that asserts the primacy of universal human rights and health and environmental standards over international or regional trade and investment agreements. International taxes or transfers that discourage harmful practices would also play a role in taming markets and redistributing income globally. The five chapters that follow sketch major facets of such an approach.

Heather Gibb, a senior researcher at the North-South Institute, proposes in chapter 5 a modest, incremental approach to reinforcing core labor standards. Owing to the adamant opposition to a labor charter in the South, she recommends that the International Labour Organization work on many fronts, and with several allies, to improve working conditions and labor rights worldwide. She considers that the international financial institutions, as well as national unions, international labor federations, and international trade secretariats, can play a positive role.

In a similar vein, in chapter 6 environmental activist and lawyer Michelle Swenarchuk reveals practical ways in which citizen groups can assert the primacy of health and environmental protection over agreements stemming from the World Trade Organization and the North American Free Trade Agreement. These strategic recommendations follow an analysis of how dispute-settlement panels have consistently interpreted trade regimes to give higher priority to freer trade and investment over these protections.

Environmental geographer Rodney White follows in chapter 7 with an ingenious, yet simple, "financial transfer scheme" that would generate powerful incentives to reduce carbon emissions in both the North and South. At the same time, this scheme would provide a mechanism for North-South redistribution that would underpin a more robust effort to reduce mass poverty in developing countries.

Garry Neil, long associated with advocacy groups promoting the arts and culture, argues in chapter 8 for preserving cultural diversity from the corrosive effects of free trade agreements. His case in point is Canada, which struggles to maintain its cultural distinctiveness in the shadow of a country, the United States, that classifies culture as just another service industry. Neil chronicles the achievements of an international movement of nongovernmental organizations that is dedicated to enshrining a legal foundation for cultural diversity in this era of global integration.

Finally, Joy Kennedy in chapter 9 concisely presents the case for a currency transaction tax (CTT), known as the "Tobin tax" after the Nobel economist who originally proposed this measure. A CTT, which is now widely regarded as technically feasible, would not only curb the speculation that fuels financial volatility and insecurity but also generate substantial funds to attack world poverty. Kennedy, an activist with ecumenical groups, emphasizes that the major hurdle to a CTT is the power of those with a vested interest in untrammeled financial markets.

Part 2, in sum, demonstrates why and how the efficiency criteria favored by global capital need to be constrained by rules and taxes that foster core social and ecological needs.

CHAPTER 5

Core Labor Standards:
An Incremental Approach

Heather Gibb

"When workers [in Central America, Mexico, and the Caribbean] try to set up unions in the [export-processing] zones, they are harassed, dismissed and their names placed on the black lists that circulate among employers," observes an ICFTU report (ICFTU 2001). "Documents belonging to the independent trade union at Duro Bags Manufacturing, in the Tamaulipas state in Mexico, disappeared when its president's house was burnt down. In Guatemala, the owner of the Cadiz maquila suspended 300 workers for forming a union, before closing down his enterprise and leaving 600 people out of work."

Although the International Labour Organization's (ILO's) 1998 *Declaration on Fundamental Principles and Rights at Work* obligates member states "to respect, to promote and to realize in good faith" workers' rights, this ICFTU report illustrates how these rights are routinely violated. It is not only ILO declarations and conventions that affirm the obligation to respect the rights of workers. The first ministerial conference of the World Trade Organization (WTO) in 1996 resolved to "renew our commitment to the observance of internationally recognized core labour standards." This commitment was again renewed at the 2001 WTO ministerial meeting in Doha. Yet action to support ILO conventions and the labor agreements that increasingly accompany bilateral and regional trade agreements remains weak,[1] and debate on the "how-to" of enforcing core labor standards continues to be heated.

Strategies proposed to ensure adherence by employers and governments to a basic set of labor rights vary considerably. Many advocate enforced compliance through the addition of a social or labor clause to trade agreements. This strategy would subject countries that violate labor standards to sanctions under these agreements. While many in the North wish to explore the potential of the WTO's dispute-settlement bodies to respond to labor rights issues, others (especially in the South) remain skeptical of this approach. The latter maintain that

61

the issues surrounding labor standards are too complex to be addressed in this punitive manner. According to this view, imposing trade-related penalties on countries that fail to honor core labor standards misses the point: poor labor conditions are associated with poverty, and poverty can only be ameliorated by addressing its fundamental causes. Eradicating global poverty demands a range of integrated strategies, including debt relief for poor countries, substantial increases in official development assistance, improved access for developing-country exports to developed-country markets, and support for adequate social protection for developing countries before they open up to foreign markets. Although core labor standards remain an important component in campaigns to reduce poverty, many fear that industrial countries would use *enforceable* labor codes as a protectionist device to exclude developing-country imports.

Agreement is growing, however, around a more broad-based, gradualist approach. This program involves a positive, employment-oriented approach to economic and social policy at national, regional, and international levels. If globalization is to be harnessed to benefit workers as well as capital, this multilevel strategy is a good place to begin. Key to this strategy is a stronger role for the ILO in the emerging global structures of financial and trade governance. The ILO is widely acknowledged as the global reference point on employment and labor standards. Its tripartite structure, drawing in employers' and workers' associations as well as governments, adds credibility and breadth to its approach.

Core labor standards are beneficial not only for workers; they may also enhance economic efficiency. A literature review by the OECD (OECD 2000) has identified a growing consensus on the relationship between core labor standards, economic efficiency, and growth. It argues that these standards enhance worker satisfaction and loyalty, which in turn increase the workers' commitment to the goals of the work group. The result can be higher productivity. Further, collective bargaining enhances the overall efficiency of the economy by facilitating income redistribution that would not occur, or would be more costly to implement, through the tax and welfare systems. The ILO presents the economic efficiency case for core labor standards as follows:

- child labor is detrimental to development, since it means that the next generation of workers will be unskilled and less well-educated;

- collective bargaining and tripartite dialogue are necessary elements for creating an environment that encourages innovation and higher productivity, attracts foreign direct investment, and enables the society and economy to adjust to external shocks;

- discrimination faced by women and minority groups are important obstacles to economic efficiency and social development.

Such arguments fortify the basic equity case for core labor standards with an important economic rationale.

But can the ILO's 1998 *Declaration* and its follow-up activities build more civilized workplaces in the global economy? This chapter surveys the main objectives of the *Declaration*, notes some of its weaknesses, and introduces the key actors and instruments involved in an employment-oriented approach to supporting core labor standards.

What Are Core Labor Standards?

What rights should be included in a list of "fundamental principles and rights at work"? The ILO and most trade unions emphasize that freedom of association and the right to collective bargaining constitute the foundation on which all other rights are built. Others disagree. For example, the World Bank, while increasingly adopting a promotional role with respect to labor standards, hesitates on the links between freedom of association and economic growth. Some argue that ILO Conventions 87 and 98 (Freedom of Association and Protection of the Right to Organize Convention, 1948, and Right to Organize and Collective Bargaining Convention, 1949) ignore the majority of workers in developing countries who are engaged in economic activity in agriculture and the informal sector. Others maintain that the right to a decent livelihood should be a core convention and fundamental human right (see, e.g., Singh and Zammit 2000).

Core labor standards should promote gender equality. Trade unions are becoming strong equality advocates, in part as a response to the rapid rise in labor force participation rates by women, the growing visibility of gender issues in the workplace, and trade union efforts to organize women workers in the informal sector. Minimum wages are particularly important to women, because women predominate in lower-paid work where minimum wages are most relevant. Further, women are less likely to be in unionized sectors, where wages are established through collective bargaining.

While the core ILO conventions do include important antidiscrimination conventions (No. 100, Equal Remuneration for Men and Women Workers, and No. 111, Discrimination Convention), they do not address certain important rights issues of particular concern to women workers. These include occupational health and safety, maternity leave, sexual harassment and physical abuse, reproductive rights, minimum wages, and maximum hours of work. As well, the conventions included in the ILO's *Declaration* do not address the needs of workers in the informal sector, where a majority of the world's workers, and the poorest workers, are to be found. This sector is growing as a result of the changing organization of production by multinational corporations; the exigencies of global competition are pushing workers out of the formal sector, governed by rules and norms, and into the unregulated, unprotected sector. Delocalization of production and the increasing use of subcontractors have contributed to the expansion of the informal sector globally. In high-income countries, about 15 percent of the population is engaged in work outside the formal sector; the figure is 40 percent for middle-income countries and 80 percent for low-income countries (Gallin 1999).[2] A majority of these workers are women.

Workers in the informal sector are in desperate need of the social protection that standards are designed to offer. The 1996 ILO Convention on Homework, for example, recognizes that home workers are entitled to minimum standards established by international law, as well as rights to accessible skills upgrading. The way forward is controversial: ideally, social protection coverage should be universal, at a cost reasonable to workers, employers, and the state. But such a universal scheme may not be realistic; the alternative is a pareddown social protection scheme to which home workers could afford to contribute. Others have warned that voluntary grassroots welfare schemes, mounted by NGOs or worker associations, may be viewed by employers as a cheap substitute for employer-funded social security, thus encouraging firms to informalize more of their activities. Instead, some argue, existing state welfare systems should be extended to all workers.

Protection for migrant workers, whether legally or illegally employed, is also urgently required, as they are frequently denied basic citizenship rights in their country of employment. Their vulnerability is exacerbated by the lack of jurisdiction of the labor-sending country once the workers leave their home country.

The Key Actors

Promoting labor standards will involve organizations working at several levels. Actors whose activities have an impact, direct or indirect, on conditions in workplaces are many and diverse.

The International Financial Institutions

Today, there is growing convergence between the ILO and the international financial institutions on the link between economic and social development, on the one hand, and the promotion of labor standards, on the other. In 1999, the ILO was admitted as an observer to the Development and Interim Committees of the World Bank and IMF, providing an institutional framework for management and staff-level cooperation. Annual meetings of senior leaders of the ILO, World Bank, and IMF provide an opportunity for discussion of pro-labor development strategies. The ILO has urged the Bretton Woods institutions and the United Nations system to speak "with a single voice" on global minimum labor standards. While not insisting that these institutions predicate their funding on whether the recipients enforce core labor standards, the ILO is urging them to integrate these standards into their policies and programs.

The multilateral financial agencies claim they are adopting certain measures to promote labor standards and determine whether their own programs and policies advance labor standards in recipient countries (Gibb and Hutchinson 2000). They include:

- sensitizing staff and management on issues involving core labor standards, including the issue of how they can address these standards in their activities and support the efforts of the ILO;

- enhancing dialogue and consultation with trade unions and nongovernmental organizations engaged in workers' rights issues; and

- considering these standards when revising relevant policy guidelines.

Trade Unions

The changing organization of work, characterized by increasing informality and own-account employment, presents challenges to both the ILO and traditional trade unions. The main challenge for them is to move beyond their traditional base in the formal sector of the economy, and thereby gain legitimacy as a truly representative voice for workers. The ILO is broadening its partnerships: it now embraces nongovernmental organizations and networks of informal workers, such as HomeNet (a network of unions and other associations representing home workers) and WIEGO (Women in Informal Employment: Globalizing and Organizing),[3] which works with women in the informal sector. The ILO, the World Bank, and WIEGO have collaborated on a study of social protection for workers in the informal economy, carried out in connection with the ILO STEP program (Strategies and Tools against Social Exclusion and Poverty) (see Lund and Srinivas 2000; ILO 1999; Gallin 1999). These steps toward more inclusive organizations that address issues of concern to workers in the informal economy are an important beginning.

As well, some trade unions are extending their activities to encompass informal workers. For example, in Canada, the International Ladies Garment Workers Union (ILGWU, now UNITE) dropped its ban on industrial homeworking to allow its Ontario region to launch an organizing campaign among home workers and establish a "pre-union" association in the Chinese-speaking community that supplied the bulk of home workers (Tomei 1999). In Australia, the Textile, Clothing, and Footwear Union organizes home workers in its sector.

And, in Bangkok, TESTU, the Transport and Export Service Trade Union, has extended its support to home-based shoe sewers (mostly wives of TESTU members) by setting up a credit union, encouraging them to lobby for welfare, and raising their concerns (low wages, intermittent work) with suppliers.

The Self-Employed Women's Association (SEWA) in Ahmadabad, India, is an example of a trade union created specifically to organize informal sector workers. Formed twenty-five years ago, SEWA organizes home workers, street vendors, paper pickers, and garbage collectors. It has created a bank providing microcredit, a vocational and trade union training program at different levels, producers' cooperatives, and service cooperatives, such as those for health and housing. SEWA played a central role in instigating the ILO's Home Workers Convention. SEWA is also active at the international level in two networks of informal sector workers: StreetNet (the International Alliance of Street Vendors) and HomeNet.

International Confederation of Free Trade Unions (ICFTU)

Founded in 1949, the ICFTU represents 124 million members in 213 trade unions from 143 countries and territories around the world. Three regional organizations comprise the ICFTU: AFRO, in Africa, APRO, in Asia; and ORIT, which draws in the Americas. The ICFTU has consultative status with the ILO, and has official status as a representative body within the United Nations, its regional bodies, and its specialized agencies, for example, its Economic and Social Committee (ECOSOC). In addition, the ICFTU represents its affiliates in meetings with international institutions such as the IMF, the World Bank, and the WTO.

In its meetings with the World Bank and the IMF, the ICFTU advocates a number of policies to enhance social safety nets, including pensions, unemployment benefits, child support, and sickness and injury benefits. The ICFTU's broader view of how the international financial institutions can promote economic growth also includes calls for programs aimed at maintaining and enhancing school participation, especially for girls; broadening the availability of health care; eliminating the worst forms of child labor; and ensuring that labor market reforms are based on respect for core labor standards.[4]

The Trade Union Advisory Committee (TUAC)

The TUAC acts as an interface between fifty-five trade unions from twenty-nine developed nations and the OECD. The TUAC holds consultative status with the OECD and various specialized agencies within the OECD structure. The TUAC's primary goals are to represent effectively the interests and views of its affiliates in intergovernmental discussions, such as the G-7/G-8

Economic Summits and Employment Conferences, and to advance the social agenda in economic policy debates. Areas of TUAC's recent work include structural adjustment and labor market policies, the impact of globalization on employment, education and training, multinational enterprises, and OECD relations with nonmember countries, particularly countries in Eastern Europe and Asia. Of growing significance is its work on the environment, sustainable development, and the globalization of information.

International Trade Secretariats (ITS)

ITSs, among the oldest international trade union organizations, are industry or sector-based. There were thirty-three international organizations at the end of World War I. Through a process of mergers, which reflects changes in the organization of work, national union mergers, and the need to rationalize scarce resources, the number now stands at around ten. The ICFTU and ITS share similar values. They frequently organize joint campaigns, and work together on complaints to the ILO concerning the violations of trade union rights in particular countries.

Tools to Enhance Labor Standards

International Conventions

The conventions of the ILO, which are negotiated through International Labor Conferences, bind all ratifying member states. The four core labor standards in the ILO Declaration are binding on all ILO members, regardless of whether they have ratified the conventions to which the Declaration refers. However, labor market institutions are at very different stages of development globally. For this reason, the ILO offers technical aid to member states to assist in their implementation of labor standards and ILO conventions.

There are no formal sanctions on countries that fail to implement ILO conventions. Since adoption of conventions is usually voluntary, different governments have committed themselves to different conventions. The ILO monitors the application of labor standards through regular reports on conventions that members have ratified.[5] Specific allegations of violations can be raised through procedures under articles 24 and 26 of the ILO constitution, and allegations concerning infringement of freedom of association principles can be brought against member states even if they have not ratified the conventions concerned. In November 2000, the ILO's governing body took the unprecedented step of calling on the international community to "review" their economic relations with Burma under ILO article 33 because of its failure to comply with Convention No.

29 (forced labor). More recently, the ILO imposed a sanction against Colombia for human rights violations and failure to protect union leaders.

National Legislation

National labor legislation, usually in the form of a labor code, is the mechanism that translates core labor standards into reality. A significant gap in national labor legislation is the lack of protection for the informal sector and some other categories of workers, such as migrant workers. This omission is linked partly to incomplete labor force statistics that omit informal sector workers, a gap that organizations like WIEGO, with the ILO, are working to bridge. Such gaps also reflect disconnects between domestic labor legislation and the changing global labor market, where trade and investment are contributing to growing migration of people within and between regions and countries.

Effective implementation of labor legislation depends on cooperation among the concerned parties—government, workers, and employers. Obviously, in the absence of sufficient numbers of trained and impartial labor inspectors, the enforcement of protective legislation becomes difficult. The ILO offers technical support to national labor ministries in drafting labor legislation that conforms to ILO conventions, and also collaborates with trade unions and NGOs in capacity-building initiatives for local trade union officials. Some developed countries foster developing-country adherence to labor standards by increasing official development assistance allocations to ILO technical assistance programs.

Government Procurement Contracts

The ILO convention 94 on labor clauses in public contracts, which has been ratified by fifty-eight member governments, enjoins governments to ensure the application of industry or national standards for wages, hours, terms and conditions, and health and safety when employing labor to service government contracts (Ladbury and Gibbons 2000). In practice, government departments adopt "harder" or "softer" approaches toward their suppliers of goods and services. Some require only that suppliers be "willing to talk" about labor standards; others apply sanctions for noncompliance with the conditions laid down by the purchasing unit.

Codes of Conduct

In January 1999, at the World Economic Forum in Davos, Switzerland, U.N. Secretary-General Kofi Annan challenged world business leaders to "embrace and enact" a "Global Compact." The compact's nine principles address issues in human rights, labor practices, and the environment. Principles 3-6 specifically focus on core labor standards. A partner in the Global Compact, the ILO has published a study that provides information to companies on how to actualize the nine principles (ILO 2000).

The ICFTU supports the Global Compact as fulfilling a critical need for global dialogue among enterprises, trade unions, and NGOs. It observes, however, that "moral authority from international institutions and voluntary initiatives from companies to protect the rights of the poor and the weak do not balance out binding rules being established at the global level to protect the rights of the rich and the powerful."[6] Some ICFTU member unions and NGOs more strongly object to a compact between the UN and corporations that, they feel, excludes civil society.

Voluntary workplace codes of conduct are another form of self-regulation by transnational corporations. They contain written statements of principles specifying the labor standards that must be enforced by their suppliers and subcontractors. Other mechanisms include social labeling programs, involving the use of a label or logo to indicate the product has been produced on the basis of certain standards. These strategies are sometimes adopted by companies that recognize they can create a niche for their "ethical products" in highly competitive markets. Fair Trade coffee and Rugmark carpets are examples.

The effectiveness of corporate codes of conduct as a mechanism to improve conditions for workers is controversial. There are several questions: how a code should be developed, and by whom; how codes should be implemented, monitored, and by whom; and the nature of the impact of one company's "good practice" in the broader economy.[7] Are there some sectors, such as high-quality sports shoes, where a code of conduct might have more impact than at facilities producing low-cost, low-skill merchandise? How can codes be used to empower workers, particularly in countries where trade unions are banned? Trade unions often stress two points: codes of conduct cannot substitute for union organization; and monitoring is done most effectively by union organizations in the workplace.

A key concern is how to implement codes of conduct so they do not jeopardize the situation of workers further down the supply chain—the informal, home-based workers, who are usually women. In an effort to conform to the terms of a code, suppliers may eliminate outsourcing to home-based workers, thereby depriving them of work. Some of the newer, better codes contain clauses requiring contractors to adopt a "continuous improvement" approach; their contracts will be canceled only when serious breaches of the code persist. These codes also require transitional economic assistance for children found working. Labor organizations and many activists also advocate that the workers themselves be involved in developing a code of conduct to ensure that the code actually addresses workers' priority concerns.

Codes of conduct can sometimes assist workers in developing and strengthening their associations. In countries that ban trade unions, voluntary participation in health and safety committees established to develop a code may precede freely established worker associations. Potential for creative and constructive partnerships among corporations, NGOs, and workers can emerge when a code of conduct is created not solely by outside experts, but with the participation of the workers themselves.

Framework Agreements

Some problems associated with codes of conduct can be overcome by distinguishing between framework agreements and unilaterally adopted company codes of labor practice. A framework agreement is an agreement negotiated between a multinational company and an international trade union organization, such as an international trade secretariat, concerning the international activities of that company. Although an international code of conduct can be part of a framework agreement, the main purpose of the latter is to establish an ongoing relationship between the multinational company and the international trade union organization.[8] For example, the International Federation of Building and Wood Workers (IFBWW) has signed framework agreements on workers' rights with transnational companies such as IKEA (furniture), Faber-Castell (pencils), and Hochtief (construction). Under the terms of the agreement with IKEA, all suppliers and manufacturing companies owned by IKEA are asked to ensure that their working conditions at least comply with national legislation or national agreements. Suppliers must also respect all ILO conventions and recommendations relevant to their operations. This means that child labor is prohibited and that workers have unrestricted rights to join trade unions and to free collective bargaining. The agreement covers almost a million workers in seventy countries.

Conclusions

Promoting core labor standards means putting workers at the center of development. It means a rebalancing of whose interests are traded off in strategies to promote economic growth. It entails a more equal partnership among workers and their associations (including trade unions and civil society organizations), employers, and governments. It also requires the ILO and national governments to extend the rights and principles contained in the ILO's 1998 *Declaration* beyond workers engaged in a traditional employer-employee relationship to include those in the informal sector.

Private companies will be under increasing pressure to comply with widely accepted labor standards. National governments should insist that their nationally based transnational corporations respect such standards in their activities in the South; indeed, there is a growing view that states have obligations to ensure that their citizens and corporations respect human rights abroad, and that international law creates direct obligations for companies. Human rights as set out in the preamble of the Universal Declaration on Human Rights are reflected in the ILO's *Declaration* of 1998. Moreover, the Subcommittee for the Promotion and Protection of Human Rights of the U.N. Commission on Human Rights is presently exploring a binding agreement relating to transnational corporations and other economic units whose activities have an impact on human rights.

Punitive mechanisms linked to trade agreements are too blunt an instrument. Polarizing the labor standards debate around sanctions linked with trade regimes such as the WTO risks sidetracking progress that could be achieved through more representative forums like the ILO, which nonetheless needs teeth and adequate funding from the international community to achieve the goals set out in the *Declaration*. Further, extreme care must be taken to ensure that measures to promote decent work for some workers do not jeopardize the livelihoods of others. A company that cuts orders from a factory failing to meet standards set out in its code may win plaudits back home. But the thousands of developing-country workers left unemployed as a result likely will have been shunted into even worse conditions. A positive, employment-oriented approach at the local, national, and global levels is more likely to prove effective.

Notes

1. Contrast the expeditious out-of-court settlement by the government of Canada to a threatened lawsuit by U.S. manufacturer Ethyl Corporation (see chapter 6) with the dithering over a complaint, filed the same year as the Ethyl complaint (1997), regarding violations of the right of workers to organize and health and safety provisions at a U.S. subsidiary's plant in Ciudad de Los Reyes, Mexico. Years later, on 11 December 2001, a press release from the U.S. Department of Labor announced that its national administrative office had recommended "ministerial consultations" on the case between the U.S. and Mexican labor secretaries!

2. The definition of an "informal sector worker" is vague and controversial. WIEGO defines the informal sector to include the self-employed (in own-account activities and family businesses), paid workers in informal enterprises, unpaid workers in family businesses, casual workers without a fixed employer, and subcontract workers linked to both informal and formal enterprises. Informal workers are not involved in a formal employer-employee relationship and thus are excluded from the social protection provided by national legislation.

3. HomeNet and StreetNet, together with the Self-Employed Women's Association (India), certain other unions, academic institutions, and international development

agencies, have formed WIEGO. WIEGO is concerned with improving statistics, research, programs, and policies in support of women in the informal sector. It collaborates with the ILO and other development agencies in various initiatives.

4. Trade Union Statement to IMF/World Bank Spring Meetings, <http://www.icftu.org>, accessed 30 October 2000.

5. For a discussion of ILO enforcement mechanisms, see ILO 1999.

6. "Global Compact Offers Opportunity for Global Dialogue Say World Union Leaders," ICFTU Online, 28 July 2000, available from <www.ilo.org>.

7. On the impact of codes of conduct on labor standards in Asia, see Adiga 2000, 4; Catholic Institute for International Relations 2000; and Yimprasert and Candland 2000.

8. See Justice 2000.

References

Adiga, Aravind. 2000. "Study Fuels Asian Worker Debate." *Financial Times,* 9 June.

Catholic Institute for International Relations. 2000. "UK Companies Operating in Indonesia." Available from: <http://www.ciir.org/ipd/iej.html>.

Gallin, Dan. 1999. "Notes on Trade Unions and the Informal Sector." Presentation to the ILO Bureau for Workers' Activity (ACTRAV) International Symposium on Trade Unions and the Informal Sector, 18–22 October, Geneva.

Gallin, Dan. 2000. "Trade Unions and NGOs: A Necessary Partnership for Social Development." Civil Society and Social Movements Program Paper No. 1, United Nations Research Institute for Social Development, June.

Gibb, Heather, and Moira Hutchinson. 2000. "Labor Standards and Poverty Reduction: International Strategies." Background Paper prepared for the Workshop on Core Labor Standards and Poverty Reduction, 4–5 December, Aylmer, Quebec. Available from: <http://www.nsi-ins.ca/download/labour.html>.

International Confederation of Free Trade Unions (ICFTU). 2001. *Americas: Annual Survey of Violations of Trade Union Rights.* Washington, D.C.: ICFTU.

International Council on Human Rights. 2001. "Business Wrongs and Rights: Human Rights and the Developing International Legal Obligations of Companies." Draft Report, Switzerland. Available from: <http://www.international-council.org>.

International Labour Office. 1999. "How Are International Labor Standards Enforced?" Available from: <http://www.ilo.org/public/english/standards/norm/enforced/index.htm>.

International Labour Office. 2000. *Companies and Core Labor Standards: An ILO Study.* Available from: http://www.unglobalcompact.com/gc/unweb.nsf/contents/printopract.htm>.

Justice, Dwight W. 2000. "The New Codes of Conduct and the Social Partners." ICFTU. Available from: <http://www.icftu.org>.

Ladbury, Sarah, and Stephen Gibbons. 2000. "Core Labor Standards: Key Issues and a Proposal for a Strategy." Report Submitted to the U.K. Department for International Development, January.

Lund, Frances, and Smita Srinivas. 2000. *Learning from Experience: A Gendered Approach to Social Protection for Workers in the Informal Economy.* Geneva: ILO.

OECD, Trade Directorate, Directorate for Education, Employment, Labor, and Social Affairs. 2000. "International Trade and Core Labor Standards." 20 September. Paris: OECD.

Singh, Ajit, and Ann Zammit. 2000. "The Global Labor Standards Controversy: Critical Issues for Developing Countries." November. South Centre.

Tomei, Manuela. 1999. "Freedom of Association, Collective Bargaining, and Informalization of Employment: Some Issues." Geneva: ILO.

Yimprasert, Junya, and Christopher Candland. 2000. "Can Corporate Codes of Conduct Promote Labor Standards? Evidence from the Thai Footwear and Apparel Industries." 24 February. Hong Kong: Christian Industrial Committee and Asia Monitor Resource Centre.

CHAPTER 6

Protecting the Environment
from Trade Agreements

Michelle Swenarchuk

In 1997, in a landmark case under chapter 11 of the North American Free Trade Agreement (NAFTA), Ethyl Corporation of the United States sued the Canadian government for $250 million. Ethyl Corporation claimed that the Canadian ban of its gasoline additive MMT—on the grounds that this additive was a dangerous nerve toxin—amounted to expropriation under chapter 11. In 1998, Ethyl won a settlement of $13 million in a case conducted in secret in accordance with the treaty's provisions. In addition, the Canadian government reversed its import ban on MMT. This settlement vividly demonstrated, to Canadians and others, how the quest for free trade could undercut hard-won health and environmental protections.

Asserting the primacy of ecological and human well-being in trade agreements is yet another facet of civilizing globalization. One-dimensional treaties have restricted the capacity of democratic governments to legislate in the public interest. Citizens associations have responded to this challenge with strategies to reassert the priority of environmental and health considerations in trade negotiations. This chapter explores both this environmental challenge and the citizen strategies to counter this challenge.

Although the removal of "barriers" to trade may sound benign, a problem arises when free-trade advocates regard national standards and regulations concerning pesticides, the safety of food, air and water, and resource management as "nontariff barriers." Trade negotiators impose "disciplines"—i.e., restrictions—on member governments' power to institute these standards and regulations. Two little-known chapters of WTO agreements and NAFTA—Technical Barriers to Trade (TBT) and Sanitary and Phytosanitary Standards (SPS)—limit member governments' domestic standard setting. We must briefly explore the import of these two highly technical chapters in order to understand the environmentally negative interpretation of existing trade agreements.

75

The Technical Barriers to Trade chapter stipulates certain requirements to which governments must adhere in establishing domestic regulations and standards:

- They should not create unnecessary obstacles to international trade; however, measures are permitted to meet legitimate objectives that include "protection of human health or safety, animal or plant life or health, or the environment."

- Emphasizing international harmonization measures, the TBS chapter requires that measures be based on science and comply with existing international standards.

- Domestic standards bodies, both governmental and nongovernmental, must comply with the TBT and related Codes of Good Practice (TBT 4).

- The International Organization for Standardization (ISO) is recognized as an international standard-setter. This organization facilitates commerce through establishing common technical requirements for many goods. Although its standards are voluntary, they are widely used by industries.

The Sanitary and Phytosanitary Standards chapter, for its part, establishes a comprehensive set of rules to govern countries' domestic SPS measures concerning plant and animal health, such as food safety and pesticide regulations. International bodies, such as Codex Alimentarius, a Rome-based UN agency, are named as standard-setters for national legislation and regulations in these areas.

Critics claim that the setting of national standards under these circumstances biases the WTO and NAFTA against environmental and health concerns and in favor of freer trade. Common complaints include these four concerns:

- The removal of standard-setting to inaccessible international bodies, such as the ISO and Codex Alimentarius, inhibits the capacity of nationally based public interest groups to improve health and environmental standards.

- Standards drafted by international bodies to ease trade barriers may be too general to permit rigorous application at the national level.

- Governments weaken environmental and health standards by increasingly forgoing national standards in favor of voluntary corporate standards, such as "codes of conduct."

- Corporate lobbyists wield considerable influence over government regulators.

Having sketched some of the technical background to the setting of national standards, we can now consider how, in practice, liberalizing trade has taken precedence over environmental and health concerns *despite* national safeguards.

GATT/WTO Cases Involving Environment and Health

An "environment and health" clause has existed in GATT since 1948. GATT article XX provides that countries may take measures necessary to protect public morals (XXa) and human, animal, or plant life or health (XXb), and to conserve exhaustible natural resources (XXg)—provided such measures are neither discriminatory nor a disguised restriction on international trade. The SPS and TBT chapters contain similar protective clauses. Yet, in practice, governments have rarely successfully justified health or environmental protections on the basis of their "necessity" to the public welfare—though they have pleaded "necessity" in numerous disputes, both under GATT prior to 1994, and since then under the WTO.

The most significant GATT decisions include these three:

- 1991 and 1994: On two occasions, U.S. prohibitions under the Marine Mammals Protection Act on imports of tuna caught with purse-seine nets that caused dolphin deaths were disallowed.

- 1990: Thailand's prohibitions on the import of cigarettes were ruled not "necessary" within GATT XX(b), though chemicals and other additives in U.S. cigarettes may have been more harmful than those in Thai cigarettes.

- 1994: The U.S. Corporate Average Fuel Economy regulation could not be justified under GATT XX(d). This regulation specified the permissible level of average fuel economy for passenger cars, both imported and domestic. However, the trade panel ruled that elements of accounting and averaging practices discriminated against foreign producers.

Four key WTO cases since 1994 follow the same pattern of freer trade trumping environmental issues:

- 1996: U.S. Regulations under the Clean Air Act designed to reduce air pollution were held to contravene GATT requirements to treat imported products like domestic ones, and were deemed not permissible.

- 1998: The European Union (EU) ban of five hormones in beef was deemed inconsistent with the SPS. (Despite this decision, the EU has not revoked the ban, and is currently subject to trade sanctions from the United States)

- 1998: U.S. prohibitions under the Endangered Species Act on shrimp imports caught without turtle-excluder devices were ruled unjustified under GATT XX.

- 2001: In the only case to uphold a defense based on "necessity," a French directive banning chrysotile asbestos, challenged by Canada, was deemed legitimate under GATT XX.

These cases demonstrate the extreme difficulty countries encounter when justifying a challenged regulation as "necessary." This generalization holds true even for an issue related to health or the environment that is deemed a "legitimate objective" in the TBT, SPS, and GATT XX. The single panel decision in favor of a challenged measure—the French directive banning chysolite asbestos—does not detract from one obvious conclusion. Claims of "necessity" do not constitute a reliable basis for defending domestic standards of public protection.

NAFTA Chapter 11 Investor-State Cases

The investment chapter (11) is NAFTA's most notorious source of conflict between environmental laws, on the one hand, and trade and investment agreements, on the other. Not even environmentalists foresaw its potential negative impact when NAFTA was negotiated in 1994. Chapter 11 prohibits governments from imposing "performance requirements" (NAFTA 1106) on foreign investors. Governments may not stipulate any of the following conditions: that foreign investors use domestic content and purchasing; that their operations generate certain levels of foreign exchange flows; or that investors transfer technology, production processes, or other business knowledge to the host country. (Technology transfer is particularly important for dissemination of green technologies.) Chapter 11 also allows foreign investors—though not domestic ones—to sue national governments directly for virtually any action that decreases their expected profits, alleging "expropriation" or "measures tantamount" to expropriation (NAFTA 1110). Countries may implement measures to achieve public goals, but only if these measures are nondiscriminatory, follow due process of law, and compensate foreign investors for lost potential profits.

At the time of the abortive negotiations for a Multinational Agreement on Investment (MAI) in 1997–98, only one NAFTA investment case was under-way—the Ethyl Corporation case discussed above. Yet even this single case provided a potent argument against the MAI. The case undermined support for MAI, because the latter's investment clauses were similar to those in NAFTA that had encouraged Ethyl to sue Canada. MAI negotiators expressed their con-sternation at a meeting with NGOs in Paris (October 1997) at the Organization of Economic Cooperation and Development. As Jan Huner, secretary to the chair of the MAI negotiations, later reported (Huner 1998), this meeting was "decisive." Certain points that environmentalists raised persuaded "many NG [Negotiating Group] members that a few draft provisions, particularly those on expropriation and on performance requirements, could be interpreted in unex-pected ways." The Ethyl Corporation dispute, Huner believed, should act as a warning. Ethyl had claimed, successfully as it turned out, that the Canadian ban on a gasoline additive on health grounds amounted to an expropriation. "MAI negotiators should think twice before copying the expropriation provisions of the NAFTA," Huner concluded.

Huner's report confirms that some governments could see the danger of even *one* problematical expropriation claim by a corporation. However, by early 2001 the number of such investment cases under NAFTA had climbed to sixteen. Decisions are reached in confidential and inaccessible arbitral proceedings (in contrast to the open proceedings in domestic courts). Thus, the information on these cases is sketchy. We do know that by 2001, four corporations (in addition to Ethyl, discussed above) had successfully sued NAFTA member-governments, claiming expropriation due to protective environmental or health measures. These cases are disheartening to those who believe that the latter measures should not take second place to the goal of enhancing free trade and investment.

1. S.D. Myers. U.S.-based S. D. Myers demanded $30 million for losses allegedly incurred during an eighteen-month ban (1995 to 1997) on the export of PCB wastes from Canada,[1] a ban justified by Canada as complying with the Basel Convention on the Control of Transboundary Movements of Hazardous Wastes and Their Disposal. In November 2000, the arbitral tribunal ruled that the ban contravened the investment chapter; it is now determining whether S. D. Myers suffered damages. Meanwhile, the Canadian government asked the (domestic) federal court to set aside the tribunal's partial award.[2] It argued two points: the case concerned cross-border trade, not a Canadian investment; and the award conflicts with a well-established Canadian policy requiring disposal of PCBs and PCB wastes in Canada in accordance with the Basel Convention on the Control of Transboundary Movements of Hazardous Wastes and Their Disposal.

2. Sun Belt Water, Inc. This California-based corporation is suing Canada for between $1 billion and $10.5 billion over British Columbia's refusal to

allow the company's bulk export of the province's water.[3] This colorful case alleges a decade of dubious actions by successive provincial governments; Sun Belt Water claims extravagant improprieties by the B.C. government and courts. In a B.C. court action, Sun Belt did not achieve its desired result. It is, therefore, using NAFTA chapter 11 to attempt to circumvent this decision.

3. Methanex Corp. This Vancouver-based company sued the U.S. government for $970 million, challenging a California state order to phase out use of the chemical MTBE (methyl tertiary butyl), a methanol-based gas additive, by late 2002. The governor of California called MTBE "a significant risk to California's environment," fearing its potential for water pollution.

In a letter of 31 January, 2001 to U.S. Trade Representative Robert Zoellick, fourteen California assembly members and senators expressed concern regarding the Methanex case, noting that both houses had passed resolutions in which they expressed their misgivings about the challenge. Of particular concern was the "second-guessing" of democratic decision-making:

> We . . . find it problematic to be told by remote and un-elected trade officials what paradigms or standards we must apply in writing environmental and public health laws for the people of our state. We further believe that since decisions about the level of risk to which a populace shall be exposed are ultimately a matter of values, such decisions are best made by elected officials in accessible and democratic fora.[4]

This case has not yet been resolved.

4. Metalclad. U.S.-based Metalclad, a waste disposal company, sued the Mexican government for $90 million. It claimed that the Mexican state of San Luis Potosi breached chapter 11 of NAFTA in refusing permission for a waste disposal facility. Metalclad began construction of the facility without having local approvals, claiming that it had assurances from the Mexican federal government. In August 2000, a tribunal found that Mexico had breached the investment chapter and awarded Metalclad $16.7 million, the amount it had spent in construction. The Mexican government appealed the award to the Supreme Court of British Columbia, on the grounds that the case was heard in British Columbia and that the Canadian government and government of Quebec had intervened.[5] The appeal was unsuccessful.

These and other recent cases have had a chilling effect on environmental protection. Of the sixteen current cases under NAFTA's purview, eight concern businesses with environmental implications: toxics, waste management, and resource management. Three cases attempt to circumvent domestic court decisions. To date, Canada has already changed two environmental laws (the MMT and PCB regulations) due to these challenges, and still faces billions of dollars in potential liabilities. Governments are unlikely to protect health and the environment if green measures entail possible multi-million-dollar price tags.

In response to the cases against Canada and NGO criticisms, the Canadian government negotiated with the U.S. and Mexican governments from 1998 to 2001 to amend the investor-state expropriation wording. Specifically, Canada attempted to restrict the scope of chapter 11; it endeavored to ensure that normal regulatory measures by government would not require compensating investors for alleged potential losses. However, these efforts failed. Then, in April 2001, the Canadian government reversed its position. Contradicting his trade minister, Prime Minister Jean Chrétien stated that the chapter is working "reasonably well" and that Canada was no longer attempting to limit these corporate claims. Despite the numerous suits against it, Canada is apparently unable to learn the lesson that other OECD members learned from the 1997 Ethyl lawsuit.

Citizen Strategies to Constrain Trade Agreements

Citizen strategies can be summarized as "dialogue within, and protests in the streets." To conduct a genuine dialogue with governmental and corporate leaders, NGOs are essentially demanding the global equivalent of domestic democratic rights. Their campaign involves, in addition to the dramatic street protests at official international gatherings, these proposals:

- the release of negotiating texts of global trade and investment agreements;
- the dissemination of informed NGO critiques of draft agreements;
- participation in trade negotiations;
- involvement in dispute-settlement hearings;
- the negotiation of new United Nations conventions to bolster protection for health, environment, and culture vis-à-vis trade law.

Access to Information and Participation by Citizen Groups

Transparency in negotiations of trade and investment agreements is fundamental to asserting a measure of popular control over trade. Uninformed citizens cannot assess the stakes involved in a particular bargaining position. Yet negotiations and dispute settlement continue to be held in camera. Fortunately, the "porous" quality of the U.S. government provided many sources of trade policy information in the 1990s; indeed, both NAFTA and MAI were leaked late in the negotiation process. Today, the number and variety of negotiations occurring globally virtually guarantee leaks.

Internationally, groups now demand the release of negotiating texts early in the process to enable citizen response prior to key governmental decisions. Across the Western Hemisphere, groups cooperated to demand the "liberation of texts" of the Free Trade Area of the Americas. These demands led to an official commitment to make them public. Citizens have closely scrutinized their governments' positions on recent preparations for negotiation of a new General Agreement on Trade in Services at the WTO. Indeed, they have pressed for access to official texts. Acknowledging the value of informed citizens' critiques during the MAI process, French officials even recommended that the government engage more lawyers and analysts to deepen its own understanding.

Citizens also require a seat at the negotiating table. The negotiation of United Nations conventions offers an alternative model of international treaty-making to the prevalent top-down, secret model of trade negotiations. The Cartagena Protocol on Biosafety, concluded in Montreal in January 2000 under the Convention on Biological Diversity, is typical. This protocol, explicitly both a trade and an environmental treaty, deals with the use and transboundary movements of living, genetically modified organisms. Trade interests played a prominent role in the negotiations. Nevertheless, in keeping with U.N. processes, the negotiations were conducted in sessions open to NGOs. They were given full access to negotiating texts, in six languages, and could speak in certain plenary sessions. Although only government officials could comment in certain negotiation meetings, NGOs could attend all the sessions. Public access was limited only by the size of rooms, not by policies of secrecy. NGOs were also free to meet with government officials outside the negotiation sessions to not only lobby but also conduct press briefings and demonstrations outside the buildings (in the minus-40-degree temperatures!). They provided many scientific and technical briefings in the U.N. building and valuable material and technical support to delegates, particularly from developing countries (Egziabher 2000). No windows were broken. No security costs were incurred. And a treaty was successfully concluded.

Access to the Dispute-Settlement Process

NGOs have attempted to intervene in NAFTA investment-dispute processes, both at the tribunal and domestic court levels. In 2001, they obtained the right to file "amicus" (friend of the court) briefs in one NAFTA case. Similarly, they filed amicus briefs in WTO dispute panels, beginning in 1998 when the WTO Appellate Body determined that dispute panels could consider such submissions. However, in late 2000, when the Appellate Body issued procedural guidelines for groups wishing to be heard on the appeal of the *Asbestos* case, Egypt and other developing countries requested a special session of the WTO General Council to oppose this decision.[6] Certain WTO member-countries felt that the extension of intervention rights to NGOs both conflicts with the government-to-government structure of the WTO, and gives NGOs rights exceeding those of WTO member-governments. General Council discussion was acrimonious, and members castigated the Appellate Body for its actions. Now, the dispute panels will hear submissions only from the parties involved—that is, the countries in which the trade dispute originates and additional countries that demonstrate a substantive trade interest in the dispute. Countries may not join the Appellate Body hearings unless they were parties before the panel whose decision is under appeal. All NGO requests to be heard on the *Asbestos* case were subsequently refused. As certain governments strongly object to NGOs making direct submissions to the Appellate Body, the prospects of this strategy of gaining citizen access to the dispute-settlement process are dim.

Restraining the Trade Regime through New International Conventions

As governments and communities increasingly experience the negative impact of free trade on environmental protection, human rights, health, and labor policy, they recognize the need to restrain trade and investment regimes. Since amending the WTO agreements would require the unanimous agreement of some 140 countries, this approach is unviable. Initiatives to limit the scope of these agreements through new international law, together with attempts to achieve the primacy of existing international conventions over WTO agreements, offer more hope. The requisite principle, as described by two proponents with particular reference to human rights, is this: "In the event of a conflict between a universally recognized human right and a commitment ensuing from international treaty law such as a trade agreement, the latter must be interpreted to be consistent with the former. When properly interpreted and applied, the trade regime recognizes that human rights are fundamental and prior to free trade itself" (Howse & Mutua 2000, 5).

Negotiations over two recent conventions illustrate what is at stake. In January 2000, negotiators for 160 countries concluded a new convention, the Cartagena Protocol on Biosafety; it established an international regulatory system to govern the use of, and trade in, genetically modified organisms such as seeds. Later that year, the Convention on Persistent Organic Pollutants (POPs), regulating the use and transfer of twelve toxic organic substances, was concluded. Both conventions authorize countries to regulate imports and exports of these substances; the goal is to protect human health and the environment. However, trade negotiators attempted to stipulate that a government's decision-making under the conventions would be limited by WTO agreements. They tried to block wording giving countries wider scope to emphasize health and the environment in decisions regarding this trade. They did not succeed, however.

No language in the final Biosafety Protocol subordinates the convention to the WTO agreements, despite efforts by the United States and Canada to include such wording. In the final hours of negotiation, however, such wording was inserted in the preamble (where it has little enforceable effect). This excerpt clearly illustrates the clash of priorities as set out in the preamble:

> <u>Recognizing</u> that trade and environment agreements should be mutually supportive with a view to achieving sustainable development, <u>Emphasizing</u> that this Protocol shall not be interpreted as implying a change in the rights and obligations of a party under any existing international agreements,
> <u>Understanding</u> that the above recital is not intended to subordinate this Protocol to other international agreements. . . .

Equally as important, the protocol adopted a higher standard of precaution in environmental decision-making. It specifies:

> Lack of scientific certainty due to insufficient relevant scientific information and knowledge regarding the extent of the potential adverse effects of a living modified organism on the conservation and sustainable use of biological diversity in the Party of import, taking also into account risks to human health, shall not prevent that party from taking a decision, as appropriate, with regard to the import of the living modified organism in question . . . in order to avoid or minimize such potential adverse effects. (Article 6)

This article is certainly positive from the viewpoint of health and environmental protection.

Similarly, in the POPs convention, the trade language appears only in the preamble: "Recognizing that this Convention and other international agreements in the field of trade and the environment are mutually supportive. . . ." But the Objective of the Convention leaves little doubt that the thrust of the agreement is to safeguard health, not establish the priority of freer trade. "Mindful of the precautionary approach as set forth in Principle 15 of the Rio Declaration on Environment and Development," states clause B, "the objective of this Convention is to protect human health and the environment from persistent organic pollutants."

The Biosafety Protocol also includes a potential strategy for protecting domestic decision-making from trade challenges. The regime it envisages for regulation of genetically modified organisms permits countries to continue governing this trade under current domestic laws. Both Canada and the EU can be expected to do so. If their decisions under national laws are challenged at the WTO—a realistic possibility, given continuing disputes between the EU and the United States of America—the defendants may invoke the Biosafety Protocol as a "safety blanket" or shield in international law, supporting its decisions vis-à-vis the WTO. In short, the multiple approaches of the protocol offer ideas for constraining the WTO's efforts to nullify democratically instituted national laws.

Building on the lessons of the Biosafety Protocol and POPs treaty, Canadian NGOs have recommended wording for negotiators of conventions on tobacco control and cultural diversity; they hope to stave off WTO-based challenges to national regulations in these areas. Ironically, citizens may increasingly need to participate in the time-consuming, expensive and unpredictable processes of international law-making in order to safeguard their democratic right to public-interest regulation at home.

Conclusion

Discussions of trade and environment issues grind on in the Committee on Trade and Environment at the WTO and at the NAFTA Commission on Environmental Co-operation; yet neither of these institutions has mitigated the accelerating global environmental decline. Few citizens' groups now expect to see such high-level policy discussions produce adequate environmental and health protections. Instead, they have turned to their own strategies of intervention in whatever forums are available to them. In such action there is scope for transcending the rigidities and nondemocratic values of the trade regimes. In particular, NGOs are focusing on building U.N. law and institutions that will ensure the priority of fundamental human rights and needs over freer trade and investment. Despite their faults, such initiatives offer some of our best hopes for civilizing globalization.

Notes

1. "Notice of Intent to Submit a Claim to Arbitration under Section B of Chapter 11 of the North American Free Trade Agreement," *Americas Trade*, 3 September, 1998; "US Firm Hits Ottawa with NAFTA Lawsuit," Toronto *Globe and Mail*, 21 August, 1998; and "US company Files Suit Under NAFTA," *Canadian Press,* 30 October, 1998.

2. Canada, Department of Foreign Affairs and International Trade, "Canada Seeks Review of NAFTA Award in S. D. Myers Case," 8 February, 2001, Document No. iwp2001_0714; and "Canada Looks to Its Courts to Limit NAFTA Investor-State Disputes," *Inside US Trade*, 23 February, 2001.

86   *Michelle Swenarchuk*

3. "Notice of Intent to Submit a Claim to Arbitration between Sun Belt Water, Inc. and Her Majesty the Queen in Right of Canada," 27 November, 1998.

4. Letter of 31 January, 2001 to Robert Zoellick, U.S. Trade Representative, from California Speaker Fred Keeley (D) and others.

5. Supreme Court of British Columbia, No. L002904, In the Matter of an Arbitration Pursuant to Chapter 11 of the North American Free Trade Agreement, Between Metalclad Corporation and the United Mexican States, ICSID Additional Facility Case No. Arb.(Af)/97/1. The appeal is based on NAFTA 1136.

6. "Amicus Brief Storm Highlights WTO's Unease with External Transparency," *Bridges Weekly Trade News Digest* 4, no. 9 (November–December 2000): 1, 4; and Appellate Body document WT/DS135/9.

References

Egziabher, T. B. G. 2000. "Civil Society and the Cartagena Protocol on Biosafety." Prepared for Forum 2000, 1–3 October, Montreal.

Howse, Robert, and Makau Mutua. 2000. *Protecting Human Rights in a Global Economy: Challenges for the World Trade Organization*. Montreal: International Centre for Human Rights and Democratic Development.

Huner, Jan. 1998. "Trade, Investment, and the Environment." Royal Institute for International Affairs, 27–30 October, Chatham House, London.

CHAPTER 7

Financing the Transition to a Low-Carbon Future

Rodney R. White

That climate change is already underway and that its impacts will be diverse and onerous are views that are now rarely disputed (Firor 1990; Strzepek and Smith 1995; Watson, Zinyowera, and Moss 1998; Harvey 2000). Hence, a scheme aimed at drastically reducing the greenhouse gas emissions implicated in this crisis is central to any "survival guide" for the twenty-first century.

Despite the stakes for all of us, this threat has not yet evoked a unified or adequate response. Governments of wealthy industrial countries refuse to contemplate significant reductions in their own greenhouse gas emissions.[1] They fear that such actions would be expensive to implement, erode their country's competitive position in the global economy, and prove unpopular with the voters. However, they do appear willing to invest in emission reduction in developing countries, on the economic grounds that it will be cheaper to do so there because energy usage is currently more wasteful than in the major industrial economies of Japan, North America, and Europe. Whatever the merits of this argument, the rich countries are at least prepared to invest something in developing countries in order to avoid, or postpone, the unpopular alternative of major emission reductions at home. But developing countries, in turn, demand that the major polluters, the industrial countries, clean up their own act before demanding remedial action by the late-developers.

How do we escape this impasse? At least a partial solution may prove feasible: a financial transfer scheme that generates powerful incentives for environmental protection in both North and South.

Dimensions of the Problem

The Sixth Conference of the Parties to the UN Framework Convention on Climate Change ended in November 2000 at The Hague, having failed to reach agreement.[2] This failure, though disappointing, surprised no one, because of the deep divisions among the delegates. (The conference at The Hague was a follow-up to the 1997 Conference of Parties to the UN Framework Convention on Climate Change [COP3] in Kyoto, which had adopted a protocol proposing national emission targets [Nicholls 2001, 16]). Few OECD members have yet ratified the Kyoto protocol.

Many factors contribute to the difficulty of reaching an agreement on reducing global greenhouse-gas emissions. Both the magnitude of the problem and the large number of participants complicate the quest for a solution. The problem is embedded in the very technology that facilitated the modernization process, specifically in the provision of cheap energy from the combustion of fossil fuels. These fuels are the major sources of power for the world's manufacturing, transport, and the heating and cooling of buildings. The technological transition to the postfossil fuel economy is the equivalent of moving directly from the Stone Age to the Iron Age. As "business as usual" is destabilizing the global climate, this change must be accomplished as swiftly as possible. A further complication is the vast number of participants; COP6 (Conference of Parties to the U.N. Framework Convention on Climate Change) involved over seven thousand participants from 182 governments, 323 intergovernmental and nongovernmental organizations, and 443 media outlets (IISD 2000). All global citizens—and the generations to come—are stakeholders in this enormous challenge.

An even more substantial obstacle to an agreement on climate change is the giant differences of opinion over how to proceed. These differences may be grouped into two major conflicts. The first, and least serious, conflict divides the industrial nations, pitting the JUSSCANNZ group against the European Union. (JUSSCANNZ comprises Japan, the United States, Switzerland, Canada, Australia, Norway, and New Zealand, usually led by the United States [Grubb, with Vrolijk and Breck 1999, xxxi]). As this group generally views climate change as less serious than does the European Union, it favors small, incremental measures to reduce greenhouse-gas emissions. These nations contend that every approach—*other than* major domestic reduction of emissions from fossil fuel use—should be used to achieve compliance with the protocol. Thus, JUSSCANNZ supports the inclusion of land-use changes that might reduce carbon emissions. These embody measures such as naturally occurring afforestation, conversion of croplands to pasture, credits for supporting emission reduction in other countries, and widespread trading of emission reduction credits—including the spurious credits known as "hot air" arising from the economic contraction of formerly communist countries in Europe. These nations deny the need for any kind of carbon tax on the grounds that raising production costs would undermine their economic competitiveness. Furthermore, the United States still presses for a commitment to emission reduction from developing countries, even though they were not signatories to the Kyoto Protocol.

In contrast, many members of the European Union have already introduced some form of carbon taxes, including the United Kingdom, which is
probably closest to the JUSSCANNZ position. The European Union generally
recognises that any serious approach to mitigating climate change must involve
a significant reduction in the domestic use of fossil fuels; this reduction must
take place before any commitment to reductions can be expected from the developing world. Observers should be leery of applauding Europe for its more
positive approach. The contrast in attitude might simply be ascribed to the extreme weather Europe has endured over the last decade.

The division within the industrial world is minor, however, compared with
the gulf between it and the developing countries.[3] This conflict springs from the
history of the last three centuries, an era during which the present-day rich
countries became rich through their own technological transformation, coupled
with their colonial exploitation. Now that the dangerous side effects of fossil-
fuel technology are obvious, industrial nations must address the consequences
of their unbridled destruction of the global resource base in the pursuit of short-
term profits. The poorer countries of the world have shown little reluctance to
exploit this irony. As Ivan Head (1991) has observed, North and South exist in
"mutual vulnerability."

Among developing countries, dissent abounds. The rich OPEC countries
of the Middle East are among the dissenters, demanding compensation for lost
oil revenues that would result from the implementation of the protocol. The
most vulnerable members are small island states and countries with large populations in vulnerable coastal zones, such as Egypt and Bangladesh. This group
also includes industrial powers like Mexico, Brazil, and Argentina—all of
which have indicated some willingness to accept responsibilities under the protocol. Most significantly, it includes China, whose carbon dioxide emissions
are predicted to equal those of the United States by the year 2020, under the
"business as usual" scenario (Logan et al. 1999, 2).

Table 7.1 illustrates an important element of the difficulty in reaching
agreement. China and India are among the largest emitters of carbon dioxide by
virtue of their huge populations. Yet, in per capita terms, China produces only
one-tenth of the emissions of the United States, while India produces only one-
tenth that of the Russian Federation.

If these divisions were not impediment enough, other contentious issues
bedevil the quest to reduce greenhouse emissions. One factor is population
growth. Population growth, largely in the developing countries, will be a major
driver behind increasing carbon dioxide emissions (White 2000). Thus, the
climate change issue is one more reason why the basic condition that supports
population growth—namely poverty—remains as urgent a problem as ever. If
rights to carbon dioxide emissions are eventually accorded to countries on an
equal per capita basis, then stabilizing the size of the national populations

Table 7.1
Carbon Dioxide Emissions by Countries Grouped by Income,
and the Six Largest Emitters in 1996

	TOTAL IN BILLION TONS		*TONS PER CAPITA*	
COUNTRIES	*1980*	*1996*	*1980*	*1996*
Grouped				
Low income	2.1	5.1	0.9	1.5
Middle income	2.8	6.9	3.3	4.8
High income	8.7	10.7	12.3	12.3
World Total	13.6	22.6	3.4	4.0
Six largest				
United States	4.6	5.3	20.1	20.0
China	1.5	3.4	1.5	2.8
Russian Fed.	. . .	1.6	. . .	10.7
Japan	0.9	1.2	7.9	9.3
India	0.3	1.0	0.5	1.1
Germany	. . .	0.9	. . .	10.5

Source: World Bank (2000), table 10. Energy use and emissions, pages 248–49.

becomes crucial. No control system will work if it is based on the per capita rights of a growing population. This very difficult issue has not yet been aired during the Conference of the Parties to the UN Framework Convention on Climate Change (COP) process.

A second requirement for success in controlling emissions is the delinking of economic growth from rising carbon dioxide emissions. In the last 150 years, these two variables have become interlocked. Some measure of economic growth is needed to reduce poverty, but growth must be based on low-carbon, or no-carbon, technology. Although all parties implicitly understand this fact, the implications have not been discussed at COP meetings.

A third untouched issue concerns the most appropriate entity to implement emission reductions. Because the debate is conducted as an international agreement, it has been assumed that national governments would implement any enforcement. Although there has been some limited recognition of the important role to play of private companies, there has been less recognition of the potential contribution of municipalities and NGOs. Unfortunately, the critical role of the choices and behavior of *individuals* has not been addressed in the COP forum.

A Modest Proposal

Certain national governments have already committed themselves to reduce their bureaucracies' energy use. For example, the Canadian federal government has pledged that 20 percent of its in-house energy use will come from renewable energy. (This undertaking is rather different from pledging to reduce greenhouse gas emissions; but it is an indicator of concern.) This vow is a reminder that emissions can only be reduced by their creators, including government services, private corporations, and individuals. Effective action to diminish emissions must reach down from the international negotiations to the actual energy user. This task might be accomplished in a variety of ways.

Figure 7.1 describes a financial transfer scheme that could lead to a steady reduction of emissions. The plan offers strong incentives for environmental protection, yet recognizes that poverty in developing countries is an abiding problem that is central to the climate change issue. It also recognizes that there are rich countries (emitting a great deal of carbon per capita) and poor countries (emitting very little per capita). Finally, it notes that, within each country, there is energy behavior that ranges from "carbon guzzler" through "carbon modest." The purpose of the scheme is to oblige all entities (governmental, corporate, individual) that emit carbon dioxide to pay something for their environmental impact. That is, they will internalize the climate change risk, and pay in proportion to their contribution to the problem. Those who emit very little relative to the norm will receive a rebate. Such a transfer mechanism would not only encourage entities to emit less, it would also encourage those who are "carbon frugal" or "carbon modest" to maintain their positive behavior.

The incentive to remain frugal is essential if we are to avoid a scenario in which the technology transfer envisaged by the Kyoto Protocol actually results in developing countries emitting *more* carbon dioxide. This situation could easily materialize when the inefficient factories and vehicles are converted to more efficient use of fuel. This development is especially likely if those savings are swamped by a rise in prosperity that encourages more consumption on the Western model. If this scenario eventuates, we would witness the type of global transformation we have seen in the transportation sector in the West; automobile engines become more efficient, but there are more of them and they are driven farther, thus producing a net increase in emissions.

Implementation of the proposal requires the following steps to be adopted at the international level:

1. Agreement must be reached on the "global carbon allowance" separating the rich countries that would pay into the Global Carbon Fund from the poor countries that would draw from the fund. For the sake of a simple illustration, this allowance is taken as one ton

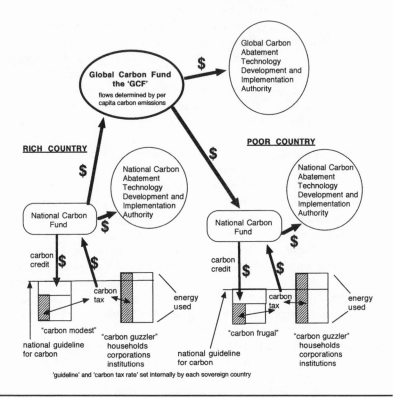

Figure 7.1
CARATS Carbon Abatement: Regulation and Transfer Scheme

of carbon emitted per person per year (see table 7.2). Countries whose per capita emissions exceed one ton would pay in, while those with less would receive payments from the fund.

2. Not all the money collected by the fund would be distributed to poorer countries. A portion—50 percent in this example—would be awarded to an international clean technology authority that would support research and implementation in low-carbon technology.

3. Agreement must also be reached on the "transfer rate" per ton of carbon above or below the amount set by the global carbon allowance. The amount a country would pay in, or receive, would

then be calculated as follows. It would equal *the product of the difference between their national per capita emission and the global allowance, multiplied by the population of the country* (set at a fixed number, such as the 1990 population, taking the same date as the baseline used for calculating carbon dioxide reductions in the Kyoto process), *multiplied by the transfer rate.*

Table 7.2 works through an example of this process for five countries—two industrial countries paying in, and three developing countries receiving compensation for their low-carbon lifestyle. Per capita carbon emissions would need to continue to be audited annually. Either the allowance or the transfer rate (or both) could be adjusted by agreement to progressively reduce global carbon dioxide emissions, while keeping the fund solvent.

The question of how the rich countries would raise money to meet their obligations to the fund, and how poor countries would allocate the money they received, is a significant one. This matter could be left entirely as an internal decision, thereby retaining an important degree of national sovereignty. For the sake of completion of the example, this proposal supports a simple replication of the international transfer mechanism at the national level. Each country could determine its own allowance level and transfer rate. The money could be collected on the major greenhouse gas–emitting activities in the country such as gasoline, home heating oil, and electricity. The "carbon modest" in the rich countries could apply for a rebate on their annual income tax form, attaching their annual receipts. In poorer countries where income tax is less common, the benefits could be distributed in the form of communal infrastructure such as schools, clinics, and water supply. The rich would pay a fee on the Western-style energy that they purchase for their automobiles and air conditioners. Again, the allowance and the transfer could be reassessed at whatever frequency desired.

Such a proposal may appear too complicated. There are two simple ripostes to this view. Firstly, the proposal is *infinitely* simpler than the mechanism currently under discussion in the COP process. Remember that much of the quarrel between the JUSSCANNZ group and the European Union revolved around the relative carbon emissions involved in various types of land use such as forest, cropland, and pasture. The measurement problems associated with these calculations are enormous, even on a scientifically managed experimental site. It is almost inconceivable that France and the United States, for example, would agree, each year, on the exact weight to be assigned to a multiplicity of carbon sinks and carbon sources. Secondly, the collection and transfer mechanisms needed to implement the proposal domestically are already in place through such instruments as value-added tax and income tax. At the international level, we would need only to agree on the 1990 figures for national populations and the annual amount of

Table 7.2
Examples of Financial Transfers under the CARATS Mechanism

Conditions
1. Global "Carbon Allowance" set at **one metric ton** of carbon per person per year.
2. "Transfer Rate" set at **U.S. $100 per ton**.
3. Contributions allocated at **50:50** between the Global Carbon Fund and the Abatement Authority (shown in figure 7.1).

Examples of Contributing Countries

Country	Population (millions in in 1995)	Metric Tons of Carbon (pp pa)	Excess over "Allowance"	Total "Transfer" × $100	To the Fund	To the Authority
CANADA	28	4.04	3.04	$8.5bn	$4.25bn	$4.25bn
USA	263	5.27	4.27	$112.3bn	$56.15bn	$56.15bn

Examples of Receiving Countries

Country	Population (millions in in 1995)	Metric Tons of Carbon (pp pa)	Below the "Allowance"	Amount Received × $50
KENYA	28	0.07	0.93	$1.3bn
CHINA	1,238	0.70	0.30	$18.6bn
INDIA	931	0.27	0.73	$34.0bn

energy used, which is published regularly. This approach would produce far less acrimony than seeking agreement on the amount of methane emitted from paddy rice and cattle that equaled carbon emitted by forest fires.

In additional to its stark simplicity, the proposal includes a number of significant advantages that would help us finance our way to a low-carbon global future. The proposal allows for the intervention of municipalities and NGOs in the field of energy conservation through encouraging building retrofits, offering low-emission transport options, and educating the public on the need for change. The best available technology could be funded through the proposed national carbon abatement technology authority. Through this mechanism, we could create two forces to move society towards a low-carbon lifestyle. The payment of the energy levy would encourage all users—corporate, institutional, and individual—to reduce energy use, while at the same time providing the funds to make the transition affordable. The price signals would be reversed from their current direction, in which most countries subsidize the production of fossil fuels and nuclear fuels, as well as subsidizing a fossil-fuel-based transport system.

Furthermore, the CARAT mechanism could operate in a complementary fashion to other emission reduction strategies such as the Kyoto Protocol with whatever combination of "joint implementation," "clean development mechanism," and emissions trading regime proves most acceptable.

Why this Proposal Might Work

The CARATS mechanism is a transfer, not a tax, because it confers visible benefits, and is not lost in general revenue. The nature of the transfer should be made as conspicuous as possible, as part of the educational program to facilitate our transition to a low-carbon lifestyle. This educational activity would be complemented by an innovative approach to funding the transition from old fuels (fossil fuels + nuclear) to new fuels (renewables + landfill methane). The transition would be accelerated by the removal of the perverse subsidies that still encourage the use of fossil and nuclear fuels.

In the context of redistributing wealth from North to South, it offers a possibly acceptable solution for the North, as it is self-funding. At the same time, it retains important decisions for national governments, such as setting the level for the national emissions. This factor is a key policy lever; it not only respects national sovereignty, but also determines the speed of the transition. It also encourages the South to adopt an active role in this key moment of human history, rather than be a passive observer of the North's folly of seeming indifference to our collective fate under the "business as usual" scenario. By converging on an equitable (per capita) endpoint for carbon emission, it demonstrates respect for the South.

Because it penalizes a high-carbon lifestyle, it should permit incomes in the South to rise, without inevitably transforming them into copies of the current Northern lifestyle. This decoupling of rising incomes from rising carbon dioxide emissions is an essential component of success. Its political attractiveness should be augmented by the fact that the mechanism is infinitely incremental; pressure can be tightened over five-year plans, annually, or through minibudgets, according to each country's appetite. Finally, the funds would be relatively easy to collect (fuel tax) and redistribute (income tax rebates and public investment).

None of this suggests that the international agreement to establish such as scheme would be easy to negotiate. For example, the transition would probably occur too late to prevent the inundation of the small island states and coastal settlements in places such as Bangladesh, Egypt, Madagascar, and Mozambique. Neither does it speak to claims such as OPEC's appeal for compensation for the disappearance of the fossil-fuel economy. It is, however, a means to transfer resources from North to South, while encouraging a lifestyle transition that reduces the impacts of climate change.

Notes

1. There are six greenhouse gases targeted in the Kyoto Protocol, each with a specific "global warming potential" per ton of gas. They are usually converted to a common metric of "carbon dioxide equivalents." A ton of carbon is the equivalent to 3.6 tons of carbon dioxide. Emissions are sometimes given in terms of tons of carbon, sometimes in tons of carbon dioxide. Hence the title of this paper: a "low-carbon future" implies a future when carbon dioxide emissions will be low.

2. The proceedings of the conference are reported in great detail on the website maintained by the International Institute for Sustainable Development at <http://www.iisd.ca/climate/index.html>.

3. One of the unremarked benefits of the Kyoto process was the voluntary distinction between the industrial world and "developing countries" as only the industrial countries signed the protocol and hence became known as "Annex 1" countries. Unfortunately, the others—developing countries—became known as "non-Annex 1" countries, which is hardly an improvement in terminology.

References

Firor, J. 1990. *The Changing Atmosphere: A Global Challenge.* New Haven: Yale University Press.

Grubb, M., with C. Vrolijk and D. Brack. 1999. *The Kyoto Protocol: A Guide and Assessment.* London: Royal Institute of International Affairs.

Harvey, L.D.D. 2000. *Climate and Global Environmental Change.* London: Prentice-Hall.

Head, I. L. 1991. *On a Hinge of History: The Mutual Vulnerability of South and North.* Toronto: University of Toronto Press.

IISD. 2000. "UNFCCC: United Nations Framework Convention on Climate Change." *Linkages: A Multimedia Resource for Environment and Development Policy Makers.* International Institute for Sustainable Development. Available from: <http://www.iisd.ca/climate/index.html>.

Logan, J., A. Frank, J. Feng, and I. John. 1999. *Climate Action in the United States and China.* Washington, D.C.: Woodrow Wilson International Center for Scholars.

Nicholls, M. 2001. "Racing for a Deal." *Environmental Finance,* December 2000–January 2001, 16–7.

Strzepek, K. M., and J. B. Smith, eds. 1995. *As Climate Changes: International Impacts and Implications*. Cambridge: Cambridge University Press for the U.S. Environmental Protection Agency.

Watson, R. T., M. C. Zinyowera, and R. H. Moss, eds. 1998. *The Regional Impacts of Climate Change. An Assessment of Vulnerability. A Special Report of IPCC Working Group II*. Cambridge: Cambridge University Press for the Intergovernmental Panel on Climate Change.

White, R. R. 2000. "Population and the Environmental Crisis." Chap. 2 in *Population Problems: Topical Issues,* ed. J. Rose. Amsterdam: Gordon and Breach Scientific Publishers.

World Bank. 2000. *Entering the Twenty-first Century: World Development Report, 1999/2000*. Washington, D.C.: World Bank.

CHAPTER 8

Arts and Culture in World Trade: Promoting Cultural Diversity

Garry Neil

Let me pretend for one moment I am a television producer, with a great idea for a new television series. It is a coming-of-age saga about a working-class kid growing up in the east end of Toronto in the 1950s—chasing the horse-drawn ice wagons in the scorching summer weather to scoop up the bits that fall; noting the appearance of the antennas on every rooftop as television comes to the city, bringing three U.S. networks and two Canadian ones; playing shinny on the outdoor rink early one morning when hockey legends Tim Horton and Allan Stanley dropped by; experimenting with cigarettes; and finding first love, in a cemetery of all places.

I budget the series at $15 million, pretty high for a Canadian production, but I have confidence. I go to CTV, Global, and CBC and back and forth and hammer out a good deal. CTV acquires five years of television rights in Canada for $4.5 million. Showcase Television throws in $.5 million for rights after CTV. I get $4 million for a cable television use in the United States, but they insist I modify the episode about the effects of U.S. television on the hero; they introduce a friend from Buffalo, so we can have some of the episodes set in a U.S. border city; and they change the sports scene to baseball. I receive $3 million from the German network ZDT, but am asked to consider relocating the series to the West, since that is what sells in Germany. The Japanese network NHK will toss in $1 million, but they require the romantic interest to have pigtails and freckles, and hail from PEI. And I've still only got 80 percent of my budget—there's $2 million to unearth.

Now, pretend I am an American television producer, with a similar idea set in New York. My series also will mark the return to prime-time television of a Canadian actor, Michael J. Fox. But now, my budget is U.S.$40 million. I pitch the idea to Fox and ABC. ABC likes it and commits to pick it up for $32 million, ITV in the United Kingdom secures it for $3 million, a sale in Japan nets

99

$3 million, and Canada's Global Television Network acquires Canadian rights for $1.5 million. Before I approach the lucrative U.S. syndication market, I am already in a profit position. You get the idea.

So, I resolve to turn my Canadian tale into a novel. But I soon discover that the average print run for a fictional work from a promising first-time author is fifteen hundred copies, compared with ten thousand in the United States, meaning the unit cost of the Canadian work is much higher. Yet the selling price must remain comparable to satisfy the Canadian consumer.

The Canadian Cultural Dilemma

This scenario highlights what I call the Canadian cultural dilemma. We are a nation of only 30 million people, spread over the second largest landmass in the world. Canadians share a border 5,500 kms long with the world's largest producer of cultural materials, and 23 million of us share a language and idiom with our southern neighbor. We can sound like we are from "Anywhere U.S.A.," except for a few idiosyncrasies, but even these can be eliminated with a little effort. Expatriate Canadians are among the leading voice performers in the U.S. commercial industry.

Canada is also an open market for cultural products. Most Canadians I know believe in the free movement of ideas, information, and entertainment, and we enjoy our access to the best of international culture. But we also need to see ourselves reflected in what we watch, hear, and read; we need to be able to view the world from our own perspective, too.

But other cultural producers enjoy a tremendous competitive advantage over Canadians. For some, the advantage arises because they have a substantially larger domestic market, like our examples from television production and book publishing; others are protected by language, or physical distance. To offer Canadian artists and cultural producers a reasonable opportunity, Canada must rely on public policies and programs. Most Canadians accept that this approach is one of the costs of maintaining our nation.

To counter the tremendous influx of foreign material that sometimes swamps us—foreign movies, television programs, books, magazines, and records—Canadian governments have taken steps. Politicians of all political stripes have implemented a series of measures, at both the federal and provincial levels, that permit our artists and cultural industries to emerge and succeed. The basic objective of these policies is to ensure that Canadians have choice in their own country. A fundamental principle underlying the measures is that Canadians are more likely to tell Canadian stories and reflect Canada's worldview.

Canadian cultural policy measures include:

- limits or restrictions on foreign ownership in most of the cultural industries;

- direct-funding programs for individual artists and cultural producers. Generally, access to most funding programs is denied to non-Canadian companies, even if they are producing Canadian content material or recording Canadian artists;

- Canadian content regulations in television and radio;

- preferential treatment of Canadian rights holders in copyright laws;

- government cultural agencies, including the radio and television services of the public broadcaster, CBC, the film and television support agency, Telefilm, and the heritage institutions;

- other regulations and programs that obligate commercial interests to direct resources to the production and promotion of Canadian material.

Megamergers are creating huge, vertically integrated multinational media companies such as AOL/Time Warner, mostly U.S.-based, with interests in all the cultural fields. At the same time, the market for English-language movies, television shows, magazines, and books is growing exponentially around the world. Cultural homogenization is becoming a key feature of the globalized world, as the same blockbuster Hollywood movies dominate the cinema screens of Canada, France, Greece, Korea, Zimbabwe, and Chile. Other states are beginning to respond in the same way as Canada, by developing programs and regulations to support their own artists and cultural producers, to give them access to their own audiences and perhaps a chance in the global markets. Like Canada's own programs, these are generally designed not to exclude the cultural creations of others, but to provide a diversity of choices for people, including local creative expressions.

Culture and the Trade Agreements

In the past fifteen years, technological change has created an explosion in the quantity of material available to consumers and a fragmentation of audiences. Other changes permit instantaneous access to these cultural works for many Westerners. The economics of film, television, and other cultural industries production also changed as budgets grew and the economic returns in the U.S. market did not keep pace. Consequently, foreign markets grew ever more important to the U.S.-based giants.

In a study reported in the 13 December, 2000 edition of the *Hollywood Reporter,* the U.S. copyright industries rule the nation's economic roost. The report states that the creative industries, including movies, television programs, software, books, and music, account for nearly 5 percent of the U.S. gross domestic product and employ 4.3 million people in the United States. Foreign sales and exports reached $79.65 billion in 1999. "The study confirms that the American copyright industries form the bedrock of the U.S. economic landscape and are this nation's greatest trade assets," said [Motion Picture Association of America] president and CEO Jack Valenti, . . . "No other sector in this new millennium can claim to play as pivotal a role in the new economy."

In the same period, globalization has brought new international trading relationships and new trade agreements. Three significant factors have emerged in global commerce:

- regional trade agreements including the European Union, the Canada/United States Free Trade Agreement (FTA), and the North American Free Trade Agreement (NAFTA);

- the Uruguay Round of the GATT that created the World Trade Organization (WTO) and brought tariff reductions, agreement on trade in services, and trade-related aspects of intellectual property rights;

- the discussions of a possible global investment treaty (dubbed a multilateral agreement on investment).

Some regard Canada's cultural policies and programs as barriers to more liberal trade in entertainment and information products and services. What we view as culture, American industry and government view as business: what we view as promoting choice, the United States views as erecting barriers. The trade agreements have created a new avenue of appeal for those who believe that cultural products are no different from other goods and services.

The importance of these industries to the American economy results in the United States aggressively supporting them in the trade talks, and in the enforcement of existing trading rules. The United States pursues this agenda both bilaterally and multilaterally. In negotiations for an investment treaty with Korea, for example, one of the key sticking points has been U.S. insistence on the elimination of the Korean screen quota system that guarantees some space for domestic television and movies. Over the past few years in Canada, we have witnessed several significant U.S. challenges to important cultural policies.

- The successful appeal before a WTO panel against Canadian measures to build the Canadian magazine industry. A split-run magazine is one that recycles U.S. editorial content, inserts a so-called Canadian section, and then sells itself to advertisers as Canadian. Importation of U.S. split-runs had been prohibited by a long-standing tariff item, which was supported by an excise tax introduced when technology allowed split-runs to circumvent the border measure. Canada had also subsidized Canada Post to provide a preferential postal rate for Canadian magazines shipped across the country. As these measures were found to violate the WTO rules, they were quashed by both the panel and the appellate body. Thus, Canada is able to support its magazine industry only through direct financial subsidy to the magazine producers.

- The U.S. threatened to challenge, under NAFTA, certain copyright provisions that favor Canadian artists, as well as those from countries with equivalent copyright regimes providing reciprocal benefits to Canadians.

- When it licensed the first set of Canadian specialty television services in 1994—including New Country Network (NCN)—the CRTC, Canada's broadcast regulator, removed from the list of services that Canadian cable companies are permitted to carry a competitive U.S. specialty channel, Country Music Television (CMT). This change was allowed under an existing policy in place when CMT was authorized initially for Canadian carriage. The CRTC decision was challenged both by the U.S. government and the company involved, but the actions were halted when NCN and CMT merged and CMT effectively entered Canada in partnership. In 1997, the CRTC quietly announced the elimination of its policy that a competitive service would be removed when a similar Canadian service is licensed.

- The European Community commenced proceedings against Canada for its refusal to permit Polygram Filmed Entertainment from expanding its film distribution business in Canada beyond proprietary products. The French company, Vivendi, may push for the action to be reopened as a consequence of its recent acquisition of Seagrams, the parent company of Polygram.

Perhaps more fundamentally, we have witnessed a change of attitude among those responsible for the development of Canadian cultural policies. When confronted with a problem that requires a public policy response, they strain for solutions in keeping with our trade obligations and ones that do not require Canada to use the FTA's cultural exemption. In other words, a whole range of policy options have been rejected from consideration because they might be contrary to trade rules. This approach is an insidious policy of self-censorship.

Preserving Cultural Sovereignty from the Trade Rules

In addressing the challenges of both the regional and global trade agreements, Canada has tried several approaches to buttress Canadian culture. But each of these options has significant problems.

Exempting Culture

While Canada agreed to modify several specific cultural policies in the talks, the FTA theoretically exempts the cultural industries from the disciplines of the agreement. However, the agreement authorizes retaliation against cultural measures "which would have been inconsistent with the Agreement," save for the exemption. It defines the cultural industries that existed in 1988. In the aborted negotiations at the OECD for a Multilateral Agreement on Investment, the French government proposed that measures adopted "in the framework of policies designed to preserve and promote cultural and linguistic diversity" should be exempt from its disciplines.

However, the language in each case is narrow and would not cover adequately all current forms of artistic expression, let alone those that emerge in this century. The French stipulation could well be limited in application to measures supporting culturally significant work, or works in minority languages. An international panel, the members of which invariably accept the wisdom of trade liberalization, could find that since Canada has already achieved "cultural and linguistic diversity," a particular measure is attempting to hide behind the cultural provision and is really an economic measure in a cultural disguise.

After the WTO panel ruled against Canada's magazine policies, the government responded by introducing Bill C-55, which would have made it illegal to sell advertising space in split-run magazines in Canada. However, the government gutted the bill when it reached an agreement with the United States on the dispute, in part because its terms may well have been contrary to the FTA. The Canada/U.S. FTA specifically includes the advertising industry within its scope.

The North American Free Trade Agreement exemption clause repeats verbatim the FTA's language. Its focus is industrial, and it defines only the forms of expression then used by creators, including film and television, publishing and sound recording. While it is a comprehensive list of those cultural industries, the list does not include the heritage sector, nor performing arts, visual arts, and crafts; even the new media may fall beyond its scope. It also excludes industries that will become culturally significant later in this century.

NAFTA also repeats the FTA's "notwithstanding" clause, thereby authorizing retaliation against Canadian cultural measures, and not limiting those retaliatory measures to the cultural realm. Since NAFTA regulates all forms of economic activity except those specifically exempted, the potential consequences of this agreement are far greater than those of the FTA. After all, new forms of artistic expression will surely emerge when artists create in media that cannot be currently envisaged.

Listing Country-Specific Reservations

There are enormous dangers to the so-called country-specific reservations route, whereby Canada can list and maintain specific measures that otherwise would be contrary to certain aspects of an agreement. Even if such reservations can be "unbound," it is impossible to list measures that have not yet been implemented, as well as safeguard all prospective cultural policy mechanisms. Further, such reservations may well become subject to principles such as "standstill," which would prohibit new or more restrictive measures, as well as "rollback," the process by which nonconforming measures would be eliminated over time. This route certainly exposes Canada to tremendous pressure on a bilateral basis; by its very nature, the reservation applies only to Canada.

Declining to Make Commitments on Culture Measures in Negotiations

In material circulated at the conclusion of the Uruguay round of GATT talks, our government insisted no commitments had been undertaken in any of the negotiating groups, including GATS, that would reduce Canada's ability to bolster its cultural sector. While the successful challenge to Canada's magazine policies relied heavily on the terms of the original 1940s GATT, as the WTO panel ruled that magazines are a "good," there is little doubt that the terms of the newer WTO agreements played a role in the panel's decision.

A New International Instrument to Promote Cultural Diversity

There is good reason to be concerned about these issues. First, in order to counter the powerful trends toward cultural homogenization, countries need to maintain sovereignty to develop cultural policy. If there is to be any hope of reflecting the world's cultural diversity in all forms of artistic expression, governments must negotiate and implement a new cultural treaty, a New International Instrument for Cultural Diversity (NIICD). The idea for

such an instrument originated in Canada, primarily because we have confronted this issue more directly than others. Such an agreement can build on
existing international declarations, such as the Universal Declaration of
Human Rights:

> "Everyone, as a member of Society, has the right to social security
> and is entitled to the realizations, through national effort and interna-
> tional cooperation and in accordance with the organization and re-
> sources of each State, of the economic, social and cultural rights
> indispensable for his dignity and the free development of his person-
> ality." (Article 22)

> "Everyone has the right freely to participate in the cultural life of the
> community, to enjoy the arts and to share in scientific advancement
> and its benefits." (Article 27)

The genesis of the concept of a new instrument to promote cultural diversity and protect the states' right to preserve their own cultures rests with distinguished Canadian actor R. H. Thomson, who talked of a global charter of
cultural rights. The February 1999 report of the Cultural Industries Sectoral Ad-
visory Group on International Trade, *Canadian Culture in a Global World: New
Strategies for Culture and Trade,* significantly boosted the concept. The key
characteristics of the proposed instrument are as follows:

- It requires equivalent status to the trade agreements. In the hierarchy
  of global agreements, those administered by the WTO, including the
  original GATT, the General Agreement on Trade in Services, and
  Trade Related Aspects of Intellectual Property (TRIPS) stand at the
  apex. To be effective, the cultural agreement would have to be at a
  comparable level.

- It must permit each nation to define culture for itself. What constitutes a culturally significant matter in one nation may be very different from that in another.

- It must permit the definitions of culture to evolve. There must be
  scope to introduce measures in new fields that emerge in this century and the next. After all, who could possibly have foreseen the
  cultural implications of television before its invention? And, of
  course, consider the Internet.

- It must contain only those commitments appropriate for culture.
  While ensuring the right of states to support their own cultural expression, artists, and cultural producers, it should work toward free

movement of cultural products as a means of ensuring diversity overall.

- Reviews of cultural policy decisions under the dispute settlement process must be done by a panel of culture experts, rather than trade experts. Where such a panel finds that a policy has been implemented for cultural reasons and has otherwise not violated obligations contained in the agreement, the policy must be sustained.

Building a Consensus for the Cultural Instrument

In 1998, a number of governments and nongovernmental organizations met in Stockholm, Sweden, to discuss culture and development at a session sponsored by the United Nations Educational, Scientific, and Cultural Organization (UNESCO). The conference grew out of concerns that many of the failures and disasters of the recent past in development work were the result of inadequate recognition of cultural differences. There was consensus among delegates about the negative consequences of globalization on culture, including the takeover of indigenous cultures by multimedia conglomerates. At the Stockholm meeting, the minister of Canadian heritage, Sheila Copps, invited her colleague culture ministers to join her in Ottawa to continue the dialogue, which they did in June of the same year. Concurrently, the Canadian Conference of the Arts (CCA), an umbrella group representing the interests of more than two hundred thousand individual artists and organizations in the Canadian cultural community, issued a call to nongovernmental groups to attend a parallel conference, entitled At Home in the World, to be held 29 June, 1998, also in Ottawa. These parallel meetings resulted in the launch of two significant initiatives.

The ministerial meeting in Ottawa became the initial meeting of the International Network for Cultural Policy, an initiative that now involves more than fifty countries. The ministers, who also met in 1999 in Oaxaca, Mexico and in 2000 in Santorini, Greece, have dedicated themselves to the following principles:

- to ensure that cultural and linguistic diversity are embraced as fundamental to global thinking on development, access, governance and identity;
- to support local and national cultures in an increasingly globalized world where information is power;
- to strike a balance that allows for full participation in the global society, while at the same time ensuring that unique identities are not lost;

- to offer a means through which countries can share their expertise, exchange views and information, and strengthen domestic and international partnerships.

In pursuing the goal of ensuring that culture is considered in international negotiations, the Network has increasingly viewed the New International Instrument on Cultural Diversity as a key to future progress. The Network is working both independently and with UNESCO in an effort to promote the idea.

On the NGO side, delegates to the At Home in the World Conference unanimously called on the world's cultural community to create an international network that could share information and develop common strategies to promote global cultural diversity. The CCA took charge of the initiative in partnership with the Swedish Joint Committee of Literary and Professional Artists (KLYS). The result was the launch of the International Network for Cultural Diversity (INCD).

While the INCD was created in 1999 and several individuals represented the Network at the WTO's Seattle ministerial meeting in November of that year, the first meeting of this new international nongovernmental organization occurred on the Greek island of Santorini in September 2000. Representatives from more than two hundred NGOs and activists from twenty-five countries attended. In a statement delivered to the world's ministers of culture following the meeting, the INCD outlined its views.

> As part of civil society, the members of the Network are nongovernmental organizations and individuals who are working for cultural diversity.
>
> We believe:
>
> - Expression through arts and culture is a fundamental part of human society;
> - Human society is diverse; and
> - Cultural diversity strengthens us all.

Among other matters, this meeting considered the challenges to cultural diversity resulting from corporate mergers, technology, and the trade agreements. Among the issues explained were:

- how promoting pluralism in the arts and culture requires sensitivity to the needs of indigenous and minority communities;
- how promoting pluralism in the arts can be a positive force for sustainable development;

- how the recording media have a pivotal role for cultural expression in today's world.

The conference reached two additional conclusions. First, "market forces alone cannot ensure cultural diversity at the national and international levels." And second, "States have a right and responsibility to implement policies and programs that support diverse artistic and cultural activities and to protect these from unwanted interventions from outside political or economic forces." Current trade agreements, it was believed, adversely affected the arts and cultural expression, and simply "exempting" culture from their terms is insufficient. Governments must retain considerable policy autonomy in the era of globalization.

The delegates argued that only a new international instrument could "give a permanent legal foundation for cultural diversity." Until that agreement is implemented, the delegates urged government ministers "to work in your own countries with all relevant ministers and civil society to ensure that no government enters into any agreement that constrains local cultures and the policies that support them."

Efforts to research and elaborate the new instrument began seriously in 2000 and picked up speed in 2001. The Canadian government has endorsed the concept and the companion declaration that, during implementation, it will refrain from making commitments in trade talks that further constrain its ability to support Canadian culture. The ministerial network has initiated substantive research, and the Francophonie and the Council of Europe have issued declarations supporting cultural diversity.

The second meeting of the International Network for Cultural Diversity, held in Lucerne, Switzerland, in September 2001, was organized entirely around a discussion of the new instrument. Delegates from thirty-two countries from around the world achieved a consensus on what they would like to see in the instrument and about how they would see it being negotiated.

At its 2001 general council meeting, UNESCO adopted a strong declaration on cultural diversity. In part spurred by the results of the Lucerne meeting of NGOS, UNESCO committed itself in its work plan to consider "the opportunity of a new legal instrument" for cultural diversity.

Discussions about the consequences for culture of globalization and the trade agreements are certain to heat up once more. The United States has tabled its proposal to include audiovisual services under the WTO's GATS agreement in the current round of talks, and new trade battles are likely to occur between Canada and the United States. But, increasingly, the Canadian experience of cultural vulnerability is being shared in other countries; technology eliminates the protections of physical distance, and more and more people are able to consume cultural products in the English language. The idea of the New International Instrument on Cultural Diversity has struck a common nerve among governments and civil society in every corner of the world.

For all of its history, Canada has been confronting the challenges of its close proximity to the world's largest producer of cultural products. Despite these challenges, over the past twenty years, we have begun to carve out a small niche for our own products. Canadians and global audiences have more access to high-quality Canadian cultural material than at any time in our history, and Canadian artists have become stars worldwide. As technology and globalization increasingly subject other nations to similar challenges, many are examining our policies and programs for ideas and inspiration. Canada's most significant contribution to civilizing globalization may well prove to be our idea for a New International Instrument for Cultural Diversity.

CHAPTER 9

Currency Transaction Tax:
Curbing Speculation, Funding Social Development

Joy Kennedy

Today, there is no reasonable impediment to solving two of our most pressing economic problems in this globalizing world: stabilizing the flow of capital, and paying the massive bills for much-needed social development. No credible reason, that is, except human greed and lack of political will, coupled with a slavish adherence to a neoliberal ideology dictating financial deregulation and capital-account liberalization.

Nonetheless, there is a new hope in the air: that taxing all cross-border currency transactions—an idea that has been circulating for some time—will resolve both problems. Although this remedy not surprisingly lacks support in the financial community, it looms as a strong contender for international agreement. It promises to be a highly significant element in civilizing globalization in our new millennium.

Dimensions of the Problem

A kind of cowboy economics is currently at play, with little regulation of the excesses of profiteering. Go for broke; gamble what you want; and winner takes all. The stakes are high in the Global Casino of Currency Speculation, where over U.S.$1.8 trillion per day is being bet around the clock. As one observer notes,

> [F]inancial markets have not behaved like other markets for goods and services. Financial markets are much more prone to instability. International financial markets are prone to go through cycles characterized by buying manias, followed by panic selling and finally market crashes. The inability of financial markets to channel resources into long-term,

111

stable investments and least of all into areas of greatest human need constitutes a prime example of market failure. (Dillon 2000)

Many of us are blindly involved in these speculative movements through our pension and mutual funds. The global community insists on a rules-based system for global trade in goods and services, yet has virtually no controls on the global trade in money. Until portfolio investment is regulated, and systemic volatility is controlled, development will be constantly threatened.[1]

This global casino does not operate with spare change, but with the resources of a country's entire population. The Asian financial crisis (1997–98), for instance, illuminates the link between the risks and instability of the financial speculation game, on the one hand, and the devastation that its failures can exact on the social development of whole populations, on the other. Countries such as Thailand, Korea, Indonesia, Mexico, Brazil, and Russia illustrate how a financial panic can eradicate decades of progress in a few weeks. Although these countries implemented policy changes to promote recovery, a solely national response offers no viable solution. The problems of governance of international finance and investment must be tackled at the global level.

True, citizens should expect national governments to protect them from the dire effects of speculative currency movements. Yet governments often plead impotence. In a remarkable speech delivered to a group of former heads of government, Canada's prime minister Jean Chrétien (1996) observed that dependence on international finance is eroding the power of nation-states. Acknowledging that "a sense of not being able to control our economic destiny . . . adds to the general anxiety about job security, our standard of living, and the world our children will inherit," Chrétien noted further problems in our world without borders:

> Tidal waves of money wash effortlessly backwards and forwards, buffeting interest rates and exchange rates [and disrupting] the best laid plans of governments. These financial waves often seem motivated by quick-changing sentiments or the short-term expectations of the proverbial 28-year-old trader in red suspenders. When a crisis erupts, a nation-state can seem powerless.

What, then, can be done?

Potential Solutions

James Tobin (1978) introduced the idea of a small tax on international financial transactions in 1972, and again in 1978, with a view to slowing down so-called hot money and its destabilizing influence. He proposed, based on

Keynes's ideas, that a tax of 0.5 percent would be sufficient to "throw sand in the wheels" of international financial market speculation without unduly interfering with trade or long-term investment. In 1996, Paul Berndt Spahn (1996) determined that an even smaller tax—0.02 percent to 0.1 percent—would be sufficient to deter unnecessary trading, since currency speculators customarily buy and sell currencies to capitalize on minuscule price differentials. The margins are sufficient for speculators to accrue substantial profits, as they typically trade in millions of dollars worth of currency contracts or bonds at a time. Thus, even a small currency transaction tax (CTT) would be sufficient to discourage so-called round trips in which speculators buy and then quickly resell large amounts of foreign currency, or tradable financial instruments such as bonds, to take advantage of small movements in exchange rates or interest rates. Since the effective tax rate under a CTT would be highest for short-term holdings and lowest for long-term investments, it would encourage investors to make long-term investments rather than engage in marauding fly-by-night ventures.

The immediate advantages of implementing a CTT are several. First, the tax would cut foreign exchange turnover by up to 50 percent. Second, half the revenues from a 0.1 percent CTT—possibly over U.S.$200 billion, according to current estimates—could be applied to poverty eradication and social development. And there would still be money in the bank for environmental protection.

Consider how far these revenues could go to ameliorate the challenges of world poverty. In 1995, the World Summit on Social Development in Copenhagen estimated what additional global spending was needed to meet *minimum* social development objectives. The tally was set at U.S.$40 billion a year for basic social services for the poorest people: $25 billion for health, $6 billion for primary education, and $9 billion for sanitation and clean water. And the 1998 United Nations Development Program's *Human Development Report* suggested that only U.S.$40 billion a year would raise 1.3 billion people, who presently earn less than a dollar a day, above the threshold of absolute poverty. Since then, the United Nations Millennium Summit (United Nations 2000) accepted an agenda for development that reiterated these pressing needs.

Although the benefits of a currency transaction tax are clear, its technical and political feasibility must be assessed. One significant factor concerns the change in procedures by which international financial markets settle accounts. Such a tax is becoming easier to administer and more difficult to evade, because financial institutions are transforming the way they conduct currency trades. Since banks conduct thousands of currency transactions every day, they use netting out rather than transferring funds for every trade; that is, they transfer only the net amounts owed. If a CTT were applied at this so-called netting stage, all the original transactions could be traced and taxed by the regulatory central banking authority. Moreover, central banks or their supervisory bodies can regulate offshore netting systems involving their currencies.

Soon, one centralized global settlement system will link all nations' domestic settlement systems. All transactions will be electronically recorded at this settlement site. Thus, tracking and taxing transactions will be relatively easy, as most netting services are already delivered by a single telecommunications system, the Society for Worldwide Interbank Financial Telecommunications (SWIFT).

Although the tracking of settlements is becoming centralized, there is no immediate need for a new supranational authority for a tax to be collected by national governments, or entities such as the European Union. Implementing a CTT at the settlement site allows a participating country's central bank to refuse to settle transactions emanating from noncooperating sites such as offshore tax havens. The central bank could collect the tax on trade transactions involving its own currency. One expert, Rodney Schmidt (2000), contends that there need be no further delay in collecting currency transaction taxes: "The technology and institutions now in place . . . make it possible to identify and tax gross foreign exchange payments, whichever financial instrument is used to define the trade, wherever the parties to the trade are located and wherever the ensuing payments are made." Furthermore, "if the tax is applied to the intermediate systems that net deals, it is feasible and can be unilaterally imposed by any country on all foreign exchange transactions worldwide" when its own currency is involved.

Then, there is the question of whether a country acting alone could collect such a tax, without suffering major penalties from threatened currency speculators. One country is unlikely to act alone, because to do so might create a negative impression among bondholders and investors that its economy is under stress, or that its macroeconomic policies are "inconsistent" or "imprudent." Accordingly, political agreement among the major currency issuers is still needed to implement a Tobin-style tax, and preferably as part of a comprehensive new financial framework. Nevertheless, the technical ability of one country to act alone has another dimension; if that country finds its currency under siege, it could unilaterally raise its CTT to a higher level to counteract the speculators, instead of raising interest rates to deter capital flight at great expense to the domestic economy.

Regardless of its merits, we should not oversell the CTT. Writing in the 1994 UNDP *Human Development Report*, James Tobin himself calls the Tobin tax "a second-best option." It would be preferable, in his view, to have a common world currency, much as Keynes proposed in his writings prior to Bretton Woods. But a common world currency would require something like a world central bank and, probably, other institutions of global governance, as well. Tobin acknowledges that it will be many decades before conditions are ripe for a common world currency. This step would demand a huge surrender of nation-states' sovereignty (see also, Tobin 1996).

A CTT alone cannot avert disasters on the scale of the Mexican crisis of 1994–95 or the Asian crisis of 1997–98. When an interviewer for the *Economist* asked James Tobin whether a Tobin tax would have prevented the Asian crisis, he conceded, "Certainly you would need other things as well." Devaluations of the Mexican peso, the Thai baht, and other Asian currencies were simply too large and too sudden to be contained by a small transactions tax. Other measures, such as the foreign exchange controls recently imposed by the Malaysian government, may be needed in those kinds of extreme situations.

While a CTT by itself might not have prevented the Asian or the Mexican crises, it could have helped minimize the contagion effects. In the aftermath of these crises, hot money flowed out of any number of other countries seeking an elusive safe haven. Chile was spared the worst of the so-called tequila effect that followed the Mexican crisis in 1994, because of its system of capital controls. Much of the hot money flowed to the United States, where it contributed to the dangerous and unsustainable overvaluation of stock market prices and set the stage for another kind of financial crisis.

A small tax is only one tool among others to ameliorate the deficiencies of unregulated financial markets. Complementary measures could include capital controls, modeled on Chile's *encaje*. Under this scheme, investors are obliged to keep their investment within the country for a minimum period of a year, or forfeit a portion of their investment that they must deposit with the central bank.

Recently, after a long history of dedicated opposition, even the International Monetary Fund (IMF) is renewing its study of the potential of a capital control scheme (see IMF 2000). This change in direction is striking, inasmuch as the IMF has insisted on liberalization of financial markets as a precondition for adjustment loans. The viability and desirability of a CTT is growing more obvious. As the proposals are tabled, governments, with the participation of civil society, must carefully consider the best place to entrust the authority both to tax and to spend.

The Politics of a Currency Transaction Tax

Today's opposition to a CTT is rooted, then, in the political power of vested interests, not in technical infeasibility. Resistance can be compared to the hostility that met the introduction of an innovation such as the seat belt. Its mechanics were accessible, and its logic clear to anyone confronting the repeated and senseless carnage. But the political resistance was enormous. Not until a government finally looked at its overall risk assessment and potential liability did it have the temerity to introduce enforceable laws. The hue and cry—charges of restricting freedom—was similar to today's protests against gun control implementation. But the change was successful. And other countries, rather than offering seat-belt-free havens, or competitive car models without seatbelts, followed suit. The success of today's almost universal seat belt requirement marks the culmination of the two factors that facilitate change: ongoing education campaigns and mobilization of support behind the new rule.

One effect of market financial crashes is that the financial sector, while it may not like the idea, now must take seriously any measures that will prevent future catastrophes. Even George Soros, that mercurial financier, has come out in favor of currency transaction taxes.

Sporadic cries for a CTT have now swelled into a chorus. First, there was the1995 G7 summit meeting in Halifax; Canadian NGOs organized to put the Tobin tax onto the international agenda. This initiative was followed by constant educational campaigns and lobbying, by the Halifax Initiative[2] in Canada (2000a and 2000b) and other NGOs elsewhere (see Tobin Tax Initiative 2000). Certain economists have joined forces with world parliamentarians and with political groups active around the globe, such as ATTAC (see ATTAC 2000a, 2000b), in building momentum behind a currency transaction tax.[3]

Today, support for the CTT is mushrooming, in Canada and abroad. In 1999, Canadian Lorne Nystrom, NDP member of Parliament, initiated a motion stating: "That, in the opinion of this House, the government should enact a tax on financial transactions in concert with the international community." Although the vote was not binding, many members of the Liberal government, including the finance minister, Paul Martin, voted for the motion. The vote was 164 in favor to 83 opposed. Subsequently, an International Legislators and Parliamentarians call for Tobin-style taxes has been successfully launched. The "Capital Tax, Fiscal System, and Globalisation" Intergroup within the European Parliament has galvanized support in member states for the introduction of Tobin-style taxes. The prime minister of India has suggested the imposition of an international levy on capital flows between developed countries and all capital repatriations from developing countries. The money could be credited to a Global Poverty Alleviation Fund

Finally, the breakthrough the CTT enjoyed at Geneva 2000, the U.N. Special General Assembly marking the five-year review of the Copenhagen World Summit on Social Development, demonstrated the importance of political mobilization. Strategic planning by the NGO CTT caucus—coupled with the Canadian government delegation's determination to sponsor a resolution for a study of the CTT—ultimately trumped resistance from the United States, Japan, Australia, and others. An agreement was brokered and the substantive intent of the motion was passed (United Nations 2000) The position of many countries, including Germany, shifted over the weeks prior to Geneva because of the decisive work of NGOs in Europe and elsewhere. The CTT became the pivotal NGO issue at this Special Session. As one Canadian delegate, John W. Foster, remarked, "Seldom does one see such a clear relationship between political organizing and a desired outcome than in the UN Special General Assembly's decision to approve the motion."

As an NGO participant in this event, I can attest to the importance of meticulous political footwork.[4] A special meeting between NGOs and the head of the American delegation revealed the real reason for U.S. intransigence on the question of even studying the CTT issue. Apparently, the American delegation was being held ransom by the powerful senator Jesse Helms, a notorious U.N. opponent. After the hard-won agreement for the United States to pay several billion dollars in back dues, they had actually paid the first of three tranches. Helms had prepared a bill for the Senate, just waiting for the word "tax" to appear, at which point he would introduce the bill and refuse to pay the rest of the debt. By accepting compromise language and holding their noses, the pro-study governments actually were agreeing to "keep the lights on in New York HQ."

The result of our lobbying was a crucial addition to the somewhat generally worded resolution. In a joint statement, Canada and Norway (final plenary meeting, 1 July, 2000), expressed[5] "[our] particular satisfaction with the consensus that has been reached, mandating the initiation of a thorough study on specific proposals for developing new sources of funding for social development and poverty eradication programs . . . [and] to take a closer look at a number of current suggestions for innovative funding-raising mechanisms, including proposals for currency transaction tax arrangements." John Langmore, director of the Division of Social Policy and Development (UN), in his round-up of achievements of the Special Session, underscored the significance of this sentence. He referred to the decision as an "astonishing breakthrough," one that could promote "more effective global public management of the international financial system" (Earth Negotiations Bulletin 2000). Further discussions and multilateral negotiations continue as the world community tries to find a way to finance sustainable development and assure a secure future.

Conclusion

The Tobin tax, or a modified version of currency transactions taxation, has many likely *advantages* (cf. Camilleri, Malhotra, and Tehranian 2000).

- It would rein in market volatility by effectively discouraging short-term speculative flows.

- It has great potential for revenue creation, especially for use in relieving poverty and distress in the South.

- It would contribute to the generation of foreign exchange reserves.

- It alters incentives to dampen speculative behavior, rather than relying on "command and control" regulatory mechanisms.

CTTs are also technically feasible. National governments could implement transaction taxes on cross-border currency exchanges, within the framework of an international cooperation agreement. Eventually, a supranational body, an International Taxation Organization, with participating member-states as its board of governors and accountable to the U.N., could assume responsibility for the allocation of the revenues. Currency transaction taxes and capital controls at the national level, especially on inflows, would be negotiated and agreed upon at national, regional, and global levels as part of a coherent and comprehensive world financial framework.

The debate over a Tobin-type tax has sparked wide international interest. It reveals much about our fundamental values (Ecumenical Team 2000a). The time is ripe to implement a CTT, to close the gap between the world's rich and poor, and to change the rules of the financial game to serve the needs of the people in both the North and the South. Let us, finally, create a civil global order.

Notes

1. A point made forcefully in the CTT NGO Caucus intervention to the III Preparatory Committee of the UN Financing for Development Conference, on 7 May 2001. See <http://www.tobintax.org>.

2. The website of the Halifax Initiative is <http://web.net/halifax/index.htm>.

3. ATTAC, which stands for Association pour la taxation des transactions financières pour l'aide aux citoyens, has more than one hundred thousand members in over one hundred French cities, and affiliates in over fifteen countries.

4. See World Council of Churches, Ecumenical Team <http://www.wcc-coe.org>.

5. See <http://www.un.org/esa/socdev/geneva2000/index.html>.

References

ATTAC. 2000a. "Appel mondial des économistes/World Economists Call for a Tobin Tax." Available from: <http://attac.org/fra/asso/doc/doc18signah.htm> and http://attac.org/fra/asso/doc/doc14en.htm>.

———. 2000b. "The Tobin Tax: How to Administer It and What to Finance?" Available from: <http://attac.org/fra/asso/doc/doc14en.htm>.

Camilleri, J., K. Malhotra, and M. Tehranian. 2000. *Reimagining the Future: Towards Democratic Governance. Report of the Global Governance Reform Project.* Melbourne: Department of Politics, La Trobe University.

Chrétien, Jean. 1996. "Notes for an Address to the Fourteenth Annual Plenary of the InterAction Council of Former Heads of State and Government, Vancouver, B.C., May 19, 1996." Office of the Prime Minister, Ottawa.

Dillon, John. 2000. "Notes for an Address to International Conference, Towards a Just International Financial System." November, Frankfurt/Main, Germany.

Earth Negotiations Bulletin. 2000. Vol. 10, 3 July. International Institute for Sustainable Development. Available from: <http://www.iisd.ca/linkages/vol10/enb1063e.html>.

Ecumenical Team. 2000a. "A Call for a Change of Heart: Some Ethical Reflections to Be Considered for the Draft Declaration." Report of the Ecumenical Team to the Thirty-eighth Session of the UN Commission for Social Development and the Second Intersessional Meeting for Geneva 2000, February, New York.

————. 2000b. "The Time to Act Is Now! Geneva 2000 and Beyond." Continuing concerns of the Ecumenical Team, to the Twenty-fourth Special Session of the UN General Assembly, June, New York.

Halifax Initiative/d'Halifax. 2000a. "The Tobin Tax: Debunking the Myths." and Fact sheet, HI, Ottawa, Canada.

————. 2000b. "We Can Stop the 'Hot Money' Casino." Fact sheet, HI, Ottawa, Canada.

Herman, Barry. 1999. *Global Financial Turmoil and Reform: A United Nations Perspective.* UNU Policy Perspectives, no. 2. New York: United Nations University Press.

International Monetary Fund. 2000. "Capital Controls: Country Experiences with Their Use and Liberalization." 17 May. IMF Occasional Paper 190, parts 1, 2, and 3. Available from: <http://www.imf.org>.

Schmidt, Rodney. 2000. "Is the Tobin Tax Practicable?" IDRC, Vietnam Office, Government of Canada, June.

Spahn, Paul Bernd. 1996. "The Tobin Tax and Exchange Rate Stability." *Finance and Development* 33 (June): 24–27.

Tobin, James. 1978. "A Proposal for International Economic Reform." *Eastern Economic Journal* 4 (July-October): 153–59.

Tobin, James.1996. Prologue to *The Tobin Tax: Coping with Financial Volatility*, ed. Mahbub ul Haq, Inge Kaul, and Isabelle Grunberg. New York: Oxford University Press.

Tobin Tax Initiative. 2000. "Factsheets," "Bibliography," and "Policy Building through Citizen Participation!" In *What Are Tobin Taxes?* Available from: <http://www.ceedweb.org/irrp/>.

United Nations. 2000. "Proposals for Further Initiatives for Social Development." Final outcome document as adopted by the Plenary of the Twenty-fourth special session of the General Assembly entitled World Summit for Social Development and Beyond: Achieving Social Development for All in a Globalizing World, July. Available from: <http://www.un.org/esa/socdev/geneva2000/index.html>.

PART 3

Reforming Global Governance and Institutions

Core Issues

How can we reform international governance and institutions to support adjusting global markets to social needs? We cannot have the latter without the former. Today, decision-making power in international organizations rests largely in the hands of the industrial countries, despite the fact that about 85 percent of the world's population resides in developing countries. For example, trade and investment negotiations involving GATT and, since 1995, the WTO have seen major issues resolved in secret gatherings of major industrial countries and a few developing countries. Moreover, the ascendancy of large corporations in many countries means that their governments primarily reflect business interests. If we seek to foster a social-democratic global order, we will have to devise more representative governance of key international institutions

Today, virtually all shades of political opinion agree on the need for reform of global institutions. The extent and nature of needed reform, however, are hotly contested. At one extreme, conservative forces in the U.S. Congress and elsewhere contemplate only a tinkering with the mandates of existing organizations such as the IMF and the World Bank. At the other extreme, radicals of both the far right and far left call for dismantling these institutions, together with the WTO, NAFTA, and the prospective FTAA. This section takes a middle path in exploring how citizen action can make global governance more democratic and less fixated on growth and efficiency criteria.

In chapter 10 political scientist Robert O'Brien guides readers through the murky process of reforming global governance. Until now, shifts in global governance have occurred in response to major crises, such as the Napoleonic Wars and the First and Second World Wars. In the absence of crisis, governance reform is likely to evolve gradually. Because states are constrained by the structural power of corporations, O'Brien contends, civic associations will play a major part in forging global institutions that preserve social values from market forces.

Extending this discussion of governance in chapter 11, philosopher Frank Cunningham asks: How can citizens gain control over decisions and actions

121

occurring outside their countries' borders that deeply affect their quality of life? He identifies four perspectives in debates on globalization and democracy: cosmopolitan, state-autonomist, neoliberal, and participative. He opts for a "pragmatic" approach that combines elements of all but the neoliberal perspective. His left-wing social-democratic viewpoint allows us, as he puts it, to "live with globalization" by safeguarding the primacy of such values as equality and cooperation in everyday life.

Chapter 12 narrows the focus to reform of a key institution promoting neoliberal globalization—the World Trade Organization. Many environmentalists and radical antiglobalization activists have called for the abolition of the WTO on the grounds that international trade is inherently exploitative or damaging to the environment and local communities. They have demanded, instead, a return to an emphasis on local self-sufficiency. However, Danish social scientist Jens Mortensen, together with most of the other authors of this volume, does not believe that either trade or the WTO is inherently bad. In fact, trade has proved to be a powerful mechanism for pulling countries out of poverty, as the experience of East Asia testifies. The goal, therefore, should be to recast the WTO to ensure that it advances the interests of the weaker, developing economies. Mortensen considers how this might be achieved.

Political scientist Cranford Pratt turns our attention to the restructuring of another important international institution in chapter 13: foreign aid. He contends that both bilateral and multilateral aid, as currently configured, largely support a neoliberal global order that militates against the interests of the poor in poor countries. Could aid be reconfigured to help humanize globalization? Although acknowledging how the structural power of capital constrains this transformation, he identifies strategies that citizens' groups can employ to move aid policy in a positive direction.

In closing, Louis Pauly, a political scientist, admonishes activists not to ignore their national governments in seeking to improve environmental, health, and other standards. Although governmental leaders in industrial countries like to blame global economic forces for their own inaction, these pleas often amount to little more than self-serving alibis. Governments in the West retain a great deal more leverage in forging an egalitarian and environmentally sustainable world than they like to admit. The message is clear: if you want a new global order, put pressure on your own politicians.

Part 3 thus suggests that a democratic reform of global governance is not only required to civilize globalization, but can be won through citizen action at the national and global levels. However, this process is likely to be conflictual and protracted, as part 4 contends.

CHAPTER 10

Paths to Reforming Global Governance

Robert O'Brien

Although we may agree upon the need to civilize globalization, what concretely does this entail? Is there something about the process of globalization that is barbarous? If this is so, how can it be brought under control and shaped for more humane purposes? These are difficult questions. This chapter provides a guide to thinking about the process of reforming global governance. It argues that an approach that pursues simultaneous and coordinated paths in the state, corporate, and civil society sectors is the most likely to produce change, but that this change will take place at a gradual and slow pace.

Because the debate on globalization is so wideranging, I begin by clarifying key terms in the chapter. These include the terms *globalization, uncivilized* and *global governance.* The following section considers how global governance actually operates. If people live in separate states, how is it possible that rules and codes of behavior might influence activity across these borders? Attention is drawn to the role of regimes, legal and financial coercion, moral appeals, and the existence of structural power. The third section turns our attention to the mechanisms that are likely to drive change in global rules. These mechanisms are states, corporations, and civic associations. The chapter concludes by considering the implications of a recent attempt at reforming global governance, the Global Compact.

Key Terms

Let us begin with the term *globalization.* It is used very widely, but people often mean different things when they use the term. For example, some people use the term to imply internationalization (an increase in the volume of economic flows across borders), others are really thinking about liberalization (the removal of restrictions on cross-border flows such as the elimination of trade or investment barriers). Both internationalization and liberalization are often used in the context of economic activity. Other people focus on universalization (particular ideas or principles being accepted by all people) or westernization (the increasing prevalence of ideas and practices originating in Europe or the United States). These terms are most often used when discussing the spread of principles, such as human rights, or the spread of culture, such as the expansion of the U.S. movie industry. An alternative use of the term globalization refers to deterritorialization.

Only deterritorialization adequately captures what is new about globalization. Following Scholte (2000a), I understand globalization to mean a process of relative deterritorialization. Territory is not disappearing, but it is becoming less important to human affairs. Deterritorialization involves the shrinking of time and space, as well as the creation of new sets of social relations and new centers of authority. We can see that time and space have become less significant obstacles to human interaction as technologies make it easier to travel across large distances or communicate with people around the world. The lowering of time and distance barriers allows people to become involved in the lives of other people in other parts of the planet much more easily. These relations can be found in engagement and response to mass media (e.g., pressure for humanitarian intervention following a CNN broadcast); they are developed through economic structures (global production and finance); and they are aroused in response to shifting centers of authority (e.g., international organizations). These relations do not eliminate the importance of the state or replace significant local social relations. However, they do add another layer to some people's social, economic, and political lives.

In what ways could this globalization process be considered as *uncivilized?* The process may take a very brutal form in which large numbers of people suffer economic deprivation or physical harm. For example, increased pollution in developed countries like the United States and Canada may contribute to global warming. The rise in temperature around the world can cause large sections of the polar ice caps to melt, flooding low-lying areas. Millions of people in Bangladesh can suffer from increased flooding, homelessness, and even famine because of economic progress in other parts of the world. In the case of people living on islands such as the Maldives (near India), their country may disappear under the rising sea levels.

Many critics of the existing form of globalization see it as being uncivilized because it allows key decisions to be made on the basis of whether or not they create a profit for businesses. In this view, all values are subordinated to the values of economic efficiency and the creation of wealth. For example, environmental measures may be weakened or abandoned, because they interfere with the profits of particular corporations. National cultures may be swamped by entertainment products from larger, more efficient foreign corporations. Labor standards may be violated, because this can result in the production of cheaper products. The chapters in part 2 of the book discuss such fears.

The criticism that it is uncivilized to have the market allocate all resources and make decisions about how life should be organized was famously put forward by Karl Polanyi (1957). He argued that the attempt to have people subject themselves completely to the market created great suffering and political turmoil in the late 1800s and early 1900s. In fact, Polanyi argued that the rise of the ideologies of Communism and Fascism and even the Second World War were a response to the social upheaval generated by an extremely liberal market. Many people today share Polanyi's fears of the effects of unregulated markets on the stability of society and the impact on people's lives. For example, the 1997 East Asian crisis saw unregulated financial markets wreak havoc on a number of countries, causing an increase in poverty, economic insecurity, and political instability.

From this perspective, the discussion surrounding civilizing globalization becomes a debate about how the process of globalization can be tempered so that a liberal market is not dictating the organization of society. Can the world continue to become a smaller place, but at less cost to the residents of the planet? Is it possible to put some limits on the pursuit of profit? Can some areas of human activity be protected from the destructive impact of competition and the exploitation of power by large multinational corporations? These questions lead us to think about the rules that are created to govern human activity across state borders. They lead us to the topic of global governance.

By *global governance*, I mean the overreaching system that regulates human affairs on a worldwide basis. Another term would be the system of world order (Cox 1996). The mechanisms and rules of global governance are created by the actions and agreements of key actors in the global system. The primary political actor is the state, but other actors such as corporations and civic associations can also influence and participate in global governance. A striking feature of global governance in the past fifty years has been the increasing role played by international (that, is interstate) organization in facilitating governance. This chapter is focused upon one particular aspect of global governance: world or international organizations and their ability to address global problems (Hewson and Sinclair 1999). These organizations are significant, because they provide both the forum for negotiating globalization rules and the mechanisms for monitoring and enforcing rules.

There are many suggestions about what needs to be done to make globalization a more civilized process. Some would stress increased citizen participation, others would point to improving labor standards, securing environment sustainability, protecting local cultures, or redistributing wealth from the winners in the globalization process to the losers. Redistribution is usually discussed in terms of transferring resources from the North to the South, but wealth can also be moved from wealthier citizens to poor citizens within a country. It is not difficult to put together a wish list of improvement, but it is much more difficult to think about how such changes could be implemented.

So how do we move from wanting change to instituting change, when we know that the obstacles to transformation are great and that national politics set limits upon what is possible? The first step is to develop a clear idea of how global governance works.

How Does Global Governance Work?

Many different factors can regulate people's behavior. Habit or custom may dictate how people behave. Religious beliefs may encourage particular forms of activity. Rules may be written down into laws that can be enforced by authority figures or policing agencies to ensure compliance. On a global scale, the rules that regulate activity and the norms that condition behavior are much looser than those that exist on a national or community level. Diversity in cultures makes agreement on modes of behavior more difficult, and the lack of a world government means that there is neither a global legislature passing binding rules nor any global police force to enforce them. States are reluctant to diminish their sovereignty by submitting themselves to higher authorities such as international organizations. Yet, despite the greater distance between global rules and local activity, there are a number of ways that global governance can function.

In the field of international relations the governance arrangements put in place by states in particular issue areas are often referred to as regimes. Regimes are "implicit or explicit principles, norms, rules and decision-making procedures around which actors' expectations converge in a given area of international relations" (Krasner 1983, 2). Regimes are ideas and rules about how states should behave. A vast literature has been created in an attempt to explain the conditions under which regimes are created, maintained, and destroyed. Most approaches see regimes as being created through state-to-state negotiations, with states acting as self-interested, goal-seeking actors pursuing the maximization of individual utility (Hansclever, Mayer, and Rittberger 1997). In other words, states create regimes, because they believe that a regular pattern of cooperation will bring them benefits. In many cases states will participate in regimes that are not ideal, because the cost of conflict outside of the regime is greater than the bad deal they get inside the regime. For example, developing states may object to many aspects of the trade regime, but they prefer to be a member than to operate outside the main trading institution.

How do these regimes influence behavior? We can identify a number of methods. Some regimes have a strong legal framework that compels states to obey rules by the threat of economic sanctions. The WTO is an excellent example. It has a strong dispute settlement mechanism that rules on trade conflicts based upon the rules contained in the agreements that created the WTO. Countries in violation of the rules must change their policies or face economic sanctions from the states they have injured. Even powerful states obey these rules, because they have an interest in a predictable system of rules that fosters increased trade and economic activity. The WTO puts the value of free trade above other goals, leading to conflict with those people who feel that free trade undermines environmental or health standards. In this case liberal values and market mechanisms are privileged over other approaches. Environmental protection must take place in the context of free trade.

The distribution of money and provision of credit can also be used to foster compliance with particular rules. This is the approach used by the World Bank and IMF. These organizations lend money to states that are in need of funds to weather an economic crisis or to further long-term development strategies. The loans are usually conditional upon having the recipients undertake certain policies. These policies have varied over time, but usually states are asked to liberalize their economies so that they earn money to pay back the loans. Institutions that disperse money are influenced by their largest financial contributors. In the case of the World Bank and the IMF, voting rights are distributed in proportion to the financial contributions of member states. Because the United States is the largest contributor to both institutions, it has the largest share of votes and influence. Thus, policies that the United States advocates are the most likely to be spread through this channel of influence in the global governance process. For example, IMF loans to South Korea during the East Asian financial crisis stipulated that Korea open up its manufacturing and financial industries to foreign investors, many of whom were from the United States.

At other times, state behavior can be influenced by appeals to morality. This is the approach used by the International Labour Organization (ILO). The ILO conducts research on labor issues and highlights the abuse of workers' rights through reports and investigations. It facilitates negotiations between states to set minimum standards for countries to follow and publicizes failure to comply with the standards. The organization's work is based upon the belief that states may change their behavior if they face international condemnation. Although the ILO has been operating for almost one hundred years, its ability to influence state behavior is limited by its lack of enforcement mechanisms. Many states ignore its reports and advice.

Expertise can also be used to convince actors that it is in their best interest to behave in a particular way. For example, organizations such as the Organization for Economic Cooperation and Development and the IMF issue reports on the economic policy of particular states and suggest how they should adapt to globalization. States are not ordered to change their policies, but they are advised that a particular change will help foster economic growth. These institutions tend to offer liberal approaches to economic restructuring and, until recently, were unlikely to advocate policies that might protect society by reducing the influence of unregulated markets.

A final element that influences behavior is the structure of the global system itself. This is known as structural power. Drawing upon theories of the privileged power position of business in a national context, Gill and Law (1993) have argued that the internationalization of economic activity has increased the direct and indirect power of business in relation to the state. The nature of the system makes some forms of behavior more likely and punishes some forms of behavior more harshly than others. For example, states must pay attention to the desires of international investors if they want to attract capital for investment or keep national wealth and businesses from fleeing to other locations. This encourages state leaders to move their economies in a more liberal direction.

In the existing system of global governance, the institutions that are tasked with liberalizing the global economy and increasing the role of the market are more influential than those seeking to protect society from market failures. On the market liberalization side, the IMF and World Bank are able to use the provision of finance for influence, and the WTO has its important dispute-settlement mechanism. However, the ILO, which protects labor standards, is confined to an advocacy role. Other institutions with social mandates such as UNICEF, which assists poor children, or the World Health Organization must work within the economic policies advocated by the liberal institutions. The structure of governance seems to favor the increasing power of the market at the expense of social values. Returning to Polanyi's view of the market, this is likely to lead to social turbulence and conflict over the rules of global governance.

Mechanisms for Change

How do you change the rules under which a particular form of global governance operates? For example, how do you shift the system in a direction that puts a higher emphasis on environmental protection? The relatively brief history of world orders or global governance warns against expecting rapid change and highlights the link between crisis and changes in governance. Dramatic transformations in governing relations between states have tended to follow large-scale wars. For example, in the aftermath of the Napoleonic Wars of the early 1800s, the European state system was managed by something called the Concert of Europe. The next large change in organizing the international system followed the terrible destruction of the First World War. The League of Nations and a number of other international organizations and treaties were created to try and improve governance and maintain peace. The Second World War marked the end of that system and ushered in a new world order in 1945.

Many of today's international organizations, such as the United Nations, the IMF, the World Bank, and the North Atlantic Treaty Organization, date back to this era. The end of the Cold War between the United States and the Soviet Union in 1989 resulted in the strengthening of existing Western institutions rather than in the creation of a new form of international organization.

Changes in reforming or replacing existing global governance structures are unlikely unless there is a devastating crisis in the international system. With the relatively peaceful end to the Cold War, the chances are low that a new world war will erupt in the near future to cause major change in global governance. More likely, wholesale change would come about as a result of a severe financial crisis that plunged the world into economic depression. Financial collapse would force decision makers to change the existing system or replace it with a new set of rules. Since such a collapse would impoverish millions and probably lead to violent conflict within and between states, it is not a method of changing global governance that many people would choose. Such a scenario is only attractive to those who have nothing to gain from the existing system. Financial collapse may come about by mistake, but not as a strategy for reform. It is unlikely to civilize global governance or relations.

Barring change on a grand and destructive scale, we must look to particular actors to foster the innovations that might gradually civilize the globalization process. The three most important actors are individual states, corporations, and civic associations.

The *state* retains a pivotal role in creating and maintaining governance in the global system because of the centrality of the connection between law and political authority. The state is the central legal actor and primary representative of individuals in the international system. Agreements binding the population of a country can only be made by a state. While its representative function is often imperfect, the state is the only institution that can make a legitimate claim to represent all of the people within its territory. Attempts to reform global governance must work through the state system.

Not all states are equally important for transforming global governance. The most developed and wealthy states are the most significant, because they can veto changes or coerce other states to follow particular sets of policies. Thus, the United States is a central actor because of its wealth and power. Changes in U.S. domestic politics can have a significant influence on the process of global governance. For example, the election of a Republican to the U.S. presidency in 2000 made the achievement of an international agreement to slow climate change much more difficult. President George W. Bush has much closer ties to the oil industry than his Democratic predecessor. Many suggestions for slowing global warming threaten the profits of U.S. oil companies and will not be welcomed by the Republican president. Since the United States is the world's largest producer of the pollutants that contribute to global warming, a treaty without U.S. participation will not be very effective. In a similar way, on different issues, the position of the European Union and its member states is crucial to securing or blocking changes in global regulation.

Other states in the system may also be important for slightly different reasons. China's views carry some weight because it represents a fifth of the world's population. In military terms it is a force to be reckoned with. In economic terms, the Chinese state controls access to what will be the largest market when it reaches a sufficient stage of development. Thus, corporations and states tread more lightly when they deal with China than with small, less powerful states. It is much easier to exert pressure on a small country such as Nicaragua to respect universal human rights than it is on China.

Another example of a developing state whose views can carry some weight is South Africa. South Africa has a great deal of legitimacy to speak on behalf of oppressed people in Africa and the developing world because of its struggle to overthrow apartheid. In addition, because South Africa is a democratic state, its views carry more weight in global discussions than the views of a similar-sized authoritarian state. An interesting example of the role that South Africa is playing in challenging the existing form of global governance is its campaign to violate the patent protection afforded to multinational drug companies that produce anti-AIDS drugs. The South Africans are trying to make a moral argument for violating the patent protection that is enshrined in the WTO.

Despite the importance of the state to global governance, some groups have moved away from concentrating all of their effort on influencing state power. The major explanation for this is that the ability of the state to offer protection from the uncivilized aspects of globalization seems to have been reduced. The populations of the weakest states in the developing world have been at the mercy of Western states and large corporations for many years. Recently, however, it appears that even advanced industrialized states seem less able to protect their citizens from increasing global competition. This has been described by one observer as the state shifting its role from providing welfare for its citizens to preparing the population for increased competition (Cerny 2000). The state does not shrink or disappear, but changes its role. The process of globalization is seen to have made it more difficult to support the traditional welfare state, which cushioned the effects of competition. In the terms of this book, the state alone is less able to civilize globalization.

The view that the state is losing power has been widely challenged. Some have argued that globalization is exaggerated; they say that the degree of internationalization as measured by percentages of trade and investment flows has precedents in the early 1900s (Hirst and Thompson 1996). Citing the persistent differences between North American, European, and Asian models of capitalism, comparative political studies dispute that there has been a movement to policy convergence (Garrett 2000). These scholars deny that the state is weaker or is unable to protect its citizens. They suggest that if political forces advocating social protection gather the political will and organize themselves properly, the government can be pointed in the direction of social protection. They suggest that globalization has very little to do with increasing inequality or decreasing social protection.

The controversies about state-corporate power continue to rage, but some trends appear undeniable. Firstly, most states around the world, in stark contrast to the 1970s, actively seek multinational investment. Secondly, in contrast to earlier decades, states seem more intent upon furnishing those companies with an attractive environment than with regulating their activity. Some have referred to states as engaging in "beauty contests" in an effort to attract foreign investment (Abbott and Palan 1996). Of course, the balance of power between any particular state and any particular firm will vary depending upon their position in the global economy.

Although a global governance system that privileges the market as an allocator of resources brings benefits to particular states and people, it is often seen to be driven by corporate strategy. *Multinational corporations* are seen as an increasingly influential factor in formulating the polices that are instituted at a global level and as an actor influencing the decision of state elites.

In the early 1990s some observers argued that the growing power of multinational corporations in relation to the state necessitated a revision of international relations and international business theory. Drawing upon a study of investment relations in Brazil, Malaysia, and Kenya, they argued that state-firm and even firm-firm bargaining was becoming more important to the international system (Stopford and Strange 1991). States are increasingly interested in attracting foreign investment, and firms are increasingly able to have governments develop policies that facilitate their investments. Thus, a key feature of how rules are created and enforced in the global economy is the negotiation conducted between states and firms.

A good example of how corporations can influence global governance is provided by the insertion of intellectual property rights (IPRs) into the WTO. IPRs include things such as copyright protection for books and music, as well as patent protection for inventions and scientific discoveries. They do not really fall under the umbrella of free trade, because their enforcement does not increase the flow of goods between states. However, in the 1980s many Western corporations in industries such as pharmaceuticals, computer software, movies, and music became concerned that competitors were copying their products. An association of leading U.S. multinational corporations (members included Bristol-Meyers, General Electric, Hewlett-Packard, IBM, Johnson & Johnson, Merk, Monsanto, Pfizer, and Time Warner) convinced the U.S. government that IPRs should be protected in trade agreements. Eventually the corporations were able to have rules that they largely drafted inserted into the WTO (Sell 1999). These are some of the rules that the government of South Africa is battling against in an attempt to provide affordable drugs to combat the large numbers of deaths from AIDS in southern Africa.

In addition to the trend of increasing corporate influence over state policy makers, one can also point to the rise of private authority. Private authority exists where firms exercise decision-making power over a particular issue area and this activity is viewed as legitimate. Cutler, Haufler, and Porter (1999) have identified six mechanisms for the exercise of private authority: industry norms, coordination service firms (e.g., bond-rating firms), production alliances, cartels, business associations, and private regimes. They argue that private firms are increasingly exercising authority in particular issue areas in the global economy. Studies of the telecommunications industry, insurance business, accountancy, and cartels support the notion of private authority (Strange 1996).

Recognizing the role and significance of corporate activity does not imply that state power is unimportant nor that all corporations behave the same way. One can acknowledge the role of corporate activity in global governance while at the same time agreeing with authors (Doremus et al. 1998) who argue that there are differences in behavior among corporations from different states and that states often support the behavior of corporations headquartered in their territory. Corporations have an interest in influencing the terms of global governance even if their particular interests are not identical.

In their pursuit of profits, corporations will attempt to influence the structures of global governance. Not all corporations will have the same immediate goals, nor follow the same tactics. Indeed, business conflict theory (Skidmore-Hess 1996) advises us to expect clashes of interest between corporations in international, as well as domestic, realms. Corporations from particular states or sectors may demonstrate distinctive characteristics. Firms that are internationally competitive will have different preferences from those that are not internationally competitive. Despite, or because of, these differences, corporations will attempt to shape governance structures by influencing state, international organization, corporate, and civil society behavior. The role of the corporation in international relations has grown to such an extent that any attempt to understand or influence global governance must take the role of corporations into account.

In addition to key states and resource-rich corporations, *voluntary citizen organizations* are playing an increasing role in influencing the principles of global governance. Indeed, since 1980, prominent civic actors have played the role of unofficial opposition to global governance agencies and interstate agreements. They have stressed an agenda that puts citizen autonomy and security at the center of governance questions. Peace groups have opposed particular weapons systems and military strategies. The campaign to ban the production and use of landmines is the most recent example. Development, women's, environmental, and labor groups have opposed the dominance of liberal policies emanating from international economic institutions. Citizen action across state borders to overcome the antidemocratic actions of their own states has been described as "democratic internationalism" (Gilbert 1999).

The global civil society sphere is the space where civic actors meet to engage in debate and political activity in an effort to shape the direction of global and national society (Scholte 2000b). It is primarily composed of voluntary, nonprofit associations. To differentiate them from profit-seeking nongovernmental organizations such as corporations, this chapter uses the term civic associations. The most visible organizations tend to be those working in high-profile areas such as Greenpeace and Friends of the Earth in the environmental field or Amnesty International in the human rights area. However, there are many other forms of organization. For example, international trade union bodies such as the International Confederation of Free Trade Unions claim a representative (127 million members), as well as advocacy, role. Religious organizations are also very active. In terms of numbers of formal organizations, the bulk of activity takes place in relatively uncontroversial forums, such as industry associations and scientific knowledge organizations (medicine, sciences, communications) (Boli and Thomas 1999, 41). Aggregating highly visible civic associations with less visible local activity, one can point to the emergence of fluid social movements around issues such as human rights, peace, and women's issues.

Although there are many groups and specific agendas, most politically active groups would describe themselves as pursuing the objectives of equity or social justice. Equity and justice could be sought in respect to gender relations (women's groups), distribution of resources (development groups), quality of life across states and generations (environmental groups), and human security (human rights). There are, of course, differences among members of civil society, just as there are conflicts among states or corporations. Organized labor is challenged by nongovernmental organizations claiming to speak on behalf of the informal sector. Women's groups in the developing world have an ambivalent and sometimes conflictual relationship with Northern feminist groups. Environmentalists seeking thorough changes to the doctrine of economic growth are in conflict with more conservative conservationist groups. Various groups claim to speak on behalf of social movements or constituencies, but the plethora of groups and lack of transparency makes it difficult to determine the legitimacy of their claims.

Although the precise nature of global civil society is debatable, it is less contentious that transnational civic actors are having an influence on world politics and interstate relations. Scholarly attention has tended to focus upon the campaigns of human rights, environmental, and women's groups to influence norms and values in the global system (Keck and Sikkink 1998). International civic associations seeking social transformation operate on a number of levels to influence global governance—they create and activate global networks, participate in multilateral arenas, facilitate interstate cooperation, act within states to influence policy, and enhance public participation (Alger 1997). Even in areas often considered to be the sole domain of states, such as international security, civil society groups can play a role in shaping the agenda and contributing to policy change (Price 1998).

At the minimum we can say that civic actors increasingly serve a role as disseminators of information, mobilizers of public opinion, and articulators of dissent and protest. Ignoring their role, as the architects of the Multilateral Agreement on Investment did (Mayne and Picciotto 1999), is likely to lead to governance breakdown. Civic associations can be instrumental in undermining the legitimacy of international organizations, even as states continue to support them.

The Global Compact—A Recent Example

If global governance is to push ahead, one would imagine some form of accommodation is required between the three different types of key actors (state, corporate, and civic). For example, a trade regime would have to simultaneously be sensitive to the interests of developing states for increased equity, to corporate interests for expansion and profit, and to social interests for restricting human and environmental exploitation. This is an enormously complicated task. An example of such an approach is the Global Compact developed by the secretary general's office of the U.N.

The Global Compact asks corporations to govern their behavior according to nine principles that are drawn from the Universal Declaration of Human Rights, the ILO's Fundamental Principles on Rights at Work, and the Rio Principles on Environment and Development. The Global Compact does not monitor corporate practice nor does it assess corporate performance. It is designed to identify and disseminate good practices (United Nations 1999). In other words, the Global Compact asks leaders of some of the world's most prominent corporations to publicly commit themselves to good labor and environmental practices.

The Global Compact addresses the concerns of some corporate, state, and civic associations simultaneously. From a developing country point of view the initiative is tolerable, because it is aimed at influencing the policy of multinational corporations rather than restricting state policy or punishing developing states for poor labor conditions. This is preferable to having the WTO enforce standards, because it removes the threat of Northern protectionism. From the corporate viewpoint, it is tolerable because the regulations are voluntary and allow continued expansion of the global economy and accumulation of profits. They can claim to be good corporate citizens without being bound by compulsory regulation. For some civic actors, it represents a limited advance in enshrining some principles of social protection. It is a small step that might lead to more binding forms of regulation.

To be sure, the social compact has severe shortcomings. Many of the companies participating in the venture are those which have been attacked as abusers of environmental and human rights or engaged in superexploitation of workers. The list includes Shell, Nike, Disney, and Rio Tinto. Each of these companies has been or is subject to boycotts or anticorporate campaigns by civic associations. One can question the degree to which such companies will actually change their stripes. Domestically, reliance only upon voluntary regulation of corporate behavior is unacceptable. Why would such activity at the global level prove any more satisfying? The ILO has hundreds of conventions but sees many abused because of a lack of enforcement powers. How would this initiative be any different? Another problem is that the selection of participating civic associations in the Global Compact was very narrow and not reflective of the wider community. The U.N. selected civic groups based on their judgment of who would be the most likely to cooperate. Reaction from many other groups has been very critical. The initiative has been condemned because it threatens the integrity of the U.N. as corporations attempt to "bluewash" their record by association with the U.N. (TRAC 2000).

The example of Global Compact is informative for our efforts to understand global governance reform for three reasons. Firstly, it illustrates that the concerns of civic actors about the uncivilized nature of globalization are being taken seriously by other actors in the system. The United Nations is responding to public unease about the costs of globalization. The Global Compact initiative follows public demonstrations against institutions such as the WTO and the IMF. The U.N. secretary general is trying to put a more humane face on globalization so that the process will continue, but in a less brutal manner. The goal is to restrain competition that is based upon the abuse of labor standards so that the public will not fight the liberal rules under which globalization is taking place. Corporations are also being forced to respond to civic pressure by setting up codes of conduct and projecting the image of moral behavior.

Secondly, it highlights the failure of existing global governance arrangements. We already have an institution that is designed to bolster labor standards—the ILO. However, the ineffectiveness of the ILO has forced labor activists to turn to the enforcement mechanisms found in the WTO to support labor standards. Many developing states oppose dealing with labor standards, because they fear that developed states might increase their protectionism through the device of labor standards. Those groups in civil society trying to improve labor standards find themselves blocked at the WTO and faced with a weak ILO. Existing global governance mechanisms seem unable to improve social standards. Thus, new initiatives such as the Global Compact are being devised in an urgent attempt to resolve difficult dilemmas.

Thirdly, the Global Compact illustrates just how difficult it is to create new governance arrangements. The costs of freer markets create more public resistance, but many states and corporations resist instruments that would require better labor, environmental, or social standards. Agreements that secure widespread corporate and state support are unlikely to satisfy the social interests that are pressing for protection. At the moment, social interests may have to accept incremental steps towards reforming institutions and policies on the global level.

The point here is not to argue the merits or demerits of the Global Compact. It is to illustrate a recent response to the difficult problem of civilizing globalization. It may be an inadequate response, but it serves as a example of state-corporate-civic associational action that can serve as a building block for civilizing globalization.

References

Abbott, Jason, and Ronen Palan. 1996. *State Strategies in the Global Political Economy.* London: Pinter.

Alger, Chadwick F. 1997. "Transnational Social Movements, World Politics, and Global Governance." In *Transnational Social Movements and Global Politics: Solidarity Beyond the State*, ed. Jackie Smith, Charles Chatfield, and Ron Pagnucco. Syracuse, N.Y.: Syracuse University Press.

Boli, John, and George M. Thomas. 1999. *Constructing World Culture: International Nongovernmental Organizations Since 1875.* Stanford, Calif.: Stanford University Press.

Cerny, Philip. 2000. "The Competition State." In *Political Economy and the Changing Global Order,* ed. Richard Stubbs and Geoffrey Underhill. Toronto: Oxford University Press.

Cox, Robert (with Timothy J. Sinclair). 1996. *Approaches to World Order.* Cambridge: Cambridge University Press.

Cutler, A. Claire, Virginia Haufler, and Tony Porter. 1999. "The Contours and Significance of Private Authority in International Affairs." In *Private Authority and International Affairs.* Albany: State University of New York Press.

Doremus, Paul, William W. Keller, Louis W. Pauly, and Simon Reich. 1998. *The Myth of the Global Corporation.* Princeton: Princeton University Press.

Garrett, Geoffrey. 2000. "Shrinking States? Globalization and National Autonomy." In *The Political Economy of Globalization,* ed. Ngaire Woods. London: Macmillan.

Gilbert, Alan. 1999. *Must Global Politics Constrain Democracy? Great Power Realism, Democratic Peace, and Democratic Internationalism.* Princeton: Princeton University Press.

Gill, Stephen, and David Law. 1993. "Global Hegemony and the Structural Power of Capital." In *Gramsci, Historical Materialism, and International Relations,* ed. Stephen Gill. Cambridge: Cambridge University Press.

Hasenclever, Andreas, Peter Mayer, and Volker Rittberger. 1997. *Theories of International Regimes.* Cambridge: Cambridge University Press.

Hewson, Martin, and Timothy J. Sinclair. 1999. "The Emergence of Global Governance Theory." In *Approaches to Global Governance Theory.* Albany: State University of New York Press.

Hirst, Paul, and Grahame Thompson. 1996. *Globalization in Question.* Cambridge: Polity.

Keck, Margaret, and Katherine Sikkink. 1998. *Activists Beyond Borders: Advocacy Networks in International Politics.* Ithaca: Cornell University Press.

Krasner, Stephen D., ed. 1983. *International Regimes.* Ithaca: Cornell University Press.

Mayne, Ruth, and Sol Picciotto, eds. 1999. *Regulating International Business: Beyond Liberalization.* Basingstoke, U.K.: Macmillan and Oxfam.

Polanyi, Karl. 1957. *The Great Transformation.* Boston: Beacon Press.

Price, Richard. 1998. "Reversing the Gun Sights: Transnational Civil Society Targets Land Mines." *International Organization* 52 (3): 613-44.

Scholte, Jan Aart. 2000a. *Globalization: A Critical Introduction.* New York: St. Martin's Press.

_____ 2000b. "Global Civil Society." In *The Political Economy of Globalization,* ed. Ngaire Woods. London: Macmillan.

Sell, Susan. 1999. "Multinational Corporations as Agents of Change: The Globalization of Intellectual Property Rights." In *Private Authority and International Affairs,* ed. A. Claire Cutler, Virginia Haufler, and Tony Porter. Albany: State University of New York Press.

Skidmore-Hess, David. 1996. "Business Conflict and Theories of the State." In *Business and the State in International Relations,* ed. Ronald W. Cox. Boulder, Colo.: Westview.

Stopford, John, and Susan Strange. 1991. *Rival States and Rival Firms.* Cambridge: Cambridge University Press.

Strange, Susan. 1996. *The Retreat of the State: The Diffusion of Power in the World Economy.* Cambridge: Cambridge University Press.

TRAC. 2000. *Tangled Up in Blue: Corporate Partnerships at the United Nations.* Transnational Resource and Action Center. Available from: <www.corpwatch.org>.

United Nations. 1999. "The Global Compact." Access at www.globalcompact.org.

CHAPTER 11

Democracy and Globalization

Frank Cunningham

Despite their many disagreements, theorists of democracy and globalization reach accord on one key argument: (1) democratic decision making in the commonly accepted sense of voting for government leaders is overwhelmingly carried out within political institutions confined to individual states; (2) people are finding their lives increasingly and importantly affected by economic, cultural, environmental, and other factors generated in parts of the world outside of the states they inhabit; therefore, (3) people are increasingly losing the potential for participation in democratic decision making (as commonly conceived) over important factors affecting them. The conclusion of this argument describes the "core problem" of relating democracy and globalization. This chapter will compare some solutions by democratic theorists. The comparison is complicated because theorists use the key terms, "democracy" and "globalization," in different ways.

Democracy

"Democracy" may be taken in a more or less robust sense, and its use in the statement of the core problem is at the anemic end of a range of definitions. From the time of Athenian democracy until into the twentieth century, it was assumed that democracy has to do with rule by the people, sometimes involving majority voting, sometimes more direct participation in common affairs, and that beyond being a convenient method for making collective decisions, democracy is also a means for arriving at policies in accord with the public good. In a famous revision of this conception, the political economist Joseph Schumpeter challenged it on both counts. If, he insisted, one looks at what actually happens in what are called democratic activities where they count, namely in affairs of state, one sees that this is almost exclusively a matter of voting for political leaders. Moreover, since even those who vote for the same candidate usually have a variety of motives, typically self-interested, it is misleading to think of democracy as rule by a unified people or as serving a common good. The result is a self-described "realist" theory according to which democracy is nothing but the ability of people to vote for or against leaders or political parties (Schumpeter [1942] 1962).

Theorists in the lineage of Schumpter are sometimes prepared to allow such behavior as political party activity to count as democratic, but at the core of all such activity is institutionalized voting. Further, it is assumed that people usually vote out of an estimation of what is in their individual interests or that when they do vote with an eye to the public good, visions of what this is will greatly diverge. Critics of this conception fault the Schumpeterians for promoting what Benjamin Barber calls a "thin" conception of democracy (1984). Absent from this conception is the direct activity that people might take in collectively conducting their own affairs in formal governmental settings and in such sites as neighborhoods, workplaces, or schools. Left out of the realist picture as well is the notion that democracy requires people collectively to deliberate about and to pursue public goods in a spirit of civic virtue, including attitudes of mutual respect and the willingness to put aside narrow self interest. These are the criticisms of "deliberative democrats" and "civic republicans" (see the essays, respectively, in Benhabib 1996 and Beiner 1995).

Aspects of democracy, thinly interpreted, figure in different approaches to globalization. However, the embrace of a more robust conception does not help one to confront the core problem, as defined above, since participation and citizen deliberation are best suited to locales even smaller than states—municipalities, workplaces, schools, and so on. So those who approach the core problem with these conceptions of democracy are in the same boat with those who confine it to voting in formal state elections. Some participationists recognize this when they argue in favor of maintaining "a state that is more self-reliant with respect to the international system" in order to preserve space for "bottom-up" political activity (Tickner 1992, 134–35). Similarly, some civic republicans maintain that the values they favor require the identification of citizens with one another, which is attainable only in national and subnational settings (see Sandel 1996, 339).

Globalization

As other chapters in this book illustrate, globalization is also a contested term. A main distinction is between pejorative conceptions, such as Claude Ake's description of globalization as "rendering democracy irrelevant and in this pos[ing] the most serious threat yet in the history of democracy" (1997, 285), and benign conceptions, as in Ulrich Beck's depiction of it as a process that "creates transnational solid links and spaces, revalues local cultures and promotes third cultures" (2000, 11–12). On Ake's view the core problem is a severely democracy-threatening one, while for Beck the problem illustrates the importance of transcending the narrow confines of the nation-state. Also pertinent to this essay are the various and overlapping "dimensions" of globalization, of which three will be addressed: *ethical, political-economic*, and *cultural*.

The *ethical dimension* has to do with who merits rights of citizenship. At a practical level this question is illustrated in the case of migration that is often involuntary due to global and local forces beyond people's control. A persuasive moral case can be made for open borders (Carens 1987); yet rights of migration, much less citizenship rights, remain restricted and at the discretion of individual states. Robert Dahl notes that this situation is a special case of the major "embarrassment of democracy"—that any boundary between those empowered to make democratic decisions and those excluded from this right will disenfranchise some people affected by the decisions. For instance, children are denied the vote though affected by the democratic decisions adults make (Dahl 1982, 97–99). Because the actions of one state are bound to affect those living in other states, confinement of democratic decision making within state borders suffers this same embarrassment. Yet, Dahl concedes, there seems no realistic alternative but to accept the limitation of democratic decision making to states (Dahl 1999).

Pertinent to a *political-economic* dimension is a distinction made by Beck (2000). "Globality" in his approach refers simply to the interconnectedness of countries, which may sometimes have mutually beneficial effects ("globalization"), but which may also have detrimental effects. The latter, Beck allows, is most dramatically the case when a transnational capitalist market limits the control most people have over their lives. For other theorists, however, it is misleading to describe a world capitalist market as one manifestation of "globality" among others, since it is the very heart of contemporary global interconnectedness. "Globalization," as Ake puts it, "is driven by a vigorous, triumphant capitalism which is aggressively consolidating its global hegemony" (1997, 282). He joins other theorists (Strange 1988; Cox 1996) in maintaining that the political-economic dimension of globalization is not just one of its aspects, but the dominant aspect. Not all theorists of globalization who share this view see a global capitalist market in a negative light, but all agree that the mobility of capital, the freedom of transnational firms from control by the governments of particular states, and the increasing power of bodies like the World Trade Organization (WTO) to dictate countries' policies greatly constrain the autonomy of states and hence the power of citizens, whose only democratic means for expressing their will is through the states they inhabit. Some theorists (like Hirst and Thompson 1996) question the additional claim that the largest capitalist players on the international scene lack a state base of support, but they agree that political-economic analyses merit pride of place in analyzing globalization.

As to the *cultural* dimension of globalization, Barber joins many critics in decrying what he sees as its effect of homogenizing the world's entertainment and news, and doing so in such a way that the indigenous habits of daily life and forms of recreation are being replaced by the common (and for Barber shallow and debased) cultures of the wealthier countries, especially the United States. He calls the resulting culture McWorld (1995; and see Held and Mc-Grew 2000, pt. 3). When combined with an anticapitalist political-economic analysis, a cultural focus also sees globalization as responsible for the diffusion of what the late Canadian political-economic theorist C. B. Macpherson called "possessive individualism." In this culture, ownership of consumer goods is seen as the end of life, and people regard their own talents and those of other people as nothing but instruments to this end (1962). According to Macpherson, beginning in the seventeenth and eighteenth centuries the growth of a competitive market bred possessive individualism in the advancing capitalist countries, and some critics of globalization see the same thing spreading now to the entire globe, including to developing countries, to former socialist societies, and even to remaining ones, such as China.

Reactions to the Core Problem

This section sketches alternative reactions to the core problem concerning democracy and globalization and relate these alternatives to each of the three dimensions of globalization just reviewed. The reactions may roughly be labeled *cosmopolitan, state-autonomist, neoliberal,* and *participationist.* My own approach combines elements of all these except neoliberalism in a left-wing *pragmatic* perspective, which will also be addressed.

Cosmopolitanism. Beck's distinction between malign and benign conceptions of global interconnectedness is meant to clear space for what he and other cosmopolitan theorists see as an exciting opportunity to extend democracy beyond state boundaries. While their conception of democracy is usually thicker than Schumpeter's, it remains close to the common conception in seeing democracy mainly as a matter of formal institutions centrally responsible to elected officials. The model pointed to by cosmopolitans such as David Held (1995) and Daniele Archibugi (1998) is the European Union, which is, as Archibugi puts it, "midway" between, on the one hand, the World Federalist vision of a single world state, which is seen as unrealistically insensitive to national differences, and, on the other hand, the sort of association represented by the United Nations, which allows too much in the way of individual state autonomy to take concerted action regarding global problems and opportunities. In this model, elected legislative assemblies and their mandated legal bodies and regulative agencies set and enforce standards with respect to economic interactions, the environment, human rights, and other such matters of trans-state concern.

State autonomism. While the cosmopolitan solution to the core problem is to weaken state sovereignty and to shift the locus of much democratic decision making to global or regional governments, an alternative solution is to resist global incursions on the powers of individual states. I am calling this approach *"state-autonomist"* instead of the more common designations, "nationalist" or "sovereigntist," to account for the fact that single states may include more than one nation and because, as Charles Beitz notes (1991, 241), a state may assign to itself a legal monopoly over all affairs within its borders ("sovereignty") but find the actual ability to exercise its sovereignty (i.e., its "autonomy") severely constrained by external forces. One motive for maintaining (or regaining) state autonomy is nationalism, whereby the state is seen as essential for protecting national integrity. Another motive, expressed by Dahl, is the belief that democracy, hard enough successfully to achieve even within states, is unrealistic on any larger scale (1999). The hope for protecting state autonomy in a shrinking world is expressed by Will Kymlicka, who maintains that, in principle, international institutions and actors can be held *indirectly* to account in a state by "debating at the national [i.e., state] level how we want our governments to act in international contexts" (1999, 123).

Neoliberalism. Each of the cosmopolitan and the state-autonomist responses to the core problem accepts some version of democracy as institutionalized voting for political leaders. The next two responses reject this conception, though for very different reasons. Milton Friedman nicely summarizes the neoliberal conception, in which, as far as possible, state action should be kept to a minimum, and human interactions should be allowed to sort themselves out through individual market transactions. There are, in his view, only two ways of coordinating the economic activities of large populations: "central direction involving the use of coercion" or "the technique of the market place" (1962, 130). Like Ake, Strange, Cox, and others, neoliberals view globalization mainly in political-economic terms, but unlike these critics, they *welcome* global capitalist marketization as an alternative to government action, whether confined to states or conducted by superstate governments. Because they specialize in criticizing socialism for being unavoidably autocratic, main neoliberal theorists like Friedman and Friedrich Hayek (1944) present themselves as champions of democracy; however, to be consistent they should be suspicious of majority voting, because it often mandates state actions that constrain markets (Nozick 1974, 268–71).

Participatory democracy. Theorists in this tradition resist the identification of democracy with voting for government leaders for the different reason that such democracy promotes political passivity. For participationists who address themselves to globalization, therefore, neither cosmopolitanism nor efforts to strengthen state autonomy are to be favored, or at least not unless subject to active scrutiny and direction by people affected by globalization. As noted earlier, participatory democrats usually focus on social settings smaller than states; however, some theorists see a role for direct collective action in what Robert Walker calls "critical social movements" that concern themselves with the effects of globalization within states and may themselves be international in composition (Walker 1988, 26–32). Anticipating broadly based and international coalitions of the sort that began in Seattle in 1999 protesting against meetings of the WTO, William Connolly sees such movements not only as reactions against capitalist-serving globalization but also as forces for the "nonterritorial democratization of global issues" (1991, 218).

Pragmatism. Not every approach to the core problem excludes all of the other approaches. For instance, Norberto Bobbio regards transstate and intrastate democratic activities as potentially mutually reinforcing (1995), and Richard Falk sees a vital role for social-movement activism as part of a cosmopolitan project (2000, 176). Although some theorists consider such eclecticism a deficiency, others of a more pragmatic bent regard it as manifesting useful flexibility. For pragmatists, political theory, like politics itself, is a matter of experimentation with alternative solutions to problems. This is why John Dewey entitled his influential book on democracy *The Public and Its Problems* (1927). Democracy for him is a matter of how people who confront common problems (social, economic, environmental, and so on) endeavor collectively to resolve them. Essential to this conception is that how problems are addressed by "publics" depends partly on the nature of the problem and partly upon the social, cultural, and political contexts within which it is being addressed. On this viewpoint, therefore, there is no one "right" way to conceive of democracy: sometimes and for some publics formal voting to empower leaders is appropriate; other times or for other publics, direct action following on deliberation to reach consensus is in order.

An application of this pragmatic method to democracy and globalization is illustrated by Michael Saward. Specifically reacting to cosmopolitanism, he recommends locating "democratic mechanisms" within a conceptual space of four quadrants depending upon whether they involve permanent structures like the European Parliament or the U.N. or are temporary measures, such as pro tem accords among countries, and whether they are undertaken by governments or, as in the case of activities of voluntary organizations, like those promoting environmental protection or human rights, by nongovernmental bodies.

Saward criticizes cosmopolitans for confining their attention to quadrant "B" to the exclusion of opportunities in "D," which include cross-border referenda and reciprocal representation (where the legislative bodies of some countries include seats for representatives from some other countries with voice or even vote regarding issues of shared concern). U.N. initiatives like the Rio,

Figure 11.1
Saward's Democratic Mechanisms Quadrants

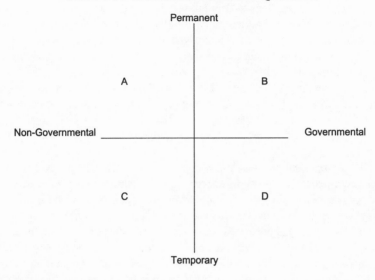

Permanent

A   B

Non-Governmental   Governmental

C   D

Temporary

Source: Saward 2000, 39.

Cairo, and Beijing conferences (regarding, respectively, development and the environment, population growth, and women's rights) can also be placed in this quadrant; while the representation of women's or environmental organizations in U.N. forums are examples from "A" or "C," depending upon whether there is provision for standing representation. With a bit of reflection a large variety of practices, institutions, and organizations can be located at various points in this chart, none of which for the pragmatist can be presumed democratically superior to the others as a general approach to globalization.

Ethical Dimensions of Globalization

One advantage to a *pragmatic* approach with respect to Dahl's "embarrassing" problem about where to draw boundaries between those empowered to make decisions and those excluded from this privilege is that the approach does not insist upon one boundary regarding all matters, and such boundaries need not be carved in stone. For instance, it would make sense for bordering Canadian provinces and U.S. states to have reciprocal representation in each other's legislatures to address environmental matters, but this would not mandate such representation regarding public education. Or a body like the European Union might establish committees to deal with economic disparities among member states that could be disbanded when the disparities shrink. As to the more deeply philosophical problem of identifying criteria by appeal to which boundaries may be justified, Susan Hurley suggests a solution in keeping with pragmatism, namely to select that boundary which is the most likely to engender or preserve democracy in the future (1999, 274). A democratic criterion is appropriate in this view not only for those who see intrinsic merits in democracy but also for those who agree with pragmatists like Dewey that the stronger democratic habits and cultures are, the better are publics able to solve problems they confront.

Setting boundaries on a *state-autonomist* perspective is relatively easy—autonomy means that the right to participate in formal democratic decision making is limited to citizens of a state. More difficult is the ethical challenge to justify such limitation. One justification is simply practical. For better or worse, the world we inhabit is portioned into states, which, when they are democratic, have established means for making collective decisions by voting. Any attempt to extend these limits—short of the impossible task of creating a thoroughgoing world government—would leave one with even more arbitrary boundaries. This seems to be Dahl's view (1999). Another defense depends upon states comprising single nations or at least as creating a nationlike common ethos among their citizens. On this assumption a "communitarian" argument for privileging members of nation-states can be given. Communitarians are skeptical about the possibility of making universally applicable prescriptions in morality and think that moral norms can only be those already embodied within the traditions of societies people inhabit (MacIntyre 1984).

Cosmopolitan and *participationist* theorists are wary of what they see, not without reason, as the parochialism and national chauvinism of such an orientation. But they are also reluctant to advocate world government—cosmopolitans for the practical reason mentioned above and participationists due to a conviction that the larger a state and attendant levels of representation and bureaucracy are, the more difficult it is for people directly to engage in self-government. A cosmopolitan solution, as already mentioned, is to settle on democratic units larger than states but smaller than the world, which in practice means regionally confined bodies, such as their favorite example, the European Union. While some participationists welcome the opportunity for cross-border coordination among social movements afforded by such bodies, their main recommendation is to encourage direct action of people wherever they confront common problems, whether within or cutting across state or regional boundaries, so this would serve as their criterion to justify a "right" to democratic participation.

The problem of who is entitled to engage in democracy-promoting activity is very easily resolved in the *neoliberal* perspective, since it is of the nature of a free market that anyone may enter into transactions within it (or at least try). The ethical problems they confront are not at the front end of democracy (who can participate) but in its outcomes, since in pure market relations there is no analogue of liberal-democratic rights to protect individuals, and even members of a majority can regularly lose out. For the neoliberal, these outcomes will and should result from the combination of entrepreneurial energy and skill, on the one hand, and good or bad luck in the marketplaces of life, on the other. From an ethical point of view, they maintain, people ought to profit from their drive and skill and not be reimbursed for inactivity or ineptitude, and to divert and administer funds to compensate for bad luck leads to objectionable plannification. Moreover, in the long run nobody need lose or lose much, since market mechanisms should function to even out advantages and rewarded entrepreneurship will create wealth, some of which will trickle down to populations as a whole.

Institutions like the WTO, the World Bank, and the adjudicative and regulative bodies of the North American Free Trade Agreement (NAFTA) are sometimes upheld by cosmopolitans as government-like institutions potentially useful for paving the way to transstate governments. On a strict neoliberal approach, by contrast, they should be seen as similar to the minimum state, that is, as instruments for setting the terms of contracts and ensuring their enforcement. On a slightly relaxed neoliberal view, measures by the World Bank to address developing world debt loads or the "side agreements" of the NAFTA for environmental protection and labor standards are in place to compensate for undesirable by-products of global competition. On a cynical interpretation, these are in fact designed as window dressing to sell global marketization to publics suspicious that the main aim is money grabs by the largest private enterprises.

Political-Economic Dimensions

After the collapse of Communism in Eastern Europe and the Soviet Union, it has become common wisdom that democracy requires capitalism—that is, an economic system where private owners of major means of wealth production (industry, natural resources, finance capital, means of distribution) are presumptively free to dispose of these assets and the profits obtained in their use as they wish. For *neoliberals* this presumption should be transgressed only in extreme cases, as to prevent fraud. Regarding globalization, they advance the further claim that trade barriers constitute an unjustified infringement on the rights of private ownership, where trade barriers are sometimes interpreted even to include public provision of education and social services.

No theorists of globalization except neoliberals wholeheartedly endorse laissez-faire—though some see beneficial economic potentials as well as pitfalls in global markets, and some consider the increasing liberalizing and globalizing of economic relations as fated, whereas others think they can be channeled or constrained.

As to how these things might be accomplished, the approaches to democracy and globalization hold out different (though sometimes complementary) prospects. *Participationists* look to social-movement activism, as manifested in the demonstrations and "countersummits" during meetings of major global market players, such as the WTO or of the leaders of the main capitalist countries (the "Group of Seven"), to force on them some sort of accountability, at least to world public opinion. More proactively, they also continue to press for effective NGO participation in international structures such as the U.N. special issue conferences or meetings of NAFTA.

Just as *cosmopolitans* seek a middle ground between world government and state autonomy, so in their political orientation they tend to favor social democracy. This stands between full-blown socialism (where political and economic institutions are structured to promote social and economic equality and cooperation) and welfare capitalism (which, being capitalistic, is structured to protect the rights of private ownership, but sanctions constraints on capitalist freedoms when required to maintain social services and tolerable working conditions). The result is to create space for social planning, including across state boundaries, as in the E.U., which is subject to popular scrutiny and voting.

In the eyes of defenders of *state autonomy*, democracy may have the potential to play quite different roles with respect to the political-economic dimension of globalization. Among the major ways that autonomy is put at risk by economic globalization is in making capital flight easier. As well, tribunals (like those of WTO) or institutions like the World Bank can overturn domestic policies deemed out of accord with the requirements of free trade. This means that in setting policies, a country must always anticipate retaliation by non-elected bodies, some not even located within it, and adjust its sights accordingly. Viewed one way, this situation is on a par with ordinary blackmail, and, as in the case of blackmail generally, there are limited options for confronting it. A powerful county like the United States can sometimes use its clout to mold international agencies to its purposes, but this option is closed to less economically powerful countries. A fatalistic reaction views the threats as unavoidable facts of life and tries to carve out a safe niche for a national economy (as in occasional entreaties by governments in Canada for people to acquire high-tech skills). An alternative is to stand up to the blackmailers. However, since the blackmailers in question are not bluffing, this means that a government challenging them must have the bulk of its population behind any acts of defiance, including preparedness to tighten belts if needs be in the event of retaliation.

One role that democracy plays in this scenario is to marshal the required support behind a government that would have to be empowered by its populace to embark upon such a risk-fraught venture. The other role is motivational. The defiant reaction called for is much like the Battle of Britain, where the German military was surprised by the determination of the British population to endure its relentless bombing. Nationalism no doubt plays a role in such popular determination, but in a less nationalistic country like Canada (and, moreover, a nationally divided one), this could not be a dependable motivation. But perhaps commitment to democracy could provide additional motivation: a people strongly enough committed to maintaining control over their own affairs will be prepared to defend democratic autonomy even if this means making some sacrifices.

If dependence on such strong commitment to democracy seems unrealistic, this is likely because of cynical attitudes toward it on the part of populations even in the developed, liberal-democratic world. In Canada, sources of this cynicism are illustrated with respect to matters of globalization itself. One source is that modern voting systems are not well suited for translating popular will into public policy. For instance, the 1988 federal election in Canada was vigorously conducted around one major issue—whether the country should join the United States in a Free Trade Agreement (later expanded to include Mexico in NAFTA). Polls showed a majority of Canadians wary of this agreement, and of the three main political parties contesting the election, only the Progressive Conservatives supported it. When, however, the votes were counted the Liberals and the New Democratic Party split a majority of the vote, allowing the Conservatives to form a government and sign the agreement. The other source of cynicism about democracy is also illustrated by debates over free trade. In the next election in 1993, the Liberal Party formed the government, having centrally campaigned on the pledge not to support the NAFTA extension of the Free Trade Agreement, but then it reversed field after the election. Later attempts by the party to reinterpret the meaning of its preelection rhetoric failed to dispel suspicion by Canadians that, as in all too many exercises in electoral democracy, majority will is thwarted by political hypocrisy.

In the face of what seems the impossibility of waging a democratically motivated Battle of Britain, the optimism for which *pragmatic* theorists (at least those in the tradition of Dewey) are famous may be in order. Part of the basis for this optimism is rejection of all-or-nothing scenarios, in which, for instance, either something is completely democratic or completely undemocratic, or a population is either entirely enthusiastic about democracy or entirely cynical. Related to this view is an activist stance whereby problems like popular discouragement with democracy invite proactive interventions to take advantage of whatever germs of democracy and democratic enthusiasm exist in a society and build upon them. This suggests that efforts to extend democracy in smaller locales than states—cities and provinces, schools and workplaces, political parties and other voluntary associations, and so on—may in the long run help to nurture commitments to democracy generally with national and international repercussions.

Democratic Culture

Campaigns to strengthen commitment to democracy are at once political and cultural. So we arrive at our final dimension of democracy and globalization. This dimension includes two concerns: that monopolization of cultural media by the more powerful countries will homogenize and debase the cultures of other countries (the McWorld concern), and that domination of the world by a competitive market will create a universal culture of possessive individualism. On a *neoliberal* perspective, neither concern is grave. Culture, in this perspective, is a commodity like any other; so if people do not want to "buy" a particular cultural product, they need not. As to a world culture of possessive individualism, two responses are available to the neoliberal. One is to challenge the claim that cultural life is shaped by economic life. An alternative response is to applaud the diffusion of a culture of economic competition. Though neither of them subscribes to full-blown neoliberalism, Russell Hardin and William Riker offer examples. Riker advocated wide popular dissemination of arguments by public choice theorists that the notion of collective self-determination (even just by majority voting) is "incoherent," in order to disabuse people of adherence to any form of democracy except the thin, Schumpeterian variety (1982, 252). Hardin thinks that a way to avoid national and ethnic conflicts is by promoting commitment to capitalistic competition as an alternative to national or social identifications (1995, 179).

For cosmopolitans, participationists, and state autonomists, however, the cultural concerns *are* grave ones, as they are for Deweyan *pragmatists*. (For Dewey, artistic production and enjoyment are important ways that "publics" come together, and his notion of democracy includes willing commitment to collective enterprises.) Of the cultural concerns, moreover, these critics should see the diffusion of a competitive market mentality as the most grave. An *autonomist* campaign to protect national cultures would be pointless were there not unique cultures to promote. Those who see democracy as, at best, a way of maximizing their chances of securing the outcome of a collective decision that is in their personal interests would not be prepared to risk hardship to defend state autonomy. *Participatory democrats* set themselves explicitly against thin and self-interest based conceptions of democracy.

These attitudes do not advance cosmopolitan aims either, as it is difficult enough to secure loyalty to a single state when the dominant political culture is built around self-interest, and this would be all the more difficult when dealing with transstate bodies. Perhaps it is for this reason that many *cosmopolitan* theorists endorse some version of civic republicanism, where citizens wish to promote the flourishing of their shared state. Cosmopolitans such as Falk (1995) and Martin Köhler (1998) believe that what Köhler (232) calls a "global civil society" is emerging, bound together by shared values including "human rights, democratic participation, the rule of law, and the preservation of the world's ecological heritage." (Evidently, such cosmopolitans discounted challenges to their optimism manifested by aggressive capitalist practices, but they did not anticipate challenges from the different direction of terrorism motivated by fanatical religious fundamentalism.)

Overlapping civic republican and participatory conceptions of democracy is one advanced by Macpherson, in which democracy aims at providing equal opportunities for individuals to develop what he calls their "uniquely human capacities" (1973, 4). The opportunities in question in this "developmental egalitarian" perspective are economic and social (for instance, access to education) but also specifically political, since meaningful participation in the conduct of public affairs is both itself a uniquely human power and required to maintain democratic support for requisite economic and social policies. An advantage of this conception is that Macpherson's list of truly human capacities is open-ended. The examples he offers are "for rational understanding, for moral judgement and action, for aesthetic creation or contemplation, for . . . friendship or love, and sometimes for religious experience" (ibid.), and he allows that the list may be extended. Therefore, this conception maintains space for the diversity of world cultures. Also noteworthy about his conception of truly human capacities is that their exercise by one person does not preclude exercise of them by others, and that beyond provision of essential social services and personal assurance of a comfortable life, development and employment of the human capacities does not require unlimited wealth. The result is that unlike the possessive-individualist picture, activity in accord with developmental egalitarianism need not be competitive or directed toward consumerist accumulation.

Living with Globalization

Contributors to this book are invited to address the question of how we can live with globalization. By now it should be obvious how I favor responding: one should strive to "live with" globalization pragmatically and in a spirit of developmental egalitarianism. The virtue of pragmatism is its flexibility. Elements of the cosmopolitan, participatory, and state-autonomist approaches to democracy may be drawn on, depending on which of the options that can be mapped in Saward's quadrants (above) is most appropriate given specific global challenges and opportunities. While rejecting the monolithic orientation of neoliberalism, this approach need not reject market solutions when appropriate.

This is not to say that a pragmatic approach is without problems. A main danger pointed out by Robert Cox (1996, 87–91) is to avoid accepting problems and resources for their solution as given, rather than critically questioning how serious a putative problem is or whether some solutions might do more harm than good.

To counter this danger, goals or standards are needed, and this is where developmental egalitarianism comes in. Those constellations of reactions to the core problem (along each of the ethical, economic, and cultural dimensions of globalization) should be selected that are most likely to promote equal development of people's human potentials. Now, on the definitions proffered above, this recommendation has distinctly socialistic (or at least left-wing social-democratic) connotations, and when procapitalist models of what is possible and desirable are dominant, any such recommendation is labeled as unrealistic at best.

My view on this matter is that the circle of people who are put off by socialist *goals* (equality, cooperation), as opposed to the *word* "socialism," is much smaller than the procapititalist pundits would have people believe. However, there is one dimension of the "unrealistic" charge that must be confronted, namely, that Macpherson and others who advocate some version of developmental egalitarianism are flying in the face of human nature. Macpherson's own reaction to this charge was to maintain that to the extent people are possessive individualists, this is not by nature but by default. In a competitive market society, most people lack the resources fully to develop their uniquely human potentials, and turn instead to self-centered consumerism and competition in an attempt to give meaning to their lives. This poses the problem that political campaigns are in order to secure and equitably distribute such resources, but such campaigns are inhibited by the very possessive-individualist values they are meant ultimately to undo.

There can be no doubt that this is a serious problem for the approach to living with globalization endorsed in this contribution. There are three, mutually compatible, reasons for hope—one appealing to *environmental* findings, another drawing on *participatory democracy*, and a third pertaining to liberal-democratic *legitimacy*. Notwithstanding efforts by those with vested interests in denying the precarious state of the world's ecology, there is growing recognition that this ecology cannot long sustain economies and lifestyles that fuel and are fuelled by possessive-individualist values. Many recognize as well that abandoning lives dedicated to competition and accumulation is not a matter of sacrifice, but holds out the possibility of a more intrinsically rewarding style of life. Macpherson drew upon the key thesis of participationists that engaging in local democratic projects, even very modest ones at first, develops people's aptitude for and appreciation of democracy with potentially spiraling effects on other of their values as well in an anti-possessive-individualist direction. He thus suggested a second cause for hope in an analogue of the slogan, also central to environmentalism, to "act locally and think globally."

The third consideration depends on a view articulated by Macpherson in his influential CBC Massey Lectures, *The Real World of Democracy*. He concluded the lectures by calling attention to what he saw as a looming crisis of legitimacy for the developed, liberal-democratic countries, whose moral stature and hence citizen allegiance and world respect are called into question by disregard of (and worse, complicity in), global inequalities. "Nothing less than massive aid, which will enable the poor nations to lift themselves to recognizable human equality," he concluded the lectures, "will conserve the moral stature and the power of the liberal democracies" (1965, 67). Those who agree with this conclusion and who are not prepared to trust the workings of a global economic market or technological wonders to redress global inequalities should, again, realize that this task must be approached in an anti-possessive-individualist, cooperativist spirit.

References

Ake, Claude. 1997. "Dangerous Liaisons: The Interface of Globalization and Democracy." In *Democracy's Victory and Crisis*, ed. Alex Hadenius. Cambridge: Cambridge University Press.

Archibugi, Daniele. 1998. "Principles of Cosmopolitan Democracy." In *Re-imagining Political Community: Studies in Cosmopolitan Democracy*, ed. Daniele Archibugi, David Held, and Martin Köhler. Stanford, Calif.: Stanford University Press.

Barber, Benjamin. 1984. *Strong Democracy: Participatory Politics for a New Age*. Berkeley: University of California Press.

Barber, Benjamin. 1995. *Jihad vs. McWorld: How Globalism and Tribalism Are Reshaping the World*. New York: Ballentine Books.

Beck, Ulrich. 2000. *What is Globalization?* Cambridge: Cambridge University Press.

Beiner, Ronald, ed. 1995. *Theorizing Citizenship*. Albany: State University of New York Press.

Beitz, Charles R. 1991. "Sovereignty and Morality in International Affairs." In *Political Theory Today*, ed. David Held. Cambridge: Polity Press.

Benhabib, Seyla, ed. 1996. *Democracy and Difference: Contesting the Boundaries of the Political*. Princeton: Princeton University Press.

Bobbio, Norberto. 1995. "Democracy and the International System." In *Cosmopolitan Democracy: An Agenda for a New World Order*, ed. Daniele Archibugi and David Held. Cambridge: Polity Press.

Carens, Joseph H. 1987. "Aliens and Citizens: The Case for Open Borders." *Review of Politics* 49 (spring): 251–73.

Connolly, William E. 1991. *Identity/Difference: Democratic Negotiations of Political Paradox*. Ithaca: Cornell University Press.

Cox, Robert W. 1996. *Approaches to World Order*. Cambridge: Cambridge University Press.

Dahl, Robert A. 1982. *Dilemmas of Pluralist Democracy: Autonomy vs. Control*. New Haven: Yale University Press.

———. 1999. "Can International Organizations Be Democratic? A Skeptic's View." In *Democracy's Edges*, ed. Casiano Hacker-Cordon and Ian Shapiro. Cambridge: Cambridge University Press.

Dewey, John. 1927. *The Public and its Problems*. Denver: Alan Swallow.

Falk, Richard. 1995. *On Humane Governance: Toward A New Global Politics*. Cambridge: Polity Press.

———. 2000. "Global Civil Society and The Democratic Project." In *Global Democracy: Key Debates*, ed. Barry Holden. London: Routledge.

Friedman, Milton. 1962. *Capitalism and Freedom*. Chicago: University of Chicago Press.

Hardin, Russell. 1995. *One for All: The Logic of Group Conflict*. Princeton: Princeton University Press.

Hayek, Friedrich A. 1944.*The Road to Serfdom*. Chicago: University of Chicago Press.

Held, David. 1995. *Democracy and the Global Order*. Cambridge: Polity Press

Held, David, and Anthony McGrew, eds. 2000. *The Global Transformations Reader*. Cambridge: Polity Press.

Hirst, Paul, and Grahame Thompson. 1996. *Globalization in Question*. Cambridge: Polity Press.

Hurley, Susan L. 1999. "Rationality, Democracy, and Leaky Boundaries: Vertical vs. Horizontal Modularity." In *Democracy's Edges*, ed. Casiano Hacker-Cordon and Ian Shapiro. Cambridge: Cambridge University Press.

Köhler, Martin. 1998. "From the National to the Cosmopolitan Public Sphere." In *Reimagining Political Community: Studies in Cosmopolitan Democracy*, ed. Daniele Archibugi, David Held, and Martin Köhler. Stanford, Calif.: Stanford University Press.

Kymlicka, Will. 1999. "Citizenship in an Era of Globalization: Commentary on Held." In *Democracy's Edges*, ed. Casiano Hacker-Cordon and Ian Shapiro. Cambridge: Cambridge University Press.

CHAPTER 12

Recasting the World Trade Organization

Jens L. Mortensen

The World Trade Organization occupies a powerful position in the world economy. It could play a major role in civilizing globalization. Alternatively, it could continue to propel an unsustainable globalization beyond democratic control. But before the WTO can assume a positive role, it will need not only to transcend the pervading elitism and secrecy that stifle its potential but also to obtain adequate resources to fulfill its responsibilities as the principal multilateral governor of the global economy.

The Power of the WTO

The WTO has evolved into the center of gravity in the governance of global economic integration. Its scope is vast. It administers agreements designed to liberalize not only trade in goods (General Agreement on Tariffs and Trade [GATT]), but also trade in services (General Agreement on Trade in Services [GATS]). In addition, the organization oversees the TRIPS agreement (Agreement on Trade-Related Intellectual Property Rights), whereby copyright and patent holders have gained extensive rights to safeguard their innovations and products across the globe. The WTO even covers certain aspects of global investments (Agreement on Trade-Related Investment Measures [TRIMS]). Perhaps most significantly, the WTO arbitrates the clash between international trade liberalization, on the one hand, and national regulations in the fields of environmental protection, health, and food safety, on the other (typically concerning the Agreement on Technical Trade Barriers [TBT], and the Agreement on Sanitary and Phyto-Sanitary Measures [SPS] on food safety). The WTO has frequently been called into action. Since its establishment in 1995, it has acted as "the world trade court" in more than 220 instances. These include the most explosive trade issues in the contemporary world economy: the European import ban on hormone-treated beef, the use of offshore tax havens by U.S. exporters, a U.S. ban on "turtle-unsafe shrimps," and banana imports into the European Union. By comparison, the WTO's predecessor, the GATT, only dealt with about two hundred disputes from 1947 to 1994. The WTO is truly redefining the rules of international economic exchange.

Not only is the organization's mandate broad, but its powers are extensive. The Uruguay Round of trade negotiations (1986–94) institutionalized a strong disputes-settlement system. This process was hailed by former WTO director-general Renato Ruggerio as "the WTO's most individual contribution to the stability of the global economy" (WTO 1998). The reform of the dispute-settlement system meant a significant shift towards a legalistic system. Three principal features characterize the new quasi-automatic Dispute Settlement System:

- *the "reverse consensus" principle* that prevents any member from blocking the establishment of a panel or adoption of the rulings;

- *the integrated dispute-settlement system* whereby all WTO agreements are enforced through one single mechanism in order to prevent "forum-shopping";

- *the Appellate Body*, providing a much needed "quality control" of the initial panel investigation.

A number of less revolutionary changes—stricter time limits, explicit requirements concerning panel composition and their impartiality—also contributed to the transformation of GATT diplomacy towards WTO legalism (see Jackson 1998; Petersman 1997).

In policy terms, this drift toward legalistic dispute resolution was a projection of the "privatization of U.S. trade politics" to the global level, moving trade issues away from the foreign policy domain towards direct corporate engagement (see Ostry 1997). The American view is that the WTO is the courtroom for trade disputes. Former U.S. trade representative Charlene Barshefsky once explained that "the WTO dispute settlement mechanism was explicitly designed to ensure that rights acquired through litigation could be firmly enforced." Others do not share that view. The Europeans and Japanese maintain a preference for a more flexible system centered on interstate diplomacy rather than on "rule of law." The *Economist* warned in 1999 of the dangers of such "a narrow legalistic view of the world," whereby the WTO has become a forum for "enforcing the letter of those 260-odd new agreements, at the expense of the bigger picture" and "keeping clients[,] such as the steel industry, happy by picking fights, going to the brink and settling at the last minute." Even large transnational corporations are concerned about the aggressiveness of WTO · dispute settlement: "Continued non-compliance, prolonged litigation, and retaliation including carousel retaliation are placing enormous economic and political strain on the transatlantic relationship and are causing significant economic harm to the American and European business communities" (Transatlantic Business Dialogue 2000, 37–38). However, the system holds firm even though cracks have appeared among the organization's supporters.

Whereas global corporations may have some reservations, the antiglobalization movement and labor organizations reject the WTO system as wholly illegitimate. A recent call to arms expressed it this way: "The WTO dispute settlement system is unacceptable. It enforces an illegitimate system of unfair rules and operates with undemocratic procedures. It usurps the rulemaking and legislative role of sovereign nations and local governments" (Public Citizen 2001). The gulf between the supporters and opponents of the WTO thus yawns wide.

Indeed, the WTO process has had its problems. Instead of providing a genuine system of law, a handful of influential firms have misused the current WTO on several occasions. As well, the WTO's organizational resources do not match its vast responsibilities. The WTO has the potential for providing a balanced and law-based regulation of globalization, but that potential has not yet been fulfilled.

The Organizational Resources of the WTO

The WTO is a system of some 260 agreements on international trade, investment, and intellectual property, whose functioning depends upon a Geneva-based organization of only some five hundred people. Its secretariat is responsible for numerous tasks that are essential for the development of a fair trade system. Most importantly, the WTO secretariat is supposed to provide extensive technical assistance to its least-developed members to aid trade negotiations, policy surveillance, and dispute settlement; in addition, it is charged with managing the relationship between the WTO and the global civil society. Any assessment of the WTO's democratic deficiencies should acknowledge that the organization, though designed to enhance multilateral governance, does not command the resources to fulfill this crucial task.

Compared to other international organizations, the WTO secretariat is a dwarf, as illustrated by table 12.1 below.[1] This comparison among the six main organizations of global economic governance illustrates well the minimalist philosophy behind the WTO. Its budget is only about 1.7 percent of the combined budget for the six international economic organizations. While WTO governance is centered around its legal activities, and thus is less in need of manpower than for instance the EU Commission, the lack of organizational resources may threaten the capacity of the secretariat to fulfill its mandate (Blackhurst 1998). The risk is not only that WTO rulings are of uneven legal quality, and thus heavily criticized (see Mortensen 2000 for details). Also, there is the problem that most of the least-developed countries cannot benefit from the legal system because they lack access to skilled legal advice. To substantiate the claim that the WTO is understaffed, consider how few staff members are assigned to key duties. For example, the Trade and Environment Division facilitates the preparatory work in the Committee on Trade and Environment. In keeping with the "Decision on Achieving Greater Coherence in Global Economic Policy-making" in 1996, other international organizations must have access to these discussions. This division is responsible for institutionalizing communication between these organizations and the WTO. It services the needs of every TREM-related dispute panel. Finally, it must offer technical assistance on trade-related environmental issues to all WTO members, report to WTO senior management and members on developments on matters concerning multilateral environmental law and politics, and maintain dialogue with the environmental NGO community and the private sector. At the same time, the division also assists with services to the TBT Working Group, and every TBT-related dispute panel. It should provide technical assistance to all WTO members on TBT matters, as well as monitor and report back to WTO and its members on developments in relation to technical standards. Absurdly, this division comprises only ten officials.

Another illustration is the Legal Affairs Division, which has been handed four specific tasks:

- to provide legal advice to members and other WTO divisions on interpretations of the WTO agreements, understandings and decisions;

- to provide legal support to accession negotiations;

- to provide training in WTO dispute-settlement procedures and legal issues; and

- to attend meetings of other international organizations on WTO-related activities.

This is a remarkable workload for the mere fifteen WTO officials working in their legal division, especially given the utmost importance of the dispute-settlement system in WTO governance.

When NGOs charge that the WTO should "Sink or Shrink" (Public Citizen 2001), it is crucial to distinguish between this body's responsibilities and its organizational resources. To shrink the WTO organization any further would jeopardize the small progress already made towards a fairer WTO system.

Underpinning these problems is a "systemically rooted funding problem" (Blackhurst 1998, 51). For instance, an initiative of the 1996 Singapore Ministerial Conference resulted in "The Comprehensive and Integrated WTO Plan of

Table 12.1
Six Agencies Compared in Size and Administrative Budget ($U.S. 1998)

Agency	Staff	Administrative budget	Costs per staff member
EU Commission	21000	3.400.000.000	162000
World Bank	5700	1.375.000.000	241000
IMF	2200	470.000.000	214000
OECD	3400	340.000.000	200000
WTO	510	97.000.000	190000
UNCTAD	440	80.000.000	182000

Source: Henderson (1998, 102)

Action for the Least-Developed Countries."[2] However, only a handful of WTO members have voluntariy financed this program. In 1999, only Germany, Denmark, Norway, Finland, and Japan contributed to technical cooperation and training activities (WTO 2000, 117). Though recent proposals support the technical assistance approach, most of them fail to mention the funding of these programs. Without automatic and adequate funding, global governance is at the mercy of domestic political games.

The regular WTO budget is funded through individual member contributions made according to a formula based on their individual share of international trade. The United States, Germany, and Japan thus contribute, respectively, 15.7 percent, 9.7 percent, and 7.2 percent of the WTO budget (WTO 2000, 117). This method is a relatively simple and fair one for sharing the WTO's operating costs. The problem, as mentioned, concerns the funding of new initiatives. These moves are also funded through the WTO Budget Committee. This committee is comprised of national representatives whose instructions are formulated by national government officials with no firsthand experience of this body. The budget is, therefore, a delicate political compromise hammered out in each capital, a compromise reached through extensive intragovernmental bargains between national bureaucracies. Budget contributions are also shaped by the competition among the various international organizations for the limited resources available. Therefore, only substantial political determination at home will generate sufficient financial resources to improve the governance of the global economy.

But will the political commitment emerge? Currently, the powerful states do not want an independent and well-financed global institution to challenge their hegemony in the trade field. Participation in the WTO process is resource-demanding, and only a few states possess the resources and expertise to participate effectively. The WTO, therefore, remains under the control of its mightiest members.

Building Democratic Legitimacy

The limited resources of the WTO are one aspect of the institutional crisis of the trading system. But a more fundamental problem for the regulation of globalization concerns the body's lack of democratic legitimacy. As two critics have trenchantly observed: "States practice no policy of transparency and consultation which permits effective NGO participation. The mechanisms of the WTO are inadequate and do not guarantee free access to information. The cleft between governments and those they represent is growing ever wider" (Bellmann and Grester 1997, 61).

The WTO remains a projection of the asymmetrical distribution of power and resources in the world economy. States and NGOs remain unevenly equipped to reap the benefits of the WTO. Therefore, future reforms must aim at counterbalancing these asymmetries in the global trade policy process.

To start, consider three principal reform models. First, there is a *bottom-up* strategy; it requires a democratization of the national trade policy–making process. Next, a *top-down* strategy calls for a democratization of WTO institutions. Finally, a *network* strategy necessitates a democratization of the entire global economic policy–making process. Yet, whatever strategy is pursued, global institution-building is a complex process. As political decision makers cannot predict a reform's precise effect, changes are risky and uncertain. That is precisely why reforming an existing organization is difficult.

An obvious solution is a bottom-up strategy: to democratize the national trade policy process. In most countries, the formulation of a trade policy remains a matter between influential lobbyists and the government. Open hearings on trade policies are rare. The WTO process would benefit from closer parliamentary involvement in member states by requiring regular briefings of parliamentary committees and allowing parliamentarians direct participation in negotiating teams. Another possibility is to grant observer or expert status to NGOs in national delegations in trade negotiations.

However, the focus here is how to recast the WTO itself. The main question is whether to embark on its comprehensive reform. On the one hand, one can envision a strong WTO equipped with an autonomous mandate to supervise trade relations, and perhaps even to initiate cases against individual members. This model would, however, invoke fears of a global superbureaucracy, especially in the United States. On the other hand, one can be intimidated by all the constraints on institutional reform, and modestly opt only for such minor reform as the elimination of redundant personnel. Such a proposal, however, is not likely to produce any notable effect. Unlike U.N. agencies, the WTO has never been accused of being a wasteful bureaucracy.

In light of these realities, perhaps the most promising plan is a network strategy—to forge more permanent ties between the WTO, other international

organizations, and the NGO community. It is necessary to combine a realloca-
tion of resources to the WTO with its democratization. The WTO must be seen
as an organization connected to its constituencies. One reform to achieve this
goal might involve the creation of independently funded pools of legal, economic, and scientific expertise for both state and nonstate actors who are currently either denied access to the WTO process, or lack the expertise to benefit
from WTO-led globalization. Other realistic reforms to enhance networking
might include: institutionalizing regular consultations between WTO officials
and NGOs, granting observer status for NGOs in relevant committees, allowing direct NGO participation in the dispute-settlement process, promoting an
interinstitutional expert group on trade and sustainable development, and ensuring automatic access to information for NGOs. Not only must the WTO acquire adequate resources to govern effectively, but the organization must earn
legitimacy to consolidate its authority.

The WTO agenda has actually headed towards the national route, the bottom-up reform that implies minimal change in the WTO itself. However, some
proposals have addressed the deeper problems. For instance, the Canadian government has proposed that a portion of the WTO secretariat budget be allocated
"to fund regular outreach initiatives, . . . to improve public and private sector
understanding of the WTO."[3] However, no WTO decision has been taken on the
funding of this initiative. Still, the very mode of thinking about NGO participation is being transformed. A recent WTO paper well illustrates this point
(WTO 2001). It proposes NGO–secretariat meetings, and occasionally
NGO–member representatives meetings, including small "lunchtime" dia-
logues. NGO representatives who have published "relevant" studies will be invited to the WTO for informal discussions with interested delegations and
secretariat officials, or to "stand-alone" NGO workshops in Geneva. The secretariat also plans to launch a comprehensive web-based program, involving
publication of NGO position papers on the WTO website. The secretariat paper
also proposed several NGO activities for the Doha, Qatar, ministerial meeting
in November 2001. Eager not to repeat the disastrous Seattle meeting, the WTO
secretariat initiated daily NGO briefings at Doha, involving the relevant WTO
secretariat directors and/or staff, and workshops organized by the WTO secretariat on issues of interest to NGOs. However, this was only a belated response
to the democratic legitimacy gap of the WTO.

Even if a political breakthrough enabled deeper reforms, at least two
problems remain. First, though improved NGO involvement in the WTO
process is desirable, such a reform must not divert the already overburdened
WTO secretariat from its principal role. It must function as the sole provider
of technical and legal assistance to the poorest WTO members, who do not
possess adequate resources to influence the new trading system. In fact, the
WTO relies too heavily on the expertise of a few governments who possess

164 *Jens L. Mortensen*

adequate institutional resources to tackle the complexities of global trade issues. Thus, the main advantage of establishing a WTO-NGO network should not be understood in terms of open dialogue, but rather as a greatly needed input of analysis into the WTO secretariat. The real significance of the WTO proposal may actually prove to be the establishment of a network of information exchange between the more resourceful NGOs and the understaffed WTO secretariat.

Secondly, the WTO–NGO network model is not without flaws. Ironically, the NGO community suffers from its own democratic legitimacy deficit. Though some NGOs are more representative than most political parties, others seem to represent only a very narrow interest. It would be extremely difficult to distinguish between genuine NGOs and those representing special-interest groups, producers, or firms. Who should decide which NGO would be permitted to participate in the network? Should the WTO itself create a roster of "serious" NGOs, and if so, according to what criteria? The risk is that the selection of NGOS becomes yet another battlefield for WTO members.

In sum, the institutionalization of a WTO–NGO network depends not only upon the political willingness to welcome societal participation in the WTO process, but also a determination to ensure genuine representativeness of the NGOs involved. Realistically, perhaps, states should remain the sole source of democratic legitimacy in the governance of globalization—"the loci from which forms of governance can be proposed, legitimated and monitored" (Hirst and Thompson 1996). But if states refuse to accept a more democratic global trade policy process, there is no alternative to exploiting fully the "supranational" governance potential in the WTO system, and call for more direct representation in the process by nonstate actors. Such a move could, however, put the WTO's very life at risk. Aggrieved governments might react with demands to "renationalize" the global governance process. Such a response would transform the WTO into a merely symbolic battleground, rather than a genuine problem-solving forum, for global economic conflicts. In short, opening up the WTO—not only to other international organizations and global NGOs but also to the citizens of each individual WTO member—is crucial, though difficult to achieve.

Conclusions

The potential of the WTO as a vehicle for civilizing globalization is limited both by its lack of resources and its lack of democratic legitimacy. The WTO process is notorious for its bias toward the interests of the most powerful firms, lobbyists, and governments. Yet, there is hope for a future democratization of the WTO. Recent initiatives lean toward fuller inclusion of NGOs, perhaps following an accreditation scheme, as with U.N. bodies. Other initiatives address the problem of providing legal expertise to the poorest WTO members. Within the

WTO itself, the Appellate Body has opened up its process. However, no permanent solutions have been found, especially with respect to the financing of initiatives. The WTO secretariat simply lacks the resources needed to perform its many tasks.

Thus, the news is both bad and good. First, the bad news: if the new WTO is not buttressed with sufficient resources, the otherwise excellent proposals for improved NGO–secretariat contacts will only exacerbate the inadequacies of its understaffed secretariat. Those governments that possess adequate legal and technical resources to benefit from the current system will further monopolize it. The good news is that the WTO is gaining a life of its own, and is thereby reinforcing the development of a global polity. Now, it is impossible for states to isolate global trade issues from the broader public debate. Thanks to the controversy surrounding the WTO, the global civil society has grown so powerful that even exporters and bureaucrats call for a democratization of the system. An accountable and transparent WTO is the best possible starting point for a democratization of global economic policymaking.

Notes

1. This comparison provides only a rough indication of the differences in size. As Henderson writes: "The figures obviously indicate only very rough orders of magnitude because it is difficult to put the figures for each organization onto a fully comparable basis" (Henderson 1998, 34). For instance, some budgets include more than operating expenses, such as grants and loans, and the hiring of temporary consultants are sometimes not accounted for in an identical manner. Still, the differences are so significant that it is safe to assume that the WTO is one of the smallest international organizations in existence.

2. "The Integrated Action Plan" aims to develop (1) *institutional capacity-building,* which calls for assistance for WTO-related activities, intragovernmental reforms, and "think-tank" capacity in LDC governments; (2) *export supply capacity* by strengthening the policy environment for trade liberalization so as to enable LDCs to exploit business opportunities by targeted support to infrastructure development; (3) *trade support services* such as improved access to finance, information technologies, and advice on standards, packaging, quality control, marketing, and distribution; (4) *trade facilitation capacity,* such as simplification of export procedures; (5) *human resource development by* organizing training courses; and (6) *supportive trade-related regulatory and policy framework,* such as strategic analysis of global economic trends for LDC governments by the six agencies involved (see WTO document WT/MIN[96]/14).

3. The Canadian proposal would insert the following language into the objectives of the Millennium Round: "*Recognizing* the need for increased transparency in order to improve public and private understanding of the WTO, we agree to improve the transparency of WTO operations by implementing more regular outreach initiatives and by ensuring that more WTO documents are made available to the public, as well as to all members, in a timely fashion" (Canada 1999).

166   *Jens L. Mortensen*

References

Blackhurst, Richard. 1998. "The Capacity of the WTO to Fulfil Its Mandate." In *The WTO as an International Organization*, ed. Anne O. Krueger. Chicago: University of Chicago Press.

Bellmann, C., and R. Grester. 1997. "Accountability in the World Trade Organization." *Journal of World Trade* 30 (6): 31–74.

Canada. 1999. "WTO and Transparency." Communication from Canada in preparation for the Seattle Ministerial Conference, 1 October .

Henderson, David. 1998. "International Agencies and Cross-border Liberalisation." In *The WTO as an International Organization*, ed. Anne O. Krueger. Chicago: University of Chicago Press.

Hirst, Paul, and Grahame Thompson. 1996. *Globalization in Question*. Cambridge: Polity Press.

Jackson, John H. 1998. *The World Trading System: Law and Policy of International Economic Relations*. 2d ed. Cambridge: MIT Press.

Mortensen, Jens L. 2000. "The Institutional Requirements of the WTO in an Era of Globalization: Imperfections in the Global Economic Polity." *European Law Journal* 6 (2): 176–204.

Ostry, Sylvia. 1997. *The Post-Cold War Trading System: Who's on First?* Chicago: University of Chicago Press.

Petersman, Ernst-Ulrich. 1997. *The GATT/WTO Dispute Settlement System: International Law, International Organizations, and Dispute Settlement*. London, The Hague, and New York: Kluwer Law.

Public Citizen. 2001. "Shrink or Sink! The Turnabout Agenda." Available from: <www.citizen.org>.

Transatlantic Business Dialogue. 2000. "Cincinnati Recommendations." 16–18 November.

Venezuela. 1999. "Promotion of the Institutional Image of the World Trade Organization: Communication from Venezuela." WTO document WT/GC/W/14, dated 5 February.

World Trade Organization. 1998. "Trading into the Future." In *An Interactive Guide to the WTO*. Available from: <www.wto.org>.

———. 2000. *Annual Report of the World Trade Organization 2000*. Geneva: WTO.

———. 2001. "WTO Secretariat Activities with NGOs." WTO document WT/INF/30, dated 12 April. Available from: <www.wto.org>.

CHAPTER 13

Can Development Assistance Help?

Cranford Pratt

What would a foreign aid program look like if its primary purpose were to help make globalization more humane? What obstacles, however, render it unlikely that such an aid program would be seriously pursued by more than a few of the developed countries? How should those in the industrial countries who wish their governments' aid programs to reflect humane internationalist values[1] respond to this challenge? These related questions guide this chapter's inquiry.

The Prevailing Official View

In recent years, international and national official aid agencies have reached a consensus about their role in promoting development in the less-developed countries.[2] From both developmental and humanitarian perspectives, this agreement marks an advance on the earlier ad hoc jostling between advocates of humanitarian objectives and those promoting self-interested economic and international political objectives. The new approach does not abandon the earlier commitment to neoliberal policies. Recipient governments are still expected to promote macroeconomic stability, deregulation, openness to trade and investment, and "lean" government. Added on to the earlier concerns, however, is a high priority accorded to poverty reduction. For example, in 1996 the aid agencies of the member states of the OECD produced a manifesto on development cooperation in which they pledged to focus their support on six priority objectives that would enable the poorest to expand their opportunities and improve their lives. As well, the donor states secured the endorsement of these targets in the U.N. Millennium Summit Declaration. Even conceding that the decisions of the OECD's Development Assistance Committee (DAC) are not binding, and that only a few states—in particular Norway, Denmark, the United Kingdom, and Ireland—have seriously adopted poverty reduction as the focus of their aid programs, the DAC pronouncement is important for the support it gives to those who have long advocated a primary emphasis on poverty reduction.

Reinforcing this focus is the World Bank's advocacy throughout the last decade of poverty reduction as a central objective of foreign aid (World Bank 1991, 1997, 2001). This advocacy perhaps constitutes not so much a belated conversion to greater ethical sensitivity as a recognition that otherwise the successful pursuit of neoliberal reforms will often be confounded by social unrest (Campbell 2000). Nevertheless, even if instrumentally intended, this shift in the World Bank's dominant outlook has generated significant changes in its policies and practices that are expected to benefit the world's poorest people (World Bank 1996, 1998, and 1999).

The new consensus includes additional components. Largely as a result of their own painful experiences, most national official aid agencies have come to agree on several important aspects of the aid process. In particular, they concur that the quality and effectiveness of foreign aid is greatly increased when

- there is close donor coordination;

- aid helps meet felt local needs;

- aid assists programs and projects that have been developed and are substantially managed by recipient governments or civil society agencies;

- aid is concentrated in a limited number of countries and sectors, thus increasing the likelihood that the aid agency will be able to acquire a fair measure of expertise on the countries and sectors in which it is active.

A further component of this new consensus is greater agency sensitivity to the hard fact that foreign aid is often valued by recipient governments because it frees up resources that can then be used for purposes of their own choosing. This fungibility of foreign aid has led aid donors to recognize that the final value of their aid to any country will be minimal, if the overall economic and social policies of the recipient government are seriously ill-conceived or the government's competence severely wanting (World Bank 1998b). Finally, it is now widely conceded that the trade, investment, and environmental policies of the developed world's governments are more important to the welfare of most less-developed countries than the foreign aid they receive. As a result, the aid agencies are seeking, and to some extent winning, a role in the decision-making processes within their own governments that shape these crucial policies.

This forthright emphasis on poverty reduction, as well as the importance attached to donor cooperation and "local ownership" of development programs, has already enhanced international aid efforts. Aid recipients, in consultation with donors and, ideally, representatives of their own civil societies, are beginning to produce Poverty Reduction Strategy Papers (PRSPs); these papers should increasingly indicate the basic strategy that donors will assist. As well, there are interesting experiments in donor-coordinated sector-wide approaches (SWAps) to development assistance in which, in theory at least, local officials take the lead. Much can be done to improve these new mechanisms. But there is widespread agreement that these initiatives have significantly increased the poverty focus of international development assistance and improved its effectiveness.

There is, however, a subtext to this consensus that complicates any assessment of its humanitarian significance. The new consensus is not a mere parroting of the neoliberal structural adjustment policies of the mid-1980s. However, it has developed out of, and still supports, the central tenets of the neoliberal ideology that has dominated the thinking and policies of the World Bank, the IMF, and many of the governments of the industrial countries for much of the last two decades. The new consensus is a pragmatic update of that earlier and more ideological neoliberalism, adding three further initiatives to the minimal state role that had earlier been regarded by the IMF and the Bank as legitimate. The first initiative is to ensure that the legal system, the governmental apparatus, and the economic infrastructure are such as to reassure both domestic and foreign investors. The second is the erection of social safety-nets. They lessen the risk that the development process will be thwarted by social unrest generated by those who would otherwise suffer severely from the consequences of globalization. The third is public investments in human capital, in particular in education and health, to accelerate development.

Thus, the interventions by governments of developing countries that official aid agencies are ready to accept, and indeed now advocate, are those that will help ensure the efficient operation and political sustainability of an open-market international capitalism. The donors remain convinced that sustained development in Third World countries requires their governments to integrate fully their economies into the international capitalist system and to leave the production and distribution of goods and services to the private sector operating within an essentially free market economy. The assumption thus remains that there is a fundamental congruity between the interest that the advanced capitalist states have in such a global economy and the interest of the world's poorest people. This pragmatic neoliberalism of the aid agencies thus continues to serve an essentially ideological function, presenting what is in the interests of the dominant capital-owning class as being simultaneously in the interests of the poorest people and countries. It may be more than that, but it certainly is that.

The continued strength of this subtext undercuts the positive humanitarian impact of the new consensus. It leads the aid agencies to focus, in particular, on the policies and capabilities of the recipient countries rather than on the inequalities produced by two international factors: the vastly unequal distribution of resources and skills between rich and poor countries; and the ability of the rich countries to influence the ways in which the benefits of growth are distributed internationally. This focus on the failures of aid-receiving governments feeds into a "what can we do, it is largely their own fault" mood of resignation. It reinforces the declining trend in total allocations for development assistance. It also provides rationalizations to discourage international redistributive and regulatory initiatives that would help ensure that the international economy operated with greater equity towards the world's poorest people and countries. Even the significance of an official aid agency participating in decision-making regarding trade and other policies of importance to the poor countries is much diminished, if agency officials endorse the complacent acceptance within government that global integration is *tout court* in the interests of the poor countries.

There is a final reason for humane internationalists to be cautious about the donors' present consensus. It shifts the rationale for foreign aid from an essentially moral concern to help the poorest peoples and countries to a cluster of neorealist rationales that claim that this aid will lessen the threats to donor prosperity and security. These threats include mass uncontrolled migration, international terrorism, the spread of communicable diseases, and mounting environmental degradation. Thus, so runs the neorealist argument, foreign aid is, in fact, in the national interests of the rich states.

Arguments of this order can very easily backfire. They may be helpful as supplementary reasons but are unreliable as the primary rationale for a generous aid program. At the core of such arguments is a fear that wealthy countries' security and prosperity are threatened by the discontent and unrest that global poverty feeds. This fear is vastly less reliable as the foundation for humanitarian policies than are sentiments of solidarity and compassion. Fear is at least as likely to generate uncomprehending antipathy and a determination to build effective barriers.

Humane Internationalist Requirements

Central to the argument of this chapter, and to that of many other contributions to this volume, is our understanding that the two different approaches to globalization—pragmatic neoliberalism and humane internationalism—hold quite different views of the economic and social consequences of a largely unregulated global market economy. Neoliberals judge that such a global economy would bring great advantages not only to the rich but also to the poor countries, and more specifically to the poorest within their societies. In contrast, humane internationalists anticipate that this global economy would widen income disparities and would neither eliminate poverty nor reduce it to morally acceptable levels. As a result, they differ in their view of the proper role of the state; pragmatic neoliberalism favors a quite limited role, whereas humane internationalism views state and international interventions as essential to the building of a more equitable and just world. If we accept the second of these perspectives, what needs to be added to the consensus now shared by most aid agencies to ensure that their development assistance will contribute significantly to the achievement of a more prosperous, more just, and more equitable global economy?

Two requirements seem fundamental. The first is that aid agencies must honestly define their objectives in humanitarian terms.[3] For decades, many governments have quietly ensured that their development assistance was used in ways that also advanced their own national economic and political objectives. A major parliamentary review of Canadian aid policies, for example, opened its report with this blunt assertion: "After almost a year of studying Canadian official development assistance, we conclude it is beset with confusion of purpose. At least three quite different impulses—commercial, political, and humanitarian—act upon the aid program" (Canada 1987, 7).

The end of the Cold War and the significant advances to freer international trade have not resulted in a greater focus on humanitarian objectives. The cruder use of development assistance to benefit national suppliers and to favor geopolitical allies has diminished. Yet most governments still attach far more importance to the strength of their economies within the international economic system and to their international political objectives than they do to aiding the world's poorest people and countries.

A humanitarian mandate for an official aid agency would place major emphasis on poverty reduction. This mandate would not preclude assistance to capital or other long-term projects, especially if they would benefit the poor. It would also permit, indeed encourage, agency involvement in countries ravaged by civil strife or drought—to help restore order, to resettle populations and assist them to rebuild their lives, to revive trade patterns, to rebuild education and health facilities, and to reestablish such basic institutions of governance as courts, police, and tax systems. However, a humane internationalist mandate would preclude the intrusion of commercial, international, political, or other objectives of public policy that, however legitimate for other government departments, would diffuse the focus of the aid agency and severely threaten its humanitarian character.

The second near-essential requirement of any agency that seeks to reflect humane internationalist values is that it must shed any uncritical acceptance of the canons of neoliberalism. It must not rely on the benefits of economic growth trickling down to the poor. Across-the-board liberalization as currently promoted by the industrialized states often widens the gap between the poorest countries and the richest and ignores vast numbers of the poorest people. An aid program that is serious about poverty reduction must search for ways *directly* to reach and assist poor people and poor communities; it needs strategies to increase their productivity, to augment their welfare, and to help empower them within their own societies to protect and advance their interests.

The impact upon the policies and programs of any agencies that reject the neoliberal assumptions so pervasive in the 1980s and 1990s would be dramatic. Such agencies would be open to projects and programs that might hamper the operation of market forces but would nevertheless aid the poorest and promote more diverse and resilient local economies. These agencies would be ready to consider and support initiatives by less-developed countries that protect workers' rights, assist local industries and local agriculture, and institute social welfare programs. They would not be dogmatic when ranking the development needs of highest priority to the countries they are assisting. They would be sensitive to the value of genuine participation by civil society in the shaping and implementation of development programs, and would stress the importance of real local ownership of aid-assisted programs. They would welcome regular independent appraisals, country by country, of the work undertaken by the national and international aid agencies.[4] They would advocate within their own governments a greater readiness to include safeguards for trade-union rights and for environmental protection in international trade agreements, though being always insistent that these not become subterfuges for rich-country protectionism. Such agencies would defend the right of poor countries to reject the neoliberal maxim that foreign investors must be conceded open access to their economies and be entitled to equal treatment therein. They would also favor effective international regulations and new international mechanisms for significant resource transfers to the world's poorest states to ensure a fairer global distribution of the growth that globalization generates.[5]

Two further features of a genuinely humane internationalist foreign aid policy are almost unavoidable corollaries of the two central requirements just presented. The first is the need to increase very significantly the budget allocations for development assistance. Instead, we are witnessing a common tendency of industrial states simultaneously to permit their aid agencies to affirm rhetorically that poverty reduction is their central preoccupation, while reducing their overseas development assistance (ODA) as a percentage of GNP further below the decades-old international target of 0.7 percent.

Finally, an agency seeking to pursue humane internationalist aid policies would genuinely involve nongovernmental organizations, both in the processes that shape its policies and in the choice of projects and programs in the less-developed countries. For many reasons, this NGO involvement is important. It facilitates greater project experimentation; it encourages within rich countries greater public involvement in the issue of global poverty; it helps identify valuable activities in the aid-receiving countries; and it strengthens civil society in these countries, thus reinforcing participatory democratic development.

A number of national agencies have long encouraged this NGO involvement and have, indeed, taken particular pride in it. However, as agencies have grown more certain that they know best how to promote development, they have tended to cease welcoming the diversity within the NGO programs that they support. Increasingly impatient towards NGOs that champion alternative development strategies, they are uninterested in the development experience of these organizations. Admittedly, the growing importance and competence of NGOs in many developing countries render more complex the question of how developed-country NGOs can most effectively contribute to the reduction of global poverty. Even so, it is difficult to regard as positive the recent tendency in some official agencies to lessen significantly their involvement with their national NGOs.[6]

The Feasibility of a Humane Internationalist Approach

Powerful influences operate to ensure that national aid agencies are sensitive to commercial and political interests and are in harmony with the dominant neoliberal view that the accomplishment of an open international market economy is an important national interest. Three of these influences have been the most important.

The first is the responsiveness of their governments to the particular interests of their capital-owning class. All member states of the OECD are capitalist countries. Even in those countries with powerful social-democratic political parties that have regularly either formed governments or been part of governing coalitions, the private sectors very largely control the production and distribution of goods and services. Thus, their governments, to varying but always significant degrees, have been sensitive to what would be advantageous to the dominant economic interests in their societies. In a few countries the recurrent pattern of coalition politics has resulted in substantial social-democratic control of the aid ministry over long periods. However, in many, aid monies have been significantly "tied"—they are spent on nationally produced goods and services—and the selection of countries and sectors in which aid is concentrated reflects in particular the interests of their exporting sectors.

More recently, as the corporate interests in the industrialized countries have come to favor open international markets, their lobbying for such special favors within the aid programs has sharply diminished. However, the strength of their attachment and that of their governments to full and open access to the countries of the world for their goods, services, and investments has become as powerful an influence on aid policies as had the earlier corporate demands for special privileges. Humanitarian considerations and civil society pressures may move governments to be responsive to immediate emergency needs of the poorest peoples and countries. But it is implausible to expect that these pressures will convert governments to humane internationalist aid strategies that conflict with these governments' foreign and international trade policies. Foreign aid policies, even if not under the direct control of foreign affairs departments, are undeniably part of the foreign policy of governments. It is one thing for an aid agency to act more compassionately and with less regard to national interests than trade and foreign affairs departments might favor. It would be quite another—and far less likely—for an aid agency to commit itself to aid strategies that would significantly challenge the neoliberal ideology that still predominates in its own government. And in any rare case where that might momentarily happen, it is difficult to imagine that the government would permit it to continue for very long.

The second key influence has been the worldview that tends to be dominant amongst senior foreign policy decision-makers. Their world is one of competing sovereign states. Operating within such a world, they see their primary responsibility in terms of expanding the influence of their state, augmenting its power, advancing its economic interests, and containing potential and actual threats from states perceived as rivals. Other possible policy objectives such as protecting basic human rights or reducing global poverty tend to be seen as "soft" policy options of lesser importance. Because the government departments that manage a country's international trade and foreign policies are typically much more powerful within government, the bureaucracy that manages the aid agency frequently either internalizes the preferences of the more powerful departments or has no choice but reluctantly to shape aid policies in ways that will advance trade and foreign policy objectives. In recent years, this dynamic has minimized any likelihood that aid agencies would seriously challenge the dominant neoliberal ideology.

The third centrally important influence that makes it unlikely that the aid policies of many OECD countries will substantially reflect humane internationalist values is the weakness within their political cultures of a responsiveness to the needs of the poor and the oppressed beyond their borders. From a humanitarian standpoint, a most encouraging development after 1945 was the emergence onto the international scene of major efforts to protect and advance basic human rights throughout the world and alleviate global poverty. However, their impact on the foreign policies of the industrial states varied greatly. Studies suggest that the responsiveness of governments to the issues of international human rights and global poverty is closely related to the strength within their countries of social-democratic movements and of those churches that are particularly concerned to give social expression to moral values (Stokke 1989; Pratt 1989).

In a few countries, most particularly in Scandinavia and the Netherlands, this moral engagement has been sufficiently powerful that its impact on public policy has been substantial. In most, however, responsiveness to the obligations that flow from a strong sense of human solidarity has been a major force only in limited sections of civil society and in the bureaucracies that administer the aid programs. Little is happening within these countries to suggest a renaissance of cosmopolitan moral commitments sufficient to overcome the controlling influence exerted by the dominant economic class and the worldview of their senior foreign policy decision-makers.

Guidelines for Advocacy

The pessimistic analysis in this chapter suggests that those who live in rich countries and are concerned to aid the world's poorest people and countries face a complex challenge. They need to press for whatever short-term improvements are politically possible in the aid policies of their governments. Simultaneously, they must challenge the uncritical acceptance of neoliberal international policies and promote a long-term public commitment to humane internationalist foreign policies. Five recommendations can be offered that should help them to balance their pursuit of these dual objectives. Many development NGOs have reached a quite similar understanding of these challenges (Reality of Aid, 1994–2000; CCIC 1999, 2001).

First, they should continue to base their advocacy of development assistance primarily on the ethical obligation to help the world's poorest people and countries. This approach means resisting the temptation to stress instead the particular and immediate national interests that might be served by foreign aid, in the hope thereby of widening public support for the aid program. It was always unlikely to be a successful tactic, and it still is. A recent report to CIDA by Bernard Wood refers to the "apparent belief that by incorporating multiple objectives, different interests can be accommodated and the base of support thus broadened." Wood declares categorically, "[T]here is no evidence to suggest that mixing objectives to emphasize short-term political or economic payoffs of aid . . . actually serves to bolster general public support. On the contrary, it appears to 'turn off' the majority of citizens . . ." (Wood 2001).

In recent years, neorealist arguments for foreign aid have given less emphasis to the commercial benefits that might flow from such aid. Rather, as noted in the preceding section, prominence is being assigned to the increased security, it is argued, generous foreign aid will help ensure. There are compelling pragmatic reasons not to rely on putative advantages such as these that foreign aid might bring to rich countries. The resources that such an aid program requires are substantial, and the alternative uses for these resources in each country would bring advantages that are immediate and real. In contrast, the advantages to any rich country of undertaking a major poverty-focused program of development assistance relate to a future that is unpredictable and, in any case, is likely to be realized only if most other rich states also implement generous aid programs. Organizations and individuals who are themselves primarily motivated by humanitarian concerns to support foreign aid should be true to their values in their public advocacy. Arguments founded on human solidarity and human compassion are likely to be far more effective than any that search for selfish reasons, personal or national, to defend foreign aid.

Second, NGOs should continue to engage in development work that directly helps poor people both to increase their productivity and to empower them to defend their interests in their own societies. Development assistance of this kind is particularly valuable. Yet it is now of less interest to many official agencies. One immediate battle is to secure the continuation of the responsive programs of their aid agencies that have in the past helped fund activities and programs proposed to them by individual NGOs. Although NGOs that urge the continuation of these programs will no doubt be accused of acting in their own selfish interests because they are themselves the intermediaries of this funding, the developmental and humanitarian value of these activities fully legitimizes this advocacy. This argument is especially valid, if Northern NGOs are careful themselves to ensure that they are assisting activities that are initiated and managed locally.

Third, even though most official aid agencies will not be won over to a full humane internationalist set of activities, it is important that NGOs continue to engage governments in constructive dialogue. The new consensus shared by most official aid agencies, as is clear from this chapter, permits and indeed encourages a wide range of poverty-focused activities. These pursuits are of value, but they do not automatically happen. Those within the agencies who wish to take advantage of this new sensitivity to the challenge of global poverty and who also seek to check the intrusion into their agencies of quite differently motivated initiatives need the political support that effective NGO lobbying can provide.

Fourth, NGOs should also argue against the complacent reassurance that the best antipoverty strategy for any poor country is to integrate its economy into an open international market economy, with its domestic economy in turn reflecting a central acceptance of the market and a hostility to government interventions. They should oppose the temptation, strong in a few agencies, to shift into activities that address common security issues or pursue objectives that are allegedly of mutual interest to both poor and rich countries.[7] The official agencies should, instead, be pressed for increased support to activities that directly increase the sustainable productivity of the poorest people and are responsive to the specific needs, capabilities, and domestic and international circumstances of each country they are assisting.

Fifth, it is important to address the wider range of government policies—especially those relating to trade, immigration, and the environment—which are often more important for the development needs of the world's poorest countries than are any advantages they might gain from foreign aid. This advocacy would include sustained opposition to government policies that act in particular against the interests of the poor countries, and support of international interventions to regulate international markets so as to advance the welfare of their poor, protect their environments, and diversify their economies.

Finally, organizations and individuals primarily engaged with development and global poverty issues need to seek out their counterparts within their own countries who are active on related issues—domestic poverty, aboriginal rights and welfare, international trade, and environmental protection. They are their natural allies in the struggle to undermine the complacency of official and dominant-class thinking about the long-term social and economic consequences of a largely unregulated open-market economy. Until the worldview that now shapes government policies is discredited, progress on each of these separate fronts is almost certain to be slow.

Notes

1. For a discussion of the concept of humane internationalism, see Stokke 1989, 10–15, and Pratt 1989, 3–22.

2. There is now a substantial literature, much of it emanating from the World Bank, on this new consensus. See, for example, Devarajan, Dollar, and Holmgren 2001. For challenges to this new orthodoxy, see Tarp 2001 and Campbell 2000.

3. Lest this seem mean-spirited, I refer to an official submission to the Canadian cabinet that, after recommending major changes to Canadian aid policies that would have greatly increased its responsiveness to Canadian commercial interests, cynically advised that the government "must repeat that 'poorest of the poor' continue to be a priority" (quoted in Pratt 1996, 378).

4. This has been vigorously advocated by Gerald Helleiner (2000).

5. Measures of this sort figure prominently in recent articles on foreign aid and global governance. (For a sympathetic review, see Van der Hoeven 2001.) They essentially advocate that resources for development assistance be raised through levies on rich countries, and be distributed to poor countries by a new international institution in which the governments and civil societies of poor countries would be strongly represented. However, these proposals are so distant from anything attainable in our contemporary world that it seemed more useful to focus here on humane internationalist reforms to the policies of national aid agencies rather than on how, ideally, aid might be managed in a new world order.

6. The long-term strategy for Canadian development assistance that is now being developed clearly intends a significant lessening of CIDA's responsive program, which provides matching funds to Canadian NGOs for aid activities initiated by them (CIDA 2001b, IV[d]).

7. That such uses of development assistance are particularly advantageous is argued in a major recent publication of the UNDP (Kaul, Grunberg, and Stern 1999). They are also singled out for special emphasis in a recent Canadian discussion paper (CIDA 2000).

References

Campbell, Bonnie. 2000. "New Rules of the Game: The World Bank's Role in the Construction of New Normative Frameworks for States, Markets, and Social Exclusion." *Canadian Journal of Development Studies* 21 (1): 7–30.

Canada. 1987. *For Whose Benefit? A Report of the Standing Committee on External Affairs and International Trade on Canada's Official Development Policies and Programs.* Ottawa: Supply and Services.

CCIC. 1999. *A Call to End Global Poverty: Reviewing Canadian Aid Policy and Practice.* Ottawa: Canadian Council for International Cooperation.

———. 2001. *Putting Poverty on the Trade Agenda.* Ottawa: Canadian Council for International Cooperation.

CIDA. 2000. "Towards a Long-Term Strategy for Canada's International Assistance Program: A Framework for Consultation." Unpublished draft, 19 October.

———. 2001a. "Strengthening Aid Effectiveness: New Approaches to Canada's International Assistance Program." Draft, 16 February.

———. 2001b. *CIDA's Sustainable Development Strategy, 2001–2003: An Agenda for Change.* Ottawa: Ministry of Public Works and Services.

Devarajan, Shantayanan, David Dollar, and Torgny Holmgren, eds. 2001. *Aid and Reform in Africa.* New York: Oxford University Press.

Helleiner, Gerald. 2000. "Towards Balance in International Aid Relationships: External Conditionalities, Local Ownership, and Development." *Cooperation South,* vol. 2.

Kaul, John, Isabele Grunberg, and Marc Stern. 1999. *Global Public Goods: International Cooperation in the Twenty-first Century.* New York: Oxford University Press.

Pratt, Cranford. 1989. "Humane Internationalism: Its Significance and Variants." In *Internationalism under Strain: The North-South Policies of Canada, the Netherlands, Norway, and Sweden,* ed. Cranford Pratt. Toronto: University of Toronto Press.

———. 1996. "Humane Internationalism and Canadian Development Assistance Policies." In *Canadian International Development Assistance Policies: An Appraisal,* ed. Cranford Pratt. 2d ed . Kingston, Ont.: McGill-Queens University Press.

Reality of Aid Project. 1994–2000. *The Reality of Aid.* London, Earthscan. An Independent review of development assistance, published annually since 1994, with subtitles that have varied with each issue.

Sandbrook, Richard. 2000. *Closing the Circle: Democratization and Development in Africa.* Toronto, London, and New York: Between the Lines and Zed Books.

Stokke, Olav, ed. 1989. *Western Middle Powers and Global Poverty: The Determinants of the Aid Policies of Canada, Denmark, the Netherlands, Norway, and Sweden.* Uppsala: Scandinavian Institute of African Studies.

Tarp, Finn. 2001. "Review of Aid and Reform in Africa.*" Journal of African Economies* 10.

Van der Hoeven, Rolph. 2001. "Assessing Aid and Global Governance." *Journal of Development Studies* 37:119–27.

Wood, Bernard. 2001. "Best Practices in Strategic Management of National Development Cooperation Programs." A study for the Policy Branch, Canadian International Development Agency.

World Bank. 1990. *World Development Report, 1990: Poverty.* New York: Oxford University Press.

———. 1991. *Assistance Strategies to Reduce Poverty.* Washington D.C.: World Bank.

———. 1996. *Poverty Reduction and the World Bank: Progress and Challenges in the 1990s.* Washington, D.C.: World Bank.

———. 1997. *World Development Report, 1997: The State in a Changing World.* New York: Oxford University Press.

———. 1998a. *Poverty Reduction and the World Bank: Progress in Fiscal 1996 and 1997.* Washington, D.C.: World Bank.

———. 1998b. *Assessing Aid: What Works, What Doesn't, and Why.* Policy Research Report. Washington, D.C.: World Bank.

———. 1999. *Poverty Reduction and the World Bank: Progress in Fiscal 1998.* Washington D.C.: World Bank.

———. 2001. *World Development Report, 2000–2001: Attacking Poverty.* New York: Oxford University Press.

CHAPTER 14

Reforming Global Governance:
The Continuing Importance of the Nation-State

Louis W. Pauly

What global governance, in fact, is there to reform? Where are the constitution, the rule-making institutions, the instruments of enforcement? Asking myself such questions, I immediately thought of my teenagers. Suppose we were called to a conference on reforming parental authority. Only a sense of curiosity would encourage me to attend, for I would surely be feeling that there were no tangible structures to reform, or that if they had ever existed, the point of reforming them was rapidly becoming moot. My children, on the other hand, could certainly be counted upon to accept the invitation with alacrity and to participate in the conference with enthusiasm. Undoubtedly, they would bring with them many proposals for changing an institution that, from their point of view, not only persists but is increasingly onerous, obnoxious, and badly in need of reform.

In that same ambivalent spirit, let me gingerly grasp the nettle put in my hands. Where is the true locus of global governance, and what could it possibly mean to reform it? I approach this question from the perspective of a citizen in a leading industrial state, and this chapter, therefore, mainly addresses contemporary concerns inside the core of the international system. From such a viewpoint, my primary contention is that the really important venue for debate and action on key issues related to global social and economic governance remains *internal* to the leading societies in the world today. In future, there will be no way to move to effective governance beyond the national level without having first achieved more effective governance at home. Secondarily, I argue that much of today's common wisdom concerning the displacement of ultimate governing authority from the public sector to the "globalizing" private sector mistakenly reflects an escapist desire to avoid practical political challenges that also begin at home.

Part of this chapter is drawn from Pauly 1999.

What do I mean by effective governance? In today's capitalist social democracies—the political-economic form that dominates the core of the world system, even in those societies where the label "liberal" democracies is preferred—effective governance implies flexible political structures that can balance social goals keyed on fairness and justice and economic goals keyed on efficiency. As they are human structures, they will always fall short of the ideal, and they will always reflect strong disagreements about the weight of the balance. Standard economic and social indicators can suggest effectiveness, as well as relative success, over time.[1] But the ultimate test of success is impossible to measure precisely, for it necessarily links performance at the national and regional levels with stability at the international level. "Success" is the broad systemic crisis that does not arise. By such a standard, the advanced industrial democracies have succeeded mainly, but not only, for themselves since the last great global cataclysm that began in 1931.

In all cases, successes or failures of mechanisms of global governance are, at best, only a part of a much larger story. At worst, they are a distraction of political energy away from the search for practicable solutions to actual problems at the national level. Antiglobalization demonstrations in Seattle, Prague, and Quebec City may well be sideshows. Shadow play may be what we really see when activists focus their energies mainly at the global level. The question is whether the lion's share of those energies could more effectively be focused at the national level in an attempt to bolster and buffer national political authority as international interdependence deepens. In this context, debates over the word "sovereignty" may obfuscate more than they clarify.

Sovereignty and Policy Autonomy

The concept of sovereignty in international relations has always been contested. Its association over time with the institution of the state, moreover, is linked with a number of material and normative transformations. Sovereignty remains an important and usually clear legal term; it connotes the internal supremacy and external independence of a given political authority. Of course, its practical evolution and elaboration over time is now, for very sound historical and philosophical reasons, generating noteworthy conceptual discussions.[2] But today, most scholars seem to reduce consequent complexities of sovereignty in political practice to the idea, and ideal, of policy autonomy. The distinction between legal sovereignty and policy autonomy is important. In a world economy that is interdependent by design, a turning away from deeper integration by legally sovereign states or by the collectivity of states remains entirely conceivable. Indeed, some did turn away in the financial realm as severe debt crises confronted them in the 1980s and 1990s, only to return to more liberal policy stances after the crises dissipated. The great post–World War II political experiment in deepening economic and social interaction among states, especially in the core of the system, was not aimed at transcending state sovereignty but at pacifying sovereign states.

To be sure, most states today confront tighter economic constraints, or clearer policy tradeoffs, as a result of a freer potential flow of capital, technology, and labor across their borders. The erosion of their absolute freedom to pursue internally generated policies—that is, an erosion of their policy autonomy, not their legal sovereignty—is the flip side of the opportunities for accelerated growth presented by those same flows. The diminution of policy autonomy is not new, and it boded no ill for state sovereignty as such. Neither did it preclude in certain circumstances the reconfiguration of political authority centered for many centuries in the state form. As in the European Union, however, states themselves would remain central to the processes through which such reconfiguration would occur, say to a multilevel polity of some kind.

There is a new and widespread perception in popular debates swirling around such processes—namely, the notion that all states, all societies, and all social groups are now equally affected by the forces of global integration. The historical record belies such a perception, and many arguments that turn on the concept of sovereignty, in effect, shroud important distinctions between and within states. Underneath much of the overt discourse on vanishing sovereignty and the inexorable logic of efficient markets, I suspect, there lies a covert agenda involving the preservation of power, the delegitimization of attempts to shift relative power balances, and the reinforcement of existing hierarchies.

The Roots of Contemporary Globalization

Following World War II, the victorious states under uncontested American leadership—and eventually without the Soviet Union and China—attempted to craft a new world order (see Ikenberry 2001). The initial American dream of a global "free" market at the center of that order was never practicable. The real order, certainly after 1947, combined a military alliance, national plans for economic development, a managed trading system, and an underlying assumption that all markets could and would eventually emulate the structure of American markets. More open markets increasingly compatible with (but never entirely convergent with) the U.S. model eventually followed.

States have responded ambivalently to global integration. They have failed to embrace unambiguously what we might call complete cross-border mobility norms—certainly with regard to labor and, less obviously, with regard to leading-edge technologies and even many forms of capital. As well, their handling of periodic emergencies in international markets in an ad hoc manner, and their preference not clearly to designate an international organizational overseer for truly integrated factor markets, reflects this ambivalence. Continuing controversies on all of these points revolve around traditional issues of national power and authority. The legitimacy of a new order tending in the direction of global integration remains highly problematic.

It grows even more problematic when we forget that a policy tendency in the direction of economic and social openness was a means to an end, and not the end itself. Globalizing economies have not yet created a global state. Nonetheless, the deepening integration of national economies into global markets has posed a continuing challenge to the architects of world order, who seek to calibrate emergent *global market facts* with recalcitrant *national political realities*.

One doesn't need to be an extremist to focus attention on the ensuing tension. One only needs to observe market and governmental reactions to the periodic crises that characterize any order relying in part on private capital markets. Such markets may be efficient in the long run, but they are always prone to bouts of mass hysteria in the short term. Since 1945, prompted by periodic emergencies, advanced industrial states regularly engaged in efforts to manage this destabilizing proclivity. In an interdependent economic and financial order, which we have created for ourselves for very good reasons, crises with potentially devastating systemic effects can begin in all but the poorest countries. In fact, from Mexico in 1982 and 1995 to Russia, East Asia, and Latin America in the late 1990s, many national economic disasters threatened to become disasters for the system as a whole.

But who was truly responsible for the necessary bailouts and for their sometimes perverse effects? Who would actually be held responsible if the panicked reaction to financial turbulence in one country actually began to bring down large commercial and investment banks and investment funds around the world? "No one," a number of practitioners and analysts now say, for the authority to manage global finance has dispersed into the supranational ether or has been privatized. I disagree. Despite the obfuscation of accountability always implied in regimes aiming to advance public policy agendas through the indirect means of private markets, actual crises in the waning years of the twentieth century continued to suggest that *national governments* would be blamed, and that they would respond to dampen these crises. If this creates what central bankers call "moral hazard," excessive private risk-taking in anticipation of public bailouts, so be it. In decent societies and a peaceful world supported by the tenuous but practical logic of democratic capitalism, this situation is unavoidable. Of course, the function of central bankers and even finance ministers is to pretend otherwise, to sow a degree of uncertainty concerning who is ultimately responsible for handling financial crises. Otherwise, investors might inadequately assess risks and invest recklessly in the belief that they would be saved by government from the consequences of their folly. Since 1931, nevertheless, governments have in fact never failed to make the distinction between pretence and necessity when the scale of such folly has brought the stability of the entire system into question.

Indeed, it is the desire to avoid the endgame of a fully transparent national emergency response—tantamount to systematically socializing investor losses while privatizing investor profits—that drives continuing multilateral and regional efforts to strengthen markets and redesign the "international financial architecture." This often means bolstering and broadening the mandates of particular international institutions, such as the IMF and the World Bank, which reside on the fault line between national politics and international markets. If this is what is meant by the term "reforming globalization," I wholeheartedly agree that scholars, students, and citizens have an important role to play. But that task is mainly the painstaking one of combining the ethical with the conceptual and the practical. We must ask not only what is right, but where have we been, what is the rationale behind existing institutions, and what new sorts of institutions might actually work more effectively.

In the best-case scenario, technocratic agencies promise to promote adequate standards of regulation around the world, design functional programs for crisis avoidance and crisis management, and provide mechanisms for states to collaborate with one another for mutual benefit. In the worst case, as we witnessed in the late 1990s in the wake of the Russian and East Asian financial debacles, those same agencies can also assume the role of scapegoats; they then serve as a political buffer for responsible national authorities. What these agencies have difficulty addressing, however, are basic questions of social justice. Not only are standards across diverse societies themselves still diverse, but those agencies are charged with helping to manage a system in which the mobility of capital is not yet, in fact, matched by the mobility of unskilled and semiskilled labor.

Political Authority in a More Open World Order

At its core, the contemporary international system reflects the fact that the governments of states cannot—or will not—shift ultimate political authority to the global level. Perhaps they do not yet need to do so, because the term "globalization" exaggerates the reality of international integration at the dawn of a new century. But surely the vast majority of their citizens do not yet want them to do so. Only in Western Europe, within the restricted context of a regional economic experiment still shaped by the legacy of the most catastrophic war in world history, was a major shift in power and authority beyond the national level in sight. And even there, the fundamental construction of an ultimate locus of authority remained highly convoluted and controversial. In the rest of the industrial world, intensifying interdependence remained the order of the day, as the citizens of still-national states sought the benefits of international factor mobility without paying the ultimate political costs implied by true integration. In such a context, unfolding tragedy in a number of so-called emerging markets seemed like a distant roll of thunder. Whether the storm it signaled will remain distant emerges as a crucially important question. But when the answer becomes clear, as on the issue of greenhouse emissions and global warming, public authorities will be called upon to respond. After all, as the entire history of the post–World War II experiment attests, markets are a tool of policy.

Today, the main global markets supporting our local societies rest on interdependent national public authorities and, increasingly, on the delegated public authority of international political institutions (see Greven and Pauly 2000). The economic face of globalization—and there are other faces—mirrors national forms of governance in leading states. These states have been led since the Second World War, albeit with varying degrees of coherence and effectiveness, by the United States. The tenuous legitimacy of those international institutions, moreover, and the evolving global order they underpin are eroded when deepening interdependence, at the core of that order, is mistakenly assumed to imply eventual political integration, or the inevitable supranationalization of public authority.[3] That supranationalization may someday come, but it will not likely be durable if it arises by stealth. Having over many decades bought into the notion that they have some responsibility for their own lives, the citizens of modern democracies cannot be counted upon passively to resign themselves to a new constitution of political authority that they did not explicitly ratify.

With regard to states and societies not at the core of that order, it is also misleading to assume that those international institutions stand only for a progressive form of mutual interdependence. Many states and many societies continue to exist in a condition of dependency. They must adapt themselves to structures of power over which they have little real influence. For them, whether those international institutions present a helping hand or a mailed fist is a matter of perception and specific circumstances.

In good times, governments of leading states can delegate the authority to stabilize markets to the private sector. Voluntary efforts, best-practice codes, even self-regulatory organizations, as oxymoronic as that term sounds, are not new. When such efforts accomplish their goals, the dog does not bark, catastrophes are avoided, and most of us don't notice. But when they fail, or threaten to fail, one of two things happen. Holders of legitimate public authority emerge from the shadows and assert their underlying power, or markets collapse. From transportation systems in England, to electricity systems in California, to environmental and social protection systems in Ontario, the emergence of private authority is a contingent and fleeting phenomenon. The fragility or the durability of international markets impinging on such systems remains entirely reflective of the interactive public authorities lying beneath their surface. In leading societies, in any event, the best place toward which to direct energy in the cause of a more just, a more coherent, and a more effective world order remains the government of their own states. Home, as the old saying goes, is where the heart is.

Openness continues to promise national prosperity and systemic peace, even as it entails the responsibility for global stewardship. Seizing those opportunities and meeting that responsibility have always required reasonably well-functioning states capable of shaping and guiding vibrant societies. The challenge of reforming global governance—of civilizing globalization—must first be met inside the leading states. It still can be. My teenagers have reason to be optimistic.

Notes

1. It is beyond the scope of this essay to survey the rapidly proliferating body of research relevant to this theme. My view is that too much popular attention has lately been accorded to the rhetoric of neoliberalism, deregulation, and the inexorably antipolitical logic of globalization. The notion of the long-term rise and resilience of social-democracy-within-internationalizing-capitalism remains eminently supportable. See, for example, Garrett 1998; Doremus et al. 1998; Ruggie 1998; Weiss 1999; and Kitschelt et al. 1999.

2. See, for example, Krasner 1999; and Hall 1999. Both of these books and many others that are related are provocatively surveyed in Philpott 2001.

3. For an expansion of this point, see Pauly 1997.

References

Doremus, Paul, et al. 1998. *The Myth of the Global Corporation*. Princeton: Princeton University Press.

Garrett, Geoffrey. 1998. *Partisan Politics in the Global Economy*. Cambridge: Cambridge University Press.

Greven, Michael Th., and Louis W. Pauly, eds. 2000. *Democracy Beyond the State*. Lanham, MD/Toronto: Rowman & Littlefield/University of Toronto Press.

Hall, Rodney Bruce. 1999. *National Collective Identity: Social Constructs and International Systems*. New York: Columbia University Press.

Ikenberry, G. John. 2001. *After Victory: Institutions, Strategic Restraint, and the Rebuilding of Order after Major Wars*. Princeton: Princeton University Press.

Kitschelt, Herbert et al., eds. 1999. *Continuity and Change in Contemporary Capitalism*. Cambridge: Cambridge University Press.

Krasner, Stephen D. 1999. *Sovereignty: Organized Hypocrisy.* Princeton: Princeton University Press.

Pauly, Louis. 1997. *Who Elected the Bankers? Surveillance and Control in the World Economy*. Ithaca: Cornell University Press.

———. 1999. "Global Markets, National Authority, and the Problem of Legitimation." Paper delivered at conference, Private Authority and Global Governance, 12–13 February, at the Watson Institute for International Studies, Brown University.

Philpott, Daniel. 2001. "Usurping the Sovereignty of Sovereignty." *World Politics* 53 (2): 297–324.

Ruggie, John G. 1998. *Constructing the World Polity*. London: Routledge.

Weiss, Linda. 1999. *The Myth of the Powerless State*. Ithaca: Cornell University Press.

PART 4

Building a Global Countermovement

Core Issues

What sort of politics will advance an agenda dedicated to civilizing globalization? The fundamental challenge is, in Richard Falk's characterization, to reconcile the operation of global market forces with the well-being of peoples and the carrying capacity of the earth. Conventional electoral politics alone is unlikely to achieve this reconciliation. It will likely require the mobilization of countervailing power through the activities of democratically inspired nongovernmental organizations and social movements at the national, regional, and global levels. Although environmentalists, feminists, human rights activists, development-oriented groups, labor unions, indigenous people's movements, and ecumenical associations all speak with their own voice on their own issues, the global countermovement is a harmony of these many voices. The chapters in this part and the book's conclusion present fragments of this evolving countermovement.

Conventional electoral politics alone is ineffectual, because politics-as-usual reflects the structural power of capital that globalization further magnifies. Social-democratic measures deemed incompatible with the efficiency criteria of global markets arouse the veto power of the owners of capital. This veto power is exercised through all-too-familiar mechanisms: capital flight, falling stock markets, decline in the value of the national currency, heavy media criticism of the offending politicians or party, and a drying up of essential campaign contributions. Only a few governments—mainly those in northern Europe—have been willing to confront such opposition, especially in an era when activist governmental action is widely regarded with suspicion.

In light of these power dynamics, international law professor Richard Falk in chapter 15 develops his notion of globalization-from-below confronting the dominant globalization-from-above. His chapter assesses the visions and political potential of the social forces associated with globalization-from-below—the civic associations promoting social and economic rights and environmental protection. Although he makes no firm predictions, his analysis is both practical in its strategic implications and hopeful.

189

Robert Weissman, a journalist, sketches in chapter 16 the events surrounding a watershed in the emergence of a global countermovement—the
Seattle protest against the World Trade Organization in late 1999. His vivid por-
trayal reveals the major protagonists in the demonstrations, and the impact that
their activities had on the deliberations of the WTO. This experience energized
and gave some organizational form to the incipient globalization-from-below.

Hans Edstrand, a young Swedish-Canadian volunteer working in Honduras, follows with a contrasting example of globalization-from-below. Chapter 17 cuts through the widespread apathy and cynicism of our age by
illustrating what individual determination and human solidarity can still
achieve. When Hurricane Mitch devastated much of Central America in 1998,
Edstrand helped spearhead the building of a new community of dispossessed
people. This community has become not only self-supporting but self-govern-
ing. Its success, according to the author, illustrates the best part of globalization: that transnational solidarity, when combined with the empowerment of
poor communities, can work wonders.

Rob Lambert and Eddie Webster provide another dramatic example of
globalization-from-below in chapter 18. Activist social scientists from Australia and South Africa, respectively, the authors chronicle the remarkable success of SIGTUR (Southern Initiative on Globalization and Trade Union Rights)
in building solidarity among union movements from both industrial and developing countries of the Southern Hemisphere. SIGTUR empowers unions to
confront transnational corporations with the same demands and grievances no
matter where they operate. The authors identify several illustrative campaigns
in which industrial protests in one country have sparked supportive actions
against the same employer in other countries.

In sum, part 4 offers a survey of the origins and nature of the global countermovement to neoliberal globalization, as well as diverse illustrations of its
development and successes.

CHAPTER 15

Globalization-from-Below:
An Innovative Politics of Resistance

Richard Falk

In this era of globalization that has reconfigured our understanding of the world, innovative and adaptive forms of political action are reshaping our understanding of world order. Until the 1990s a state-centric map of world politics, although not empirically accurate in all respects, did depict the main patterns of international conflict and cooperation, but no longer. Part of why it is useful to accept the terminology of globalization is that it encourages a conceptual reassessment of global policy processes, and especially an appreciation of nongovernmental arenas of influence and transnational social forces that can no longer be seen as mere extensions or instrumentalities of states. On the contrary, the state has, to a significant degree, been hijacked to serve the goals of international trade and investment, and has lost much of its autonomy by being instrumentalized to serve financial and business centers of power.

It is within this setting that the main ideological energies of globalization have succeeded in establishing a political climate dominated by neoliberalism. In such an atmosphere, world business leaders have fashioned their own arenas of influence to circumvent the dysfunctional priorities of the traditional state. One early attempt in this direction was made in the mid-1970s by the Trilateral Commission, established at the time to coordinate elite opinion in North America, Europe, and Japan so as to counter the economic challenges being mounted by the Third World. An even more influential and enduring initiative is that of the World Economic Forum that holds its meetings in Davos, Switzerland each year, involving the most important private sector leaders and receiving intense media coverage. These transnational initiatives have been extremely effective in conditioning the behavior of international financial institutions, especially the IMF, World Bank, and WTO, thereby helping to project the neoliberal consensus onto the world stage. This globalization of policy formation has the advantage of not seeming to be an undertaking of the former

191

colonial powers or rich states in the North to reestablish the kinds of control that could be used to regain an exploitative grip on the world economy. In this sense, globalization is generating a less state-centric world order responsive to the priorities of economistic geopolitics, but one that increasingly is being called into question as unrepresentative of the peoples of the world and detrimental to their well-being.

These doubts about the antidemocratic operating style and detrimental societal and environmental impacts of globalization have stimulated opposition of both a grassroots and transnational composition. This opposition had its precursors in civil society movements that worked transnationally to support human rights and environmental protection, and locally to oppose specific megaprojects in the Third World such as large dams or nuclear power plants.

Only in the late 1990s did this cascading civil society activism shift the main focus of its attention to the perceived distortions and inequities associated with the current functioning of the world economy. The alarm bells of discontent with globalization sounded in Seattle in the wake of media-resonant militant street protests that succeeded in obstructing an annual WTO meeting in December 1999 (see chapter 16). This outburst of popular opposition to mainstream globalization was followed by a series of similar demonstrations of opposition on those occasions in cities around the world where the managers of corporate globalization and their governmental allies held their most important meetings. It may be that such displays of discontent with globalization signal the start of a worldwide political movement that is unique in character, combining grassroots constituencies, transnational social forces, and political activism without a territorial base.

In this chapter, these innovative modalities of resistance are understood as constituting "globalization-from-below" (GFB), and are in active dialogue and tension with the corporate globalizers that are here regarded as constituting "globalization-from-above" (GFA).[1] This broad-brush distinction is only a first approximation of this encounter. The lines of actual conflict are shifting and far more convoluted. There are governments committed to more humane and environmentally sensitive guidelines for the world economy, and increasingly, there are corporate voices warning about the dangers of "market fundamentalism" (Soros 1998). And there are underway widely publicized efforts to engage leading corporations in pledging voluntary adherence to international standards pertaining to human rights, labor practices, and environmental protection.[2] At present, there is a mood of uncertainty bearing on the sustainability of globalization without some form of legitimating compromise emerging from the struggles between GFA and GFB. As we look ahead, then, the main motif of GFB is to humanize and democratize globalization, not to oppose in neo-Luddite fashion technological innovations, especially those association with information-processing, that are capable of promoting human well-being.

Of notable significance is that the main antagonists and sites of struggle can no longer be accurately comprehended by reliance on a statist view of the world. The main antagonists are market forces on one side and civil society associations on the other. The main sites of struggle are the urban settings where the managers of GFA gather. Even if these managers are leaders of the advanced industrial states, as is the case at the so-called annual World Economic Summit or the Group of Eight (G-8) meetings, their principal role is now to carry out the policy directives that promote world trade and investment, that is, to act as facilitators for GFA. It is these new framings of conflict and struggle in innovative policy-making arenas of growing influence, as well as the impact of information technology and networking forms of organizational structure, that justify attaching the label "globalization" to the current era. World order can no longer be interpreted and understood as exclusively an affair of sovereign, or "Westphalian," states.[3] As succeeding sections will make clear, the state remains the most significant political actor in this early phase of globalization, but it must share the stage with other actors, and its own role has been adapted to these new realities.

A Normative Assessment of Globalization

Globalization, with all of its uncertainties and inadequacies as a term, does usefully call attention to a series of developments, including reorienting the role of the state and altering the ethos of government, which are associated with the ongoing dynamic of economic and political restructuring at the global level. The negative essence of this dynamic, as unfolding within the present historical time frame, is to dispose governments to accept to varying degrees a discipline of global capital. Such a discipline takes the form of a coherent body of ideas and promotes economistic policymaking in national arenas of decision, subjugating the outlook of governments, political parties, leaders, and elites to the logic of the global market that privileges the efficiency of capital above all else. This economistic preoccupation tends to accentuate the distress of vulnerable and disadvantaged regions and peoples, and has resulted in widening disparities between rich and poor within and among countries and regions.

Among the consequences is a one-sided depoliticizing of the state and electoral politics as neoliberalism (in some form) becomes "the only game in town," according to widely accepted perceptions that are dutifully disseminated by the mainstream media to all corners of the planet. This sense of ideological closure is reinforced by interpreting the Soviet collapse as caused by its bureaucratic rigidities, and the Chinese success as associated with its leaders' opportunistic encouragement of private investment and predatory capitalism. This neoliberal mind-set is dedicated, above all else, to relying on private sector solutions for societal problems. As such, it seeks to minimize socially oriented public sector expenditures devoted to welfare, job creation, environmental protection, health care, education, and even the alleviation of poverty—unless the specific programs are convincingly reconciled with efficiency criteria currently favored by world capitalism. Education of certain types can be made to appear consistent with cultivating the skills needed to achieve successful access by a society to the opportunities offered by the world economy, and thus increased expenditures on education, if so validated, may be supported by a neoliberal political leadership. However, because of the neoliberal tendency to minimize the contributions of government, even the infrastructure of education is becoming increasingly privatized in many settings. Fortunately, many of the expenditures on social goods are entrenched, and difficult for politicians to reduce dramatically because of legal and bureaucratic obstacles and citizen backlash, especially the existence of varying degrees of electoral accountability in constitutional democracies that inhibit implementing a neoliberal vision. Nevertheless, the political tide is definitely running in the neoliberal direction, and will continue to do so as long as the citizenry of leading states can be induced to ingest the pill of social austerity, sweetened for the middle and upper classes by tax cuts, without reacting too vigorously. To date, the mainstream of these societies has been generally pacified, especially as represented by principal political parties. Political debate on economic policy is often avoided by swallowing propaganda on behalf of globalization to the effect that the best route to material betterment for all strata of society is by relying on economic growth, and that growth proceeds most rapidly when the efficiency of capital is as unencumbered as possible. With this perspective, globalization becomes the solution rather than the problem, and those who resist are hurting what it is they purport to help. The prior climate of social-democratic opinion is placed on the defensive, advocating a variety of "third ways" that endorse the core policies of neoliberalism, while promising to sustain a humane society. Such contradictory affirmations invite cynicism and despair when the social benefits are not forthcoming.

Moreover, the experiences of the 1970s and 1980s led to a revised assessment of investment climate conditions in countries of the South. In the period after 1945, there tended to be a natural confrontation between vested economic interests associated with Northern investments and nationalism in the South. The latter fostered efforts to gain control over foreign-owned property rights through nationalization. These challenges, aggravated often by Cold War concerns, led to an interventionary diplomacy that tended to favor authoritarian governments. Such governments seemed to serve best the interests of business, keeping labor under tight controls, avoiding strict regulation, and receptive to an exchange of economic concessions for military equipment and diplomatic support. The CIA-supported interventions in Iran in 1953 and Guatemala in1954 were emblematic of this approach, which was also evident in U.S. diplomatic encouragement given to antidemocratic military leaders in South America up through the mid-1980s. But then business and government thinking began changing. Greater stability and economic opportunity seemed to arise in settings where constitutionalism and political moderation prevailed. As well, this more consensual atmosphere tended to foster a more educated and skilled citizenry and a competent style of political leadership that was better positioned to take advantage of the global marketplace. An embrace of formal democracy also removed much of the stigma for corporate officers and managers of dealing with governments that were being severely criticized for violating the human rights of their own citizens.

But such a revised outlook does not engage the subject matter of economic and social rights, which if treated as constraining global economic policy would require modifying the major premise of neoliberal globalization. This set of circumstances that constitute GFA, if not transformed, presages a generally grim future for human society. This future includes a tendency to make alternative orientations toward economic policy appear dysfunctional or utopian, which, to the extent believed, generates overall resignation and despair. Some normative goals associated with human betterment continue to be affirmed within political arenas, but with an accompanying spirit of deference to private-sector solutions. Such goals as human rights and environmental protection receive rhetorical endorsement of a ritual character from world leaders, but the substantive claims of such activities on resources are minimized. The primacy of economistic factors tends to focus policy attention on the grand objectives of growth and competitiveness, making societal undertakings appear as a humanitarian luxury that is becoming less affordable and acceptable in an integrated, market-driven world economy.

One of the most definite spillover effects of the mind-set induced by globalization, as suggested, is to exert a downward pressure on public goods expenditures. The financial strains being experienced by the United Nations and development assistance, despite the savings associated with the absence of strategic rivalry of the sort that fueled the Cold War arms race, is emblematic of declining political and financial support for global public goods. This weakening of financial support for the U.N. runs counter to the widespread realization that the growing complexity of international life requires increasing global capabilities for coordination and governance, at least for the sake of efficiency.[4] An augmented U.N. is also needed for the sort of humanitarian peacekeeping that does not engage the strategic interests of leading states. The inability to mobilize the capabilities to address the crises of sub-Saharan Africa during the 1990s exhibits the inadequacy of the U.N., given the constraints arising from inadequate funding and political support, to mitigate humanitarian catastrophes. The United States is both the leading ideological champion of neoliberal globalization and the most severe critic of the U.N., positions that seem linked.

In the context of international trade, both domestic labor and minority groups in rich countries of the North have been mounting some influential pressure to attach human rights and environmental conditionalities to trade policy, often for self-serving goals. Such efforts in the North to object to such labor abuses as child labor or unsafe working conditions are often insensitive to the stark realities of life in developing countries, where an untimely imposition of international standards could worsen human suffering. At the same time, business and financial élites tend to resist such advocacy for their own selfish reasons. Implementing international standards diminish some of the advantages of "outsourcing" and, hence, the attractiveness of investment in the South. International standards interfere with capital-driven efforts to situate business operations where labor costs are low and regulatory regimes anemic.

Economic globalization has also produced some major positive benefits, including a partial leveling-up impact on North-South relations if conceived broadly and a rising standard of living for several hundred million people in Asia, which has included rescuing many millions from poverty. According to recent UNDP figures, the proportion of the poor globally, but not their absolute number, has been declining modestly during the past several years. As well, the dynamics of globalization has accelerated the diffusion for technological innovation, making it possible for poorer societies to take creative advantage of some of the most advanced technologies and thereby to improve rapidly the material circumstances of its population.

There are some indications that, when countries reach a certain level of development, an expanding urban middle class exerts pressure to improve workplace and environmental conditions. Governments of such countries also become more confident actors on the global stage, challenging inequities and biases of geopolitical structures. Malaysia typifies such a pattern in many ways during the past two decades despite authoritarian leadership. There is every reason to encourage economies of scale, reliance on technological innovations, and the pursuit of the benefits of comparative advantage so long as policymakers also take detrimental social, environmental, political, and cultural effects into sufficient account. What is objectionable is to indulge a kind of market mysticism that accords an unconditional policy hegemony to the promotion of economic growth, dismissing adverse social harm as tolerable or uncontestable side effects of a laissez-faire approach. To rely on ideological certitudes that neglect the realities of human suffering is morally unacceptable. Such is especially the case since empirical evidence does not support the claim that growth will automatically reduce poverty and distress.

Globalization also has been influenced by several contingent historical factors that intensify these adverse social and environmental costs. Globalization is proceeding in an ideological atmosphere in which neoliberal thinking and priorities go virtually unchallenged, especially in the leading market economies.

- The collapse of the international socialist "other" has encouraged capitalism to insist upon market logic with a relentlessness that has not been evident since the first decades of the industrial revolution. Capitalism was subsequently moderated in its social impact by the challenge of socialism. It is the current absence of countervailing forces posing a threat to the established order, together with the historical understanding of the ending of the Cold War, that has encouraged the ideologues of capitalism to revert to predatory forms of practice (Falk 1999).

- This neoliberal climate of opinion that seems so insensitive to societal hardship is reinforced by an antigovernment mood that tends to oppose state-led social interventions and public-sector solutions. This mood contains many disparate elements, including a consumerist reluctance to pay taxes, an alleged failure by government to promote social objectives, technological changes that emphasize the transformative and deterritorialized civilizational role of computers, and a declining capacity of political parties to provide forward-looking policy proposals.

- The policy orientation of governments grows steadily more business-focused as organized labor declines as a social force. This development has resulted in the serious erosion of the perceived threat of a potential revolutionary opposition from what Immanuel Wallerstein identifies as "the dangerous classes" (Wallerstein 1995, 1–8, 93–107).

- Globalization is unfolding within an international order that exhibits gross inequalities of every variety, thereby concentrating the benefits of growth upon already advantaged sectors within and across societies, and worsening the relative and absolute condition of those already most disadvantaged. The experience of sub-Saharan Africa during the last two decades confirms this generalization.[5]

Thus it is that globalization in this historical setting poses a particular form of normative challenge that is different from what it would be in other globalizing circumstances. The challenge is directed, above all, at the survival of, and maybe the very possibility of sustaining, the compassionate state, as typified by the humane achievements of the Scandinavian countries and the optimistic gradualism of social-democratic approaches.[6]

Yet certain problematical aspects of globalization have surfaced that have led some thoughtful neoliberals to recommend adjustments in GFA. Even prior to the Seattle protest, the complacency of GFA was shaken by the 1997 Asian financial crisis and its reverberations in Japan, Russia, and Latin America. Re-acting to such developments, the neoliberal consensus at Davos began to adopt a more normative tonality about the self-regulating character of the world econ-omy. It was now acknowledged that the business world should affirm "a re-sponsible globality" and "globalization with a human face." This change of mood was also accompanied and reinforced by calls by the U.N. secretary gen-eral, Kofi Annan, for self-regulation by the global business community, espe-cially in upholding international standards in their overseas operations. This reevaluation also led such visible international institutions as the IMF and World Bank to step back from their prior unconditional endorsement of the pre-cepts of neoliberalism. Such institutions adopted a more socially engaged rhetoric and advocated less dogmatic policies that accorded a much higher pri-ority to the reduction of mass poverty and unemployment. In effect, the forces of GFA were seeking to disarm their critics, or at least meet them halfway, so as to achieve greater public acceptance throughout the world. And in 2000–2001, the bursting of the dot.com stock market bubble in the United States, inducing a global recession, sharpened criticisms of those who would treat the world economy as self-organizing, that is, without any need for significant institu-tions and procedures of overall economic governance. There is a more self-reflective mood now present among leadership groups associated with GFA.

Given this background, it seems appropriate to ask the complementary question—what is the normative potential and political leverage of the social forces associated with GFB? Do these forces have an alternative coherent vi-sion to that favored by advocates of GFA? Globalization exhibits various ten-dencies of unequal significance, the identification of which helps us assess whether GFB is capable of neutralizing some of the detrimental impacts of GFA, and moving from a purely defensive and critical posture of opposition to one that is more creative and affirmative.

The New Politics of Resistance

Political oppositional forms in reaction to GFA have been shaped by six conditions. These conditions together define the new politics of resistance that constitutes globalization-from-below.

First, there is the virtual futility of concentrating upon conventional elec-toral politics, given the extent to which the principal political parties in consti-tutional democracies have subscribed to a program that defers to the discipline of global capital. This development may not persist if social forces can be mo-bilized to press social-democratic leaderships effectively to resume their com-mitment to the establishment of a state that is internally and internationally compassionate, and if such an empathetic outlook proves to be politically viable. So far, to the extent that its power has been tested, the demands emanating from GFB have been successfully rebuffed at the level of the state. A few years ago, Germans in their national elections mandated tougher regulation of the private sector, including higher taxes on business and more attention to social justice. However, the financial community effectively vetoed the mandate of German citizens, through the mechanisms of a falling stock market, threatened capital flight, and much media criticism directed at Finance Minister Oskar Lafontaine. It did not take long for Lafontaine to be asked to submit his resignation, and for the Schroeder government to abandon its challenge to GFA. This de facto veto power of the financial community exerts a chilling, if indirect, effect on electoral politics.

Although the severity of this constraining influence varies in relation to the ideological stance of a country's leadership, its efficiency in handling the social agenda, disparities in wealth and income, the coherence and outlook of organized labor, and the overall growth rates of the national, regional, and global economies, the main conclusion remains valid. Resistance to economic globalization is not likely to be effective if it relies on mere criticism of existing beliefs and practices shaping the world economy. Only the mobilization of countervailing power seems capable of generating an effective challenge.

Second, the groups that oppose GFA have recognized that the struggle against economic globalization is unlikely to have a major impact on public opinion until they fashion a credible alternative economic approach. Such an alternative must have enough of a mobilizing effect on people to induce a new perception of the "dangerous classes" on the part of those shaping the policies associated with GFA. This role cannot be played by the industrial working class, which has suffered a serious decline arising from the discrediting of socialism, the displacement of industrialism by electronics as the leading economic sector, and the co-option of skilled labor via stock options and a seeming stake in capitalist success. To be effective, GFB must attain a weight and density that is capable of making existing economic and political elites so nervous about their managerial ability to contain opposition that they begin seriously to explore a politics of accommodation. Such an accommodation would entail the adoption of policy options that depart significantly from the precepts of neoliberalism. In such an altered atmosphere it is easy to imagine the negotiation of social contracts that restore a balance between the interests of people and those of markets, at the regional or even global level.

Third, aside from the reemergence of dangerous classes, *the prospect of ecological constraints will induce the market to send signals calling for a negotiated transition to managed economic growth and increased institutional governance in the interest of sustainability.* With limits on certain forms of growth and on energy policy being required for both environmental reasons and middle-term business profitability, it may be possible at some now unforeseen point to reach agreements on a regional or even global basis amounting to an environmental contract. The objective of such an instrument, which would not need to be formally agreed upon or written in the form of a treaty, would be to reconcile anxieties about the carrying capacity of the earth with a range of social demands to secure the basic needs of individuals and communities.

One sign of movement in this direction is the attention being given to the radical idea of supplementing, if not altogether replacing, the traditional emphasis on "national security" with a new outlook based on "human security." The political language of human security gained international attention through the annual Human Development Reports of the United Nations Development Program, and even more so through its endorsement and use by Lloyd Axworthy during his tenure as Canada's foreign minister in the last half of the 1990s. At present, the idea is being widely discussed in various global civil society networks, and through the medium of an independent international commission headed by former high commissioner of refugees Sadako Ogata and a Nobel Prize winner for economics, Amartya Sen. This commission will issue a report in 2003.

Fourth, GFA has inadvertently encouraged a resurgence of support for right-wing extremism, which expresses a territorialist backlash hostile to globalization. These reactionary antiglobalization challenges take the form of a varied and evolving array of national political movements that have scared governments still dominated by moderate outlooks, and led them to rethink their acquiescence to the discipline of global capital. Electoral results in several European countries, including Austria and France, reveal both considerable support for the political right and a rightwards swing by the mainstream leadership. A significant minority of citizens faced with the fiscal symptoms of economic globalization—cutbacks in social services, high interest rates, capital outflows, and instability in employment—have been drawn to ultranationalist ideologues who place the blame on GFA or foreigners. Will national political parties and governments be able to recover their authority by responding effectively to this challenge without successfully civilizing globalization?

Fifth, the leverage of GFB depends to some extent on the future of organized labor, and its still uncertain response to globalization. A central question arises. Will labor militancy become somewhat more effective and socially visible as it shifts its focus from industrial-age priorities of wages and workplace conditions to such emerging concerns as downsizing, outsourcing, child labor, and job security? There are also possibilities of engaging wider constituencies than organized labor in this struggle by including individuals and groups who are feeling some of the negative effects of globalizing tendencies. Jacques Chirac seemed sufficiently shaken by the December 1995 large-scale work stoppages and demonstrations in France that he partially reversed ideological course, at least rhetorically and temporarily. Chirac, previously known as a dogmatic ad-

herent of neoliberal thinking, abruptly issuing a dramatic call for the establishment of "a social Europe." Clearly, the affirmation of such a goal represented a
retreat for Chirac from a basic tenet of neoliberalism and thus provided a psychological victory for GFB. But rhetorical victories do not necessarily produce
adjustments in policy, particularly if the structures that underpin the neoliberal
approach are strong and elusive, as is the case with the world economy. In retro-
spect, Chirac's conversion to the cause of a social Europe seems little more than
a tactical maneuver that was designed to gain more operating room.

Another indicative development within the setting of GFB involves a renewed recourse to the strike weapon as a means for working people to resist some
of the impacts of globalization. Organized labor, despite economic growth in the
North, has not been able to share in the material benefits of a larger economic pie
because of the impinging effects of competitiveness and fiscal austerity. In numerous economic sectors it has been losing jobs and facing a continuous threat of
industrial relocation. The General Motors strike of October 1996 in Canada
seemed at the time to be a harbinger of both a new wave of labor militancy and a
new agenda of grievances. The strike focused precisely on issues of job losses
and industrial relocation, involving a direct challenge to the approach of the managers of economic globalization. It suggests a new emphasis in the labor movement that has the potential for transnational cooperative activities among
workers. There is also present in these developments an emerging recognition
among labor leaders of their need to collaborate with civil society organizations
in shaping their struggle for greater fairness in the global economy.

*Sixth, a highly visible setting for resistance to GFA has been a series of
global conferences held under the auspices of the United Nations on a variety of
policy issues.* Although denied formal access because of their lack of statist cre-
dentials, nongovernmental organizations exerted a considerable impact on the
agenda and substantive outcomes of these intergovernmental meetings. These
representatives of civil society used these events to strengthen transnational networking links, thereby building a movement of global proportions from the
ground up. Starting with the Rio Conference on Environment and Development
in 1992, through the 1993 Vienna Conference on Human Rights and Development, the 1994 Cairo Conference on Population and Development, the 1995 Social Summit in Copenhagen, and the Beijing Conference on Women and
Development, to the 1996 Istanbul Conference on Habitat and Development,
parallel gatherings of transnational activists prefigured what is here being called
GFB. These events were early experiments in a new sort of participatory global
politics that had little connection with the traditional practices of politics within
states, and could be regarded as fledgling attempts to establish "global democracy." However, these efforts were not able to continue on the paths cleared by
the United Nations, for leading states were not receptive to such challenges to
their authority and preeminence and to the ideological hegemony of GFA.

These developments, representing an effort to engage directly both statist and market forces, produced their own kind of backlash politics. At first, at Rio and Vienna, the response by leading states was a co-optive one, acknowledging the participation of GFB as legitimate and significant, yet controlling policy outcomes through intergovernmental diplomacy. But later, at Cairo, Copenhagen, and Beijing, these democratizing forces were perceived as adversaries of the neoliberal conception of political economy, as unwelcome champions of social change on such issues as gender rights and self-determination for indigenous peoples, and as subverters of a statist world order. The format of a global conference open to both types of globalization began to be perceived by elites as risky, and possibly was regarded as an early sighting of the next wave of revolutionary challenge, an unwanted rebirth of dangerous classes in the sense earlier reserved for working people during industrial-era capitalism.

This assessment of action and reaction has been generally validated in subsequent years. To begin with, there has emerged a refusal by leading states to finance and organize global conferences on sensitive issues under the banner of the United Nations. There has been, in reaction, a search for new formats by citizen groups associated with GFB, with a predictable increase in the oppositional and militant character of global civic politics. The main attempt of GFB has been to organize a populist presence at meetings of the Group of Eight or at annual, and even regional, meetings of the board of governors of the IMF, World Bank, and WTO. Also, there have been various efforts to set up tribunals of the people to consider allegations of social crimes attributable to GFA.

If the challenge of GFB is to become formidable enough to prompt those representing GFA to seek accommodation, these and other new tactics will have to be further developed. One direction of activity that may be easier to organize is to concentrate energies of resistance at regional levels of encounter, especially in Europe, Asia-Pacific, and the Americas, at intergovernmental gatherings devoted to expanding growth in the region by implementing neoliberal policies. The Third World Network, based in Penang, has been very effective in educating the cadres of resistance to GFA about adverse effects and encouraging various types of opposition. Otherwise, resistance to GFA and the ascendancy of market forces is likely to be ignored.

Concluding Reflections

Above all, the leadership of GFB needs to formulate a more coherent program of goals and tactics to clarify the sort of globalization it is seeking for the peoples of the world. At the core of this clarification needs to be a compromise between the logic of the market as the foundation of global economic governance, as associated with the World Trade Organization and the Bretton Woods institutions, and a vision of cosmopolitan democracy held by many activists dedicated to a more equitable and sustainable world order.[7] There is also the matter of appropriate tactics. Militant tactics may be selectively employed to supplement the regulatory efforts, feeble at best, of national governments. Such an approach was successfully initiated by Greenpeace several years ago, to reverse a decision by Shell Oil approved by the British government to sink a large oil rig named Brent Spar in the North Sea.[8] The issue here was one of environmental protection, but the tactic of consumer leverage is potentially deployable in relation to any issue that finds its way onto the transnational social agenda. What induced the Shell turnaround—although it never conceded the possible environmental dangers of its planned disposal of the oil rig—was the focus of the boycott on Shell service stations, especially those located in Germany. Indeed, the impact of this initiative was so great that both the *Wall Street Journal* and the *Financial Times* editorialized against Greenpeace, complaining that it had become "an environmental superpower." Shell itself has made a notable effort to upgrade its image, publishing ads in the *Economist* and elsewhere that proclaim its interest in upholding human rights and environmental standards, even if it hurts the bottom line of its quarterly profit reports.

The politics of resistance in this emergent era of globalization are still in formation. Because of their global scope and of the specificities of local, national, and regional conditions, the tactics and priorities of gobalization-from-below will inevitably be diverse. Just as GFA tends towards homogeneity and unity, so GFB tends towards heterogeneity and diversity. This contrast highlights the fundamental difference between top-down, hierarchical politics and bottom-up, participatory politics. Yet this conflict is not a zero-sum rivalry; it is rather one in which the transnational democratic goal is to reconcile global market operations with both the well-being of peoples and the carrying capacity of the earth. Whether this reconciliation is possible and how it will be achieved are likely to be the most salient political challenges of the new millennium.

Notes

1. For my earliest reliance on this terminology with respect to globalization, see Brecher, Childs, and Cutler 1993, 39–50. For a more comprehensive consideration of such perspectives, see Brecher, Costello, and Smith 2000. For a useful and sophisticated overview of globalization-from-below in the setting of transnational environmentalism, see Wapner 1996.

2. See the U.N. initiative encouraged by the secretary general, and called "The Global Compact: Shared Values for the Global Market," with a website at <www.unglobalcompact.org>; Regelbrugge 1999.

3. However, when it comes to authority with respect to the use of force in relation to the sovereign rights of states, the Westphalian reality persists. For a collection of essays exploring the post-Westphalian hypothesis from this angle, and generally concluding against its main claim, see Lyons and Mastanduno 1995.

4. See two recent reports of global commissions of eminent persons: Commission on Global Governance 1995; and Independent Commission on Population and the Quality of Life 1996.

5. Effectively argued in Kothari 1997.

6. This position is elaborated in Falk 1996.

7. A comprehensive and important effort to formulate such a perspective is to be found in Held 1995, 267–86.

8. See discussion of this case by Prins and Sellwood 1998.

References

Brecher, Jeremy, John Brown Childs, and Jill Cutler, eds. 1993. *Global Visions: Beyond the New World Order.* Boston: South End Press.

Brecher, Jeremy, Tim Costello, and Brendan Smith. 2000. *Globalization from Below: The Power of Solidarity.* Boston: South End Press.

Commission on Global Governance 1995. *Our Global Neighbourhood.* Oxford and New York: Oxford University Press.

Falk, Richard. 1996. "An Inquiry into the Political Economy of World Order." *New Political Economy* 1:13–26.

———. 1999. *Predatory Globalization.* Cambridge: Polity Press.

Held, David. 1995. *Democracy and the Global Order: From the Modern State to Cosmopolitan Democracy.* Cambridge: Polity Press.

Independent Commission on Population and the Quality of Life. 1996. *Caring for the Future.* Oxford and New York: Oxford University Press.

Kothari, Smitu. 1997. "Where Are the People? The United Nations, Global Economic Institutions, and Governance." In *Between Sovereignty and Global Governance: The United Nations, the State, and Civil Society,* ed. Albert J. Paolini, Anthony P. Jarvis, and Christian Reus-Smit. New York: St. Martin's Press.

Lyons, Gene M., and Michael Mastanduno, eds. 1995. *Beyond Westphalia? State Sovereignty and International Law.* Baltimore: Johns Hopkins University Press.

Prins, Gwyn, and Elizabeth Sellwood. 1998. "Global Security Problems and the Challenge to Democratic Process." In *Re-imagining Political Community: Studies in*

Cosmopolitan Democracy, ed. Daniele Archibugi, David Held, and Martin Köhler. Stanford, Calif.: Stanford University Press.

Regelbrugge, Laurie, ed. 1999. *Promoting Corporate Citizenship: Opportunities for Business and Civil Society Engagement.* Washington, D.C.: CIVICUS, World Alliance for Citizen Participation.

Soros, George. 1998. *The Crisis of Global Capitalism: Open Society Endangered.* New York: Public Affairs.

Wallerstein, Immanuel. 1995. *After Liberalism.* New York: New Press.

Wapner, Paul. 1996. *Environmental Activism and World Civic Politics.* Albany: State University of New York Press.

CHAPTER 16

Seattle: Global Protest Comes of Age

Robert Weissman

"It is best at this time to take a 'time out,'" U.S. Trade Representative Charlene Barshefsky advised the assembled group of country delegates to the World Trade Organization meeting late on the night of Friday, 4 December 1999. "Therefore we've agreed to suspend the work of the Ministerial," said Barshefsky, who served as chair of the meeting of trade ministers. As Barshefsky closed the meeting in total disarray—without even a final formal declaration by the world's trade ministers—a roar erupted from the back of the convention hall. Nongovernmental organizations that had been granted admission to the closing session of the WTO meeting cheered the failure of the trade talks.

Many of the country delegate seats, however, were empty. Frustrated, tired, and disgusted with the negotiation process, many delegates skipped the final session altogether—a visible manifestation of the breakdown in fraternal relations at the WTO.

This scenario was a surprise ending to a week of stunning developments, in which the opponents of WTO-facilitated corporate globalization exerted more influence over the negotiating process than anyone anticipated.

Democracy Spills into the Streets

Monday set the tone for the week of WTO meetings, when approximately ten thousand demonstrators organized by the Jubilee 2000 Northwest Coalition linked arms to surround an opening reception for WTO participants. Apparently fearful of the demonstrators, most delegates, journalists, and other guests, sponsored by the corporate-funded Seattle Host Organization, bowed out. No more than fifteen hundred sampled the fine foods—a far cry from the minimum of five thousand that organizers expected.

207

Early Tuesday morning, thousands of people, mostly students and young people, gathered in two locations to march toward the convention center where the WTO talks were scheduled. With most organized into affinity groups coordinated through the Direct Action Network, they strode toward the convention center, located in the city center, unimpeded by Seattle police. As they neared the convention center, they split up into multiple groups.

Eventually, the protesters occupied every intersection that provided access to the convention center. In a highly disciplined action, core groups sat down and blocked the intersections. In some access ways, groups "locked down," joining arms inside pipes so the police could not drag them away. At certain intersections, there were hundreds of people, at others a thousand or more. "Just Say No to the WTO," the protesters chanted as they danced. They linked arms to prevent any delegates to the WTO, or anyone else, from entering the convention center where opening sessions were planned.

While the direct action participants anticipated arrest, initially the riot-gear equipped Seattle police only formed lines to block them from advancing all the way to the convention center. As the morning wore on, the crowd participating in the direct action grew to approximately ten thousand.

The eventual police response was erratic. In many intersections, the police did not move against the demonstrators. In others, they responded not with arrests, but with extraordinary amounts of tear gas, almost always fired without prior warning. In some areas, the tear gas cleared the demonstrators, but in others the crowds were simply too dense and those with gas masks remained unmoved. In some cases, police fired rubber bullets into the crowd and roughed up protesters with their batons.

While the police eventually cleared limited access ways to the convention center and the adjacent Paramount Theater where formal opening ceremonies had been scheduled, the vast majority of delegates could not reach the convention center or the theater. Delegates who tried to walk through the protesters' lines were turned away. Many, including high-ranking members of the U.S. delegation, were locked down in their hotels, denied the right to exit by police. WTO proceedings were canceled in the morning, and only a small number of delegates were able to participate in the afternoon sessions. By and large, Tuesday was a lost day for the negotiators.

Meanwhile, as ten thousand young people stood face-to-face with police in gear that resembled the Storm Troopers armor in *Star Wars*, tens of thousands of people participated in a labor-led rally and march against the WTO. Representatives from labor unions in more than one hundred countries banded with the leadership of the AFL-CIO in denouncing the WTO's failure to respect basic labor rights. Members of the steelworkers and teamsters unions who turned out in force teamed up with substantial contingents of longshoremen, ironworkers, and workers from other unions. But many participants—including thousands of environmentalists, farmers, consumer activists, religious people, and women's activists—were not allied with labor.

The labor-led march turned around before reaching the convention center, remaining physically apart from the direct action. But many of the marchers broke off and joined the direct action, providing reinforcement in the early and midafternoon.

In the later afternoon and evening, the crowd of demonstrators thinned and the police ratcheted up their response. Growing increasingly aggressive, they resorted to tear gas, rubber bullets, and violence, though they refused to make arrests to clear the streets. A small number of protesters broke storefront windows, primarily but not exclusively of major chain stores. Those engaging in property destruction were easily identifiable—many were dressed in black as part of a Black Bloc that considers itself anarchist—but the police chose not to arrest them or take action to prevent them from engaging in further property destruction. In contrast, many of those participating in the direct action did try to stop the property destruction, engaging in heated discussions and chanting "Nonviolence."

The police violence would escalate on Wednesday; that evening the police—bolstered by National Guard troops and reinforcements from areas surrounding Seattle—chased protesters out of the downtown area (declared a "protest-free" zone) and into the Capitol Hill residential neighborhood. The police fired huge amounts of tear gas, made arbitrary arrests, and brutalized protesters and even certain nonprotesters. Many of those arrested alleged that they were beaten and mistreated in jail. Until ordered by a court to allow those arrested to see legal counsel, police at the jail seemed to maintain an overt policy of denying prisoners access to legal representation.

The Wednesday police violence largely eventuated away from the convention center and the notice of WTO delegates. But the police actions, plus alleged mistreatment in jail of those arrested in connection with the protests, were serious enough to prompt calls for investigations not just by Seattle's mayor but by Human Rights Watch and Amnesty International. "The use of chemical sprays, restraint chairs and beatings appear to violate international human rights standards," Amnesty International said.

Notwithstanding city efforts to clamp down on all public dissent in the downtown area, protests continued throughout the week, with thousands of environmentalists, farmers, steelworkers, and women demonstrating at separate marches and rallies. All of the demonstrations were high-energy and featured focused attacks on the WTO and the corporations that have drafted and lobbied for its rules. Protesters enthusiastically chanted, "This is what democracy looks like"—a pointed contrast to the proceedings inside the WTO—as they marched in the streets.

On Friday, perhaps ten thousand people united in a spirited labor-led march—organized on about twenty-four hours notice—once again to protest the WTO and the city's infringements on civil liberties through the creation of a "no protest" zone.

The Collapse

Inside the convention center, negotiations began on Wednesday, after riot-gear-equipped police and National Guard forces cordoned off the downtown from most protesters. The trade ministers were seeking to achieve a final Ministerial Declaration that would establish the framework for a new round of trade talks to expand the power and authority of the WTO.

WTO Director General Mike Moore and Barshefsky had announced that negotiations would be conducted in five working groups. Each group was open to any interested government delegation. They were to discuss a variety of subjects:

- agriculture;

- market access (the extent to which industrialized countries have opened their markets to developing countries);

- implementation (how industrialized and developing countries should implement their obligations under existing WTO agreements);

- the Singapore work program (continuing issues discussed at the previous WTO ministerial meeting, including the possibility of new agreements on investments and competition);

- transparency and openness.

It is unclear why the working groups failed to produce compromise agreements. After negotiations collapsed, Barshefsky noted "a general view that we need processes with a greater degree of transparency and inclusion." However, she observed that "this process became exceptionally difficult to manage."

When it became clear the working group format would fail to produce a compromise deal in the limited time available, the United States sought to forge a deal through the WTO's heavy-handed old-style tactics. Charlene Barshefsky and the rest of the U.S. negotiating team picked a handful of countries to commence negotiations in a closed "Green Room." The idea was for the selected group to hammer out a comprehensive deal, and then present it to the entire WTO membership as a fait accompli for adoption.

Developing country delegates were outraged at the return to Green Room negotiations. On Thursday, more than seventy African, Caribbean, and Latin American countries—a majority of the WTO members—issued statements warning that they would not be steamrollered into joining a "consensus" statement.

Early Friday morning, a draft compromise text was released. The compromise seemed to embody a modified negotiating agenda, which did not include controversial EU proposals for talks on investment and competition agreements. The EU apparently withdrew its demand for recognition of "multifunctionality" in agriculture—the idea that agricultural regulations should be governed not only by narrow market considerations but also by food's central role in national cultures and the importance of protecting farmers. The United States agreed to a review of antidumping rules. Dumping is the practice of countries selling goods in foreign markets at below-cost; many developing countries argue the United States uses antidumping rules to exclude their goods illegitimately. U.S. unions in certain sectors, especially steel, believe the rules are crucial to bar unfair competition.

A proposal for a draft working group on biotechnology remained in brackets—used for areas where agreement has not been reached—as did much of the text. Biotechnology had sparked contention within the European delegation. The European Commission, composed of the top officials who represent the entire European Union, agreed early in the week to a WTO working group on biotechnology. This position provoked outrage among numerous European environmental ministers—members of elected, national governments—for whom the announcement was a surprise.

But the Friday morning draft was not to be the basis for a final compromise. By mid-afternoon, rumors flew that the entire negotiation might collapse. Published reports indicate that Charlene Barshefsky, seeing the writing on the wall, decided to pull the plug.

In a news conference following the close of the meeting, Barshefsky asserted that most contentious issues never reached final negotiation stage, implying that the talks had foundered solely on the basis of agriculture, and the European Union's refusal to compromise on its support for export subsidies. Export subsidies is an issue over which the United States is allied with developing countries against Europe. For Barshefsky, this explanation was, in part, an attempt to attribute the collapse to EU resistance to global demands.

In contrast, Pascal Lamy, the EU trade minister, blamed the collapse on "the complexity of the negotiation" and developing countries' dissatisfaction with the negotiating process. The EU, he said, "stood as a bridge between the United States and developing countries on most topics."

Barshefsky and Lamy were probably both right to some degree, though Barshefsky's claim that the agricultural dispute was solely to blame is almost certainly too narrow a reading of events. Other factors leading to the breakdown included:

- the revolt of the Third World countries against the Green Room negotiation process;

- the Third World government resistance to the U.S. call for formation of a working group to study the relationship between trade and labor issues (intensified after Bill Clinton told the *Seattle Post-Intelligencer* that he hoped the WTO would eventually enforce core labor standards with sanctions);

- and the potential domestic political costs of U.S. agreement to the Friday morning compromise proposal.

On each of these issues, the street protests heightened contradictions and conflicts. The simple fact of preventing negotiations on Tuesday helped impede agreement in the agricultural sector by limiting the time negotiators had to cut a deal. The street demonstrations clearly stiffened the spines of the Third World negotiators. As the talks collapsed Friday night, a delegate from Zimbabwe explained that the street demonstrations emboldened the Third World negotiators to object to the exclusionary processes inside the WTO.

By the end of the negotiations, the Third World ministers' bitterness was palpable. George Yeo, head of the Singapore delegation and the chair of the controversial agricultural working group, said that a "quiet revolt" emerged against rich country backroom deal-making. "We know we will not get anywhere with this [negotiating] arrangement where things are hidden," Mustapha Bello, head of the Nigerian delegation, declared to a reporter. Bello echoed the sentiment of many other developing country delegates in self-consciously expressing almost complete ignorance over what "they"—the rich countries— were offering in the real negotiations.

But the street demonstrations also simultaneously antagonized many Third World negotiators, who objected to demands by some critics for inclusion of labor and environmental standards in the WTO.

Meanwhile, U.S. labor movement demands that the WTO respect efforts to enforce core labor standards—backed by mobilized rank-and-file members—backed the Clinton administration into a corner. An administration cave-in on its minimalist labor rights demands, or on the dumping issue, would clearly have domestic political costs, especially for the presidential candidacy of Al Gore. And so the vocal protests drove the country negotiators apart, contributing to the collapse.

Seattle's Legacy

For those who opposed the Seattle agenda of expanding the WTO's power, the events of 29 November to 4 December 1999 exceeded their most optimistic expectations. While Barshefsky and Moore suggested that future WTO talks could build on the progress made in Seattle, once the member countries had caught their breath following the "time out," two years would pass before these talks moved ahead.

The protesters were jubilant. "I believe that the global economic order will define its history as the time before Seattle and the time after," said Han Shan of the Ruckus Society, one of the main organizers of the Seattle direct actions. "History has been made in Seattle as the allegedly irresistible forces of corporate economic globalization were stopped in their tracks by the immovable object of grassroots democracy," said Lori Wallach, director of Public Citizen's Global Trade Watch, as the talks disintegrated. "The momentum from tonight's victory will enable us to move from successfully resisting a new round of WTO expansion to starting a turnaround."

But what was achieved in Seattle was a delay, not a turnaround. Sheltered from protesters by inaccessibility and tight security in Doha, Qatar, in November 2001, the next WTO meeting of trade ministers endorsed a new round. Launching a new negotiating round was nearly as important to corporate interests as maintaining existing WTO rules and the prevailing model of corporate globalization. Nevertheless, the struggle had been joined in Seattle: global protest had clearly come of age.

CHAPTER 17

Globalization-from-Below:
Letter from Honduras

Hans Edstrand

Fresh out of university, I arrived in Central America in December 1997. I was young, idealistic, invincible—on a personal crusade to find my life's purpose and, I hoped, rediscover the beauty in human nature. With a spring in my step and a pocket full of common sense I embarked on my quest and stumbled into an opportunity to contribute in a challenging yet fulfilling way. The two phases of my journey have not only put a human face on global development, but also demonstrated that when people work together anything is possible. For me, globalization-from-below means people from the North and the South united in grassroots projects to empower poor communities.

Perhaps destiny, or pure luck, or perhaps just the will to serve guided my path. It quickly led me through Mexico, Guatemala, and Belize, only to dump me in what a friend calls "the exhaust pipe of Central America," Tegucigalpa, Honduras. With little Spanish and no contacts, I was just another gringo in this stormy sea. Pollution, crime, intense poverty, and overall social chaos don't encourage a newcomer to put down roots, but that's just what I did. Landing work at a local orphanage operated by the international humanitarian organization Nuestros Pequeños Hermanos (NPH) marked the first step in my odyssey.

The orphanage, called Rancho Santa Fe, has a fairy-tale quality; it is a magical city of over five hundred children, with homes, school, workshops, church, and recreational facilities. At any given moment, you'll find children doing what they do best: playing, laughing, singing, studying, inevitably fighting, but most of all growing up in a very loving environment. Rancho Santa Fe offers these Honduran orphans emotional and spiritual support, along with education and practical training to become productive Honduran citizens.

Over the next nine months, this facility became my home as I worked, played, laughed, and cried with my new family. During this enchanted time, I learned to appreciate the good fortune implicit in growing up in Canada and

215

Sweden, and discovered how to share that fortune with my Honduran counterparts through teaching them a myriad of practical and personal skills ranging
from carpentry to cooking. All the while, I was inspired by being a member of
an international organization that could weave such a beautiful web of worldwide collaboration; it offered life-saving benefits to these victims of Third
World poverty.

　　Nonetheless, the extent of Honduran underdevelopment shocked me. Neither my university studies in geography, economics, and politics, nor my travels
through Guatemala, El Salvador, and Nicaragua prepared me for Honduran realities. If a country like El Salvador can be considered Third World, then Honduras would seem to be in the Tenth. From highways to telecommunications,
from police and government to business and industry, Honduras just falls further
and further behind. The United Nations Development Programme ranks Honduras 113th out of 174 countries in its Human Development Index; it cites the
low average income as the most significant factor delaying development. Not
very informative, really, unless you've lived with this level of poverty and can
somehow internalize what 113th translates into: chronic unemployment and low
wages; systemic governmental inefficiency and widespread corruption; hunger
and disease for the general populace. Nor does it take U.N. statisticians to determine the root problem: quite simply, the Honduran economy is stagnant and
too externally oriented. Lacking a widespread tax base, the government is per-
petually bankrupt. The story is the same every year. Children lose approximately
a third of their schooling, as teachers are on strike negotiating subsistence
wages; the police don't have the tools (vehicles, gasoline, radios, firearms) to be
effective; the roads and bridges disintegrate; modern communication, especially
by telephone, remains a constant challenge and inaccessible to the majority.
Thus, Honduran society is utter chaos and the population endures chronic
poverty. As one "privileged" university graduate confessed tearfully, people
watch helplessly as they sink further into poverty each year. It seemed as if life
could not get much worse for the average Honduran.

　　But it did with the unwelcome arrival of Hurricane Mitch. And, ironically,
this further devastation of October 1998 led me to the second phase of my
quest. Although it destroyed bridges, roads, businesses, and agriculture, the
damage to Rancho Santa Fe was minimal. NPH was in a good position to assist the rest of the country in the emergency relief. All through November, I
worked with a small group of NPH volunteers delivering water, medicine, food,
and clothing to the isolated communities around Tegucigalpa. Everywhere, we
met the uncomprehending stares of refugees who had watched their homes,
their livelihoods, their loved ones swirl away in the raging torrent of Rio
Choluteca. There seemed to be no end to these people's suffering and little hope
of a better future. As the immediate emergency subsided and other organizations—the United Nations, USAID, and occasionally the Honduran govern-

ment—assumed control of water, food, and medicine, our focus shifted towards this better future through a long-term reconstruction effort.

One step led to another and, for the next two years, I was the executive director and cofounder of Nueva Esperanza, the resulting Honduran foundation. Our primary objective was the autoconstruction of two hundred homes with the refugees from Hurricane Mitch 47 kilometers outside of Tegucigalpa in Moroceli, El Paraiso. Nueva Esperanza organized, administered and financed the construction while beneficiary families supplied the low-to-medium skilled labor. Nueva Esperanza facilitated development with dignity by empowering marginalized people through access to resources (primarily education and financing).

In Moroceli, with two hundred houses finished and inhabited in 2001, the real *community development* began in earnest. The focus shifted from housing autoconstruction towards education, health, job creation, security, and recreation. Community participation and leadership is now the primary objective at every level. As the technical staff of Nueva Esperanza slowly phases out, control is being passed to the community, the Honduran government, and other Honduran NGOs working in human development.

That education is the basis of any type of genuine, sustainable development is a guiding principle on which Nueva Esperanza was founded. Primary education for the young, coupled with practical training for the adults, has been the primary focus since 2000. This effort has demanded close cooperation with the Honduran government (Ministry of Education and INFOP, the government training organization). Currently a primary school, including a kindergarten and grades 1–6, operates with the assistance of five government-appointed teachers. A library and study hall have been constructed to facilitate the studies of the community. Adult training includes courses in sewing, handicrafts, and shoemaking. INFOP plans to establish a regional training center in Nueva Esperanza offering cosmetic/beauty training, small appliance repair, and tailoring. Formal adult education is being offered through a unique Honduran radio program, *Maestro en Casa,* which allows working adults the opportunity to complete their primary education (the equivalent of grade 9), through home study night classes broadcast over the radio.

Further domestic education is provided by the Honduran NGO Calidad de Vida, which focuses on human development and the promotion of family values. Calidad de Vida has also begun a successful bakery; it plans to expand its operations to include a small sewing workshop, as well as a youth center.

Nueva Esperanza is fortunate to share the Santa Rosa de Lima health center with the neighboring community of Nuevo Paraiso. Primarily an outpatient center, it furnishes invaluable medical attention to the twenty thousand people in the Moroceli region. A new building incorporates maternity, emergency, laboratory, and dentistry facilities. While equipment and staff are still being negotiated, Santa Rosa de Lima has become the most comprehensive medical establishment within 50 km, attending an otherwise very isolated population. On 27 December 2000 the first baby was born at Santa Rosa de Lima, a tiny girl from Nueva Esperanza. She was named Rosa Victoria, honoring both the clinic where she was born, and the doctor who delivered her. Since then, further children have been delivered, averaging one baby per week in the year 2001.

Microenterprise has been a parallel objective since the beginning of the housing construction at Nueva Esperanza. At present, the community includes a sewing workshop (micromaquila), a bakery, and handicraft and shoe workshops, as well as a cooperative-run supermarket. INFOP along with Calidad de Vida have been very active in these efforts to stimulate local employment/enterprise over the past year and are currently examining how to expand their operations.

Microcredit has long since been available through a system of community banks sponsored by the Rotary Club of Tegucigalpa, and individual credits can be accessed through the Padre Guillermo Arsenault Cooperative. Nueva Esperanza residents are using this financing to develop small businesses in fields ranging from agriculture and farming to carpentry and artisanal crafts.

The long-term economic development of Nueva Esperanza is focused on a mixed cooperative organized with the members of the community. This cooperative, Rios de Agua Viva, is a legally recognized Honduran institution with a board of directors elected by the general assembly of all members. Currently, Rios de Agua Viva operates a small discount supermarket at Nueva Esperanza providing both the residents and surrounding communities with basic goods at affordable prices. The cooperative will soon implement a direct bus route between the community and Tegucigalpa to facilitate the flow of people and commerce. Additional plans include the installation of a community telephone service and the expansion of certain production workshops.

As the technical team slowly phases out, Cooperativa Rios de Agua Viva is stepping in and assuming control of the investment of Nuestros Pequenos Hermanos in microenterprises and housing construction. The beneficiaries of the houses in Moroceli are repaying the material value of their homes ($1,700/25,000 Lps.) financed over a period of eight years. These payments are deposited in a rotating communal fund controlled by the cooperative and dedicated to the continued growth of Nueva Esperanza. These funds are regulated through what could be considered the constitution of Nueva Esperanza (20 percent Health, 20 percent Education, 10 percent Waste Management, 15 percent Security, 15 percent Infrastructure/Business, 10 percent Legal Reserve, 5 percent Variable, 5 percent Audit). The mortgage payments are the equivalent of a tax that the beneficiaries pay for the continued growth and development of Nueva Esperanza. As this constitution is framed with the people, they learn about its interpretation and implementation, in an attempt to promote future transparency and internal regulation.

The success of this experiment in global development can be measured through people such as Doña Genoveva who embody its vitality and promise. Sixty-eight years old, she is the mother of ten, grandmother of twenty-five, and great-grandmother of countless more. Dona Genoveva came to Nueva Esperanza with two of her granddaughters and their seven great-grandchildren in March 1999 when the project was still just an idea. Since then she has solidified her role as the communal grandmother through her unfailing optimism, kind words, and hugs.

From her first days in Moroceli, living in a ten-square-meter plastic temporary shelter, Genoveva set about establishing her *Pulperia* and restaurant. Indefatigable in every respect, her fame spread quickly as the workers and beneficiaries flocked to her kitchen for food, drink, advice, or just a little warmth. Her indomitable spirit was one of the pillars that helped this community's pioneers to overcome the enormous adversity involved in a project of this nature.

As the community has grown, so has the competition, but Genoveva has kept pace learning new skills such as baking and handicrafts. Her success at the project has prompted three more of her daughters, also displaced by Mitch, to join the project in subsequent phases. People urge her to slow down—"Let the others in the family shoulder the burden," they declare. She replies she doesn't know how—and even if she did, she wouldn't be happy. Her resilient spirit and relentless hard work epitomize what Nueva Esperanza as a community development is all about: coming together to overcome adversity and find new hope.

As a volunteer planning a Hurricane Mitch reconstruction project from Rancho Santa Fe, I could never have dared to imagine the magnitude of Nueva Esperanza's growth. But the objective was never size, always quality. Common sense dictates, and experience has shown, that two hundred houses built well are far more valuable than five hundred built poorly. Our initial focus in March 1999 was to build sixty houses well. That number swelled to an additional sixteen, then twenty-three, and so it grew.

There's no shortage of international support for good projects. That verity has been the single most wondrous aspect of Nueva Esperanza: the coordination of a tremendously diverse range of international resources with Third World people's needs in a dignified, sustainable way. From a Third World perspective, this collaboration is globalization's greatest gift. Dona Genoveva will never know the international benefactors who made her new home or this new dream possible, nor will any of them ever know her. That the solidarity demonstrated by the international community following Hurricane Mitch could find meaningful expression in Nueva Esperanza gives globalization a human face.

CHAPTER 18

Transnational Union Strategies for Civilizing Labor Standards

Rob Lambert and Eddie Webster

Globalization-from-below is arising with force and vigor. Inevitably beset by serious obstacles and questions of strategy, the myriad of initiatives also reveals unprecedented opportunity. While cyberspace heralds capitalism's increased dominance through facilitating and consolidating the power of corporations and international financial institutions, it also signals an age of movements that are *potentially* more genuinely global in scope and in action. Cyberspace can be used to advantage in building these movements as activists harness the Internet, websites, and databases to build resistance campaigns. As well, the lessening of Cold War ideological division has created new space for global organizing (O'Brien 2000).

SIGTUR (the Southern Initiative on Globalization and Trade Union Rights) is an example of such a movement that aspires to be global in scope and action. This chapter describes the genesis of this new Southern union formation and considers the challenges, difficulties, and opportunities that exist. This new labor internationalism embodies a connected strategic focus: building the capacity to resist globalization's severe impacts, while simultaneously initiating debate and policy formulation on an alternative model to civilize globalization.

SIGTUR is a network organization that was formally launched at a meeting in Australia in March 1999.[1] Its formation is the product of a decade of intense activity that linked democratic unions from Asia (South, Southeast, and East), Australia, New Zealand, Southern Africa, and Latin America.[2] The significance of the venture is that it has successfully created a strategic alliance between the most powerful labor unions in the South, many of which are in an expansionary phase, contradicting the general union membership decline so prevalent in the current era. These mass-based democratic unions include the Congress of South African Trade Unions (COSATU), the Australian Council of Trade Unions (ACTU), the Center of Indian Trade Unions (CITU), the All-India

Trade Union Congress (AITUC), the Korean Council of Trade Unions (KCTU), and the Kilusang Mayo Uno (KMU) in the Philippines. SIGTUR has also embraced newly emerging democratic unions in Indonesia, Malaysia, Thailand, Sri Lanka, Pakistan, and China. The CUT in Brazil has recently committed itself to the venture. Trade union democracy and independence rather than ideological orientation are the essential foundation of SIGTUR.[3] "South" is defined *politically*, not geographically. That is, SIGTUR is one initiative to bring together some of the world's most exploited working classes, where union rights are negated or constrained under authoritarian political systems.

The drive to create this new component in the architecture of trade union internationalism was the anticipated impact of globalization. The left leadership of the Australian trade unions was concerned that the rapid transition to open economies and trade would lead to the demise of labor standards globally, given the negation of these rights in major regions of the global economy such as Asia. Here, low-waged, export-oriented national economies were shaped in part by the denial of standards through various forms of state- and employer-controlled labor unions. In most instances, democratic unionism was weak, struggling simply to survive.

Economic deregulation was viewed as an attack on civilized labor standards, which embrace union recognition, the freedom to organize and to bargain collectively. These political gains, principally in certain industrial countries, had led to significant social advance. This advance contrasted markedly with the Southern labor situation, which was characterized by all that undermines civilizing processes. To "civilize," according to the *Oxford English Dictionary*, is to move towards a "more advanced stage of social development"; it is a "bringing out of barbarism," whereas barbarity is a "savage cruelty, causing pain and suffering." Ironically, globalization forced a deeper awareness of the barbarous labor standards that Southern workers endure. Instead of turning inward and defensive, left Australian unions committed themselves to building alliances in the South. What were the conditions of labor that became a spur to action?

Dark Satanic Mills

SIGTUR delegates manifest a perception of globalization that deviates from neoliberal orthodoxy.[4] Their perspective exhibits these main features:

• Globalization's logic challenges civilized labor standards.

• It does so by subordinating all other political and economic freedoms to a single freedom—free trade, free markets, the freedom of corporations to roam the globe in search of the cheapest, most docile labor, the highest subsidy, and the lowest possible company tax.

- Corporate need is paramount in the new global economy; human need does not enter the calculus. Workers appear expendable (downsized, outsourced, casualized) in the greater cause of promoting liberal economic transformation.

- The "miracle of growth" in the newly industrializing nations masks the corresponding spread of cruelty, pain, and suffering in labor relations. This facet is all but unnoticed in the media.[5] Nowhere is this more evident than in those Asian nations promoted as models, illustrators of the effectiveness of integration into the global trading system. Prior to the 1997 Asian financial crisis, Indonesia was held up as one such example.

Indeed, the conditions of the industrial working class in Asia today mirror those that Engels famously recorded in Manchester a century and a half ago. However, this reality is obscured by neoliberal economic ideology, which argues, for example, that the military regime of Soeharto transformed a "poverty-stricken country" into another potential "Asian tiger economy" through engaging globalization and relying on market forces.[6] Such analysis presents no picture of workers' lives in the new factories. Ethnographic research furnishes such a picture, one that graphically illustrates globalization's savage cruelty. Brevity demands we present only one such illustration from Indonesia; however, this instance reflects labor conditions throughout all the newly industrializing economies in Asia.

Hobsbawm noted of mid-nineteenth-century English proponents of change, "[They] clearly had no clue as to what industrial capitalism actually did to peoples' feelings as well as to their bodies" (Hobsbawm 1964, 105). Similarly, globalization advocates choose to avoid this issue, paying no attention to psychological and social impacts. They ignore the reality of Samina's daily life. Samina is a thirteen-year-old Indonesian factory worker. She works a ten-hour shift, from seven in the evening to six the following morning, with a midnight break of an hour. When the company has export orders to clear, she works twenty-hour shifts.[7]

Samina explains the impact of such demands upon her physical and mental health:

> On the night shift the air is cold. I can't stand it when the night air is cold. When I work at night I don't feel well. When I go home I'm unable to sleep because my companions haven't yet gone to work. How is it possible for me to sleep? I'm compelled to wash my clothes first, take a shower, and after that I can go to sleep because by then my companions have all left for work. I sleep for only two hours, get up, have something to eat, and then go back to sleep again. What has

happened to me? I'm sick and I still feel cold even though it is the middle of the day.

It is not only me that is undergoing this. All of my friends are experiencing the same thing. I feel sorry for my friend, who is the same age as me—thirteen—she has been crying, probably because she can't do without sleep and the night air is too cold.

Exhausted after endless weeks of these long shifts, an angry Samina contends, "Why should the manager be allowed to sleep while I have to work?" She devised a plan to escape the watchful eye of the supervisor and gain some sleep after one in the morning. Samina and her friends placed newspapers on the toilet floors and then took turns to sleep, having locked the door. Others minded the machine of the "off-shift" friend. Sometimes this grueling overwork continues for a week or more, with predictable results:

When we work for a whole week like this, we get angry and all of us sometimes stay away from work on Sunday. When I work for these long periods, I often get fever, becoming hot and then cold. I suffer from coughing and colds a lot. My parents don't know that I work in this cruel factory. It makes me sad to have to lie to them. If they knew that I worked here it is quite likely that I would be ordered to return to the village. So, I just don't say anything. If I send a letter home I always say that everything is just fine.

Working these long hours, my feet feel as though they are broken. They feel weary to the point that it is as though they feel that it is necessary to ask forgiveness for whatever they have done. If I sit down to get relief and I'm discovered by the foreman, then I'm scolded. He says, "Do you want to work, or do you want to play around? You are not allowed to sit before the bell rings. No one is permitted to leave the job."

So, these are the sorts of things that I have suffered while I have been working at this factory. Is there still any hope to change this fate of mine? And outside the walls of this cruel factory, who can hear my screams and the crying of my friends who are the same age as me?

These conditions were the spur to the formation of democratic unions. A factory worker explains:

I was concerned because the company treats its workers badly and without compunction. Now I'm beginning to stand up and think about changing the situation. I joined a group to learn about labor matters. I kept studying for more than a year and I gradually understood labor legislation. At this point I began to approach my friends providing them with broader perspectives. I invited them to join me in the learning process that I had been through. For this I had to be patient and diligent in confronting obstacles, because it wasn't easy to invite my friends to change the situation at the company. Yehhh. . . . A bitter experience, phew. . . . but I didn't care, because human beings have to struggle. Eventually, we formed a union. (*Cerita Kama*, January 1992)

Disconnecting Africa

While children are drawn into the Asian economy, a growing number of workers in southern Africa are losing their jobs and joining the informal sector in a struggle to survive. It is leading, in the words of James Ferguson, to a process of "disconnection" (Ferguson 1999).

Unlike delinking, disconnection is a relationship in which one side hangs up on the other without necessarily cutting the links. The image of this process is captured in the liquidation of Zambian Airways in 1996. British Airways replaced their flights to London, hence the link remained. Ferguson argues that globalization has come to mean a sense of disconnection—a process of "red lining." It is as if, Owen Sichone (2000) argues, the region is being cast back to the second-class status independence inherited. This sense of going backwards, what Burawoy calls "involution" in his research on northern Russia, is a retreat of the majority of the population onto their own resources, intensifying household production and elevating women's previous role as organizer and executor of the domestic economy (Burawoy, Krotor, and Lytkina 2000).

Sitas has identified three coping strategies that unemployed workers use in order to survive in the port of Durban, South Africa:

> Firstly, new hunter-gatherer type societies among the urban poor come into being. They accumulate anything that can be accumulated from waste products to gadgets and sell it for their survival. Many members of these societies are homeless. Secondly, new forms of servitude, of dependent labor, are growing. If casual labor refers to occasional labor activity to do formal jobs, these activities are *subcasual*. These people are at the beck and call of individuals who demand chores, duties, sexual favors, and services. Thirdly, the most visible form of work relates to the growth of street traders and hawkers. They sell basic commodities to Black poor, memorabilia to tourists and food to urban workers. (Sitas 2001, 13–14)

These are the challenges that SIGTUR faces. SIGTUR presents an opportunity to forge a relationship between workers in different regions of the South, who are experiencing globalization in different ways. Struggles to form democratic unions in Indonesia and South Africa are a case in point. COSATU, CUT, KCTU, and KMU, for example, have had to devise union-building strategies in a hostile environment. SIGTUR is a forum for exchange of information, strategy, and tactics, thereby accelerating democratic union growth in the union-free zones of the global economy. This process of building a new Southern internationalism will now be considered.

Globalization-from-Below

A survey of SIGTUR's brief, decade-long existence demonstrates the potential, and the obstacles encountered, in inventing a globalization-from-below. SIGTUR had to transcend the debilitating divisions of Cold War politics, and learn how to use cyberspace as a vital ally.

Consider first the impact of Cold War divisions. Left Australian unions played a key role in SIGTUR's emergence. Their unique history of politicized international solidarity explains their motivation. Immediately following the Second World War, Australian dockworkers refused to handle Dutch ships carrying soldiers to reestablish colonial rule in Indonesia. Unions were also intensely engaged in the antiapartheid struggle, which involved disrupting shipping.

Several unions organized a modest meeting in Perth, Western Australia, in May 1991, to explore the possibility of creating a new Southern formation. There were twenty-four delegates, evenly divided between Australian and regional participants. The latter included leaders from the KMU in the Philippines, the newly established Solidarity trade unions in Indonesia, as well as democratic union activists from Malaysia, Sri Lanka, Pakistan, and Papua New Guinea. South Africa's COSATU sent a senior delegation of four who played a vital role in sharing experiences of how democratic unionism could be built in a hostile environment. They emphasized the importance of forging collective power in the workplace, *before* engaging in resistance in the form of strikes and demonstrations. Caution and discipline were deemed essential. Organizational space needed to be identified and contradictions exploited. This first meeting demonstrated the value of Southern unions meeting. The issue of unions as a counterpower to the forces of globalization was at the forefront of the agenda.

This tentative step was challenged. Despite the symbolism of the Berlin Wall crumbling in 1989, Cold War politics lingered. A right-wing national organization in Australia with strong Catholic Church links, the National Civic Council (NCC), launched a scathing attack on the initiative, which had serious implications because of their influence within the right wing of the Australian Labor Party and union movement. In a feature in the Autumn 1990 edition of their national magazine, *Social Action*, the NCC claimed that

> The initiative for the conference came from the far left of the trade union movement in Western Australia, and appeared to have a distinct WFTU flavor about it. The Soviet-backed World Federation of Trade Unions (WFTU) has been anxious to build regional initiatives between unions allied or favorable to it and unions associated with the International Confederation of Free Trade Unions (ICFTU).

But the established unions who attacked SIGTUR's initiative were influenced by U.S. anticommunism. The founding of a Communist regime in China engendered a U.S. containment strategy. Workers had to be shielded from communism, either through unrepresentative employer-dominated company unions, or through state-controlled organizations. SIGTUR had little option, therefore, but to search out struggling democratic unions in opposition to such client unions. In repressive Indonesia, the only choice was linkage with NGOs organizing in the factories by stealth. A similar situation pertains in China today, and indeed the 1970s rebirth of democratic unionism in South Africa was based in part on the intervention of university students who set up Wages Commissions to organize factories. These new formations are the product of struggle; hence the criticism was in fact a demand to abandon this commitment and accept the status quo—weak, ineffectual unions representing employer and state interests. Despite these attacks, SIGTUR's determination to work with *any* democratic union, regardless of political orientation, remained central. This orientation was later formulated in a *Principles for Participation* statement based on ILO conventions 87 (Freedom of Association) and 98 (Collective Bargaining).

SIGTUR reflects a commitment to civilizing globalization. This goal requires new forms of global *action,* which was beyond the scope of client unionism created as a Cold War stratagem. Consequently, the International Confederation of Free Trade Unions (ICFTU), its Asia branch, the Asia-Pacific Regional Organization (APRO), and a number of the International Trade Secretariats (ITS) opposed SIGTUR, which in turn strengthened right-wing opposition in Australia. However, this failed to stifle the initiative, because of powerful support from both COSATU and the left Australian unions. Consequently, a much larger congress attended by 140 delegates in Perth in November 1992 followed the successful launch of the venture. The base of the network expanded to include Thailand, Vietnam, Korea, and India. The Center of Indian Trade Unions sent a large delegation, which contributed significantly to the debates. COSATU was again strongly represented. At their instigation, the first formal structures were established at this meeting. A Regional Coordinating

Committee (RCC) was created, giving formality to the new entity. A third meeting of 140 delegates was held in Perth in November 1994.

Global Action: The Turning Point

The turning point for SIGTUR arrived in 1995, when the conservative government in Western Australia introduced amendments to the Industrial Relations Act that undermined freedom of association. This action radicalized the Western Australian union movement, which then launched a local campaign that threatened power cuts, a trade blockade of Western Australia, and strike action. A twenty thousand-strong protest march endorsed the local action and responded enthusiastically to COSATU's public commitment to globalizing the dispute through instituting shipping boycotts in South Africa.

This threatened action reinforced commitments to action by other SIGTUR unions in the region. Protest action outside Australian embassies was organized. This transnational solidarity was historic: it was the first time workers from developing nations acted in concert with workers from a developed liberal democracy whose labor rights were being stripped away. Philippines unionists spoke, at an August 1995 Perth rally, of the "parliament of the streets": "In our experience it is not enough to merely lobby in the halls of parliament. We took our issues out into the parliament of the streets, factories, and fields, with militant mass actions. We are one with you in the streets of Western Australia."

These responses were not unnoticed by the mainstream financial press. The *Far Eastern Economic Review* (19 October, 1995, 23) carried an article headlined, "Role Reversal: State Attracts Asian Criticism on Workers' Rights."

This fusion of the local and the global won the day. The amendments to the labor law were withdrawn. As well, a weakness in globalization had been detected: trade dependency between nations meant that shipping and communications boycotts could cut vital trade arteries, and thus force compromise.

Crucially, this campaign also transformed SIGTUR's relationship with the established union internationals. They now had to acknowledge that the venture's prime objective was to forge an effective resistance to globalization, not replay Cold War politics. Hostility and division gave way to a coalition-building commitment in the interests of strengthening a globalization-from-below. This consensus has led to an active cooperation between the International Trade Secretariats and SIGTUR.

Despite the initial defeat, the conservative attack on Australian trade unions continued unabated. In early 1997, antiunion laws were again introduced, leading to another round of intense local resistance backed by global action. In September, dockworkers from every port in South Africa went on strike and marched through the port cities in protest against Australian government action. When the federal government tried to de-unionize the Australian waterfront in April 1998, the COSATU transport unions instigated shipping boycotts, as did the American longshoremen on the West Coast.

Through these waves of action, SIGTUR continued to evolve as a global campaign–oriented network organization. This orientation was consolidated through further congresses, which were held in Calcutta in 1997, in Johannesburg in 1999, and in Seoul in 2001. The focus is on developing and refining global action. Cyberspace has proven a vital ally in this venture.

Cyberspace and Networked Action

Internet communications facilitated these campaigns and defined SIGTUR's character as a *network organization*. SIGTUR is an initiative grounded in traditional union organization; it is not simply a network. Rather, it is a campaign-oriented *network* of democratic unions in the South, grounded in, and accountable to, traditional union organization. SIGTUR therefore exhibits a novel combination of the old and the new. This contradicts Castell's notion that unions "seem to be historically superseded" as they "dwindle down in much of the world" (Castells 1997, 360). In his analysis, the new networks supersede the old organizational forms. Our argument is quite the reverse: networks have the potential to transform, empower, and extend union organization. They attain the fullness of their transformative potential only when grounded in organization.

New informational networking has obvious strengths. In the absence of hierarchy, structure, and control, debate opens up, and action decentralizes and becomes flexible and participative. The weaknesses of networks are the result of its socially disembodied character. Networking may generate protest politics, as happened in Seattle in November 1999. However, to translate these significant and possibly defining moments of protest into effective power politics requires grounding in established unions and civil society organizations. This linkage is the only way in which a network can be sustained. Formal organizations, which are democratic, accountable, committed to a "globalization-from-below" and open to change, allow for a socially embedded networking. These organizations also provide a financial base to build a new global movement that integrates these organizational forms—social organization and networking—into a coherent whole that draws on the respective strengths of each.

Nowhere is this synergy more apparent than in the transformation of traditional labor internationalism, as illustrated in table 18.1.

SIGTUR integrates traditional Southern unions into the dynamism of networking. All organizations are Internet connected, establishing intersecting nodes. Furthermore, SIGTUR is generating cyberspace campaigning and organization (not just networking) that connects the old and the new in a

Table 18.1
The Transformation of Traditional Labor Internationalism

Old Labor Internationalism	New Labor Internationalism
hierarchy	network
centralization	decentralization
command	participation
control	empowerment
restricted debate	open debate
slow decision making	quick decision making
large bureaucracy	de-layered
formal	flexible
diplomatic orientation	mobilization orientation
focus on workplace and trade unions only	focus on coalition building with new social movements and NGOs
predominantly North	predominantly South

transformative project to civilize globalization. This process is best illustrated through a current global campaign.

Exploring Globalization's Vulnerability

SIGTUR actively supports the International Chemical, Energy, and Mining (ICEM) ITS in its global campaign against the antiunion, antienvironment practices of one of the world's most powerful mining multinationals—Rio Tinto Corporation. Rio Tinto has sixty operations in forty nations.[8] This British-dominated corporation demands total managerial control over production. It constantly downsizes its workforce, creating serious workload, health and safety, and environmental problems for workers and their communities.[9]

The Construction, Mining, Forestry, and Energy Workers Union (CFMEU), a powerful Australian union and an ICEM affiliate, has been locked in intense struggles at Rio mine sites to end these problems. Lengthy, bitterly fought disputes at Rio Tinto's Hunter Valley mine indicate both Rio's corporate strategy and the union's determination to resist it. A five-week strike was triggered at the Rio Tinto coal mine when the company tried to introduce Australian Workplace Agreements (AWAs) to the workplace, to promote more flexible work practices and thus allegedly "get into the 20th Century" (*Australian*, 18 July 1997). These agreements included freedom to use contractors, part-time, temporary, or casual labor on any work as required; individual performance assessments; the right to allocate overtime at management's discretion, rather than through a union seniority list; and finally, the right to hire and fire on merit (as decided by the company) in place of recruitment from a union list of retrenched miners, and retrenchment on a "last on, first off" basis. The company offered a substantial $10,000 a year pay inducement, as well as improvements in superannuation and medical benefits, to any who volunteered for individual contracts. All but seven workers refused the contracts, insisting instead on a collective agreement. Despite long, determined strike action, the leadership recognized that local struggles had to be globalized if the issues were to be resolved, particularly since Rio had the backing of the Conservative government and their new antiunion, individual contract legislation.

In response, ICEM followed a cyberspace-empowered strategy. It formed the Rio Global Union Network (RGUN) in California. RGUN's campaign against Rio Tinto uses the Internet to coordinate actions even in the remotest corners of the globe. ICEM has demanded of Rio:

- a commitment to core ILO conventions that protect worker rights;

- a global agreement giving effect to these principles, including effective monitoring mechanisms;

- that disputes with workers will be resolved in the light of these principles.

The strategy illustrates our argument on the importance of a grounded network. RGUN's first task was to embody the network *within* organization. Two forms were distributed via the Internet. One was directed to unions on Rio sites, and the other to community organizations and individuals willing to commit to the Rio global campaign. With regard to the former, individuals are chosen by the union to be the Rio Tinto Global Campaign work-site organizer. In taking on this position, they accept the responsibility

- to communicate with workers on site about the global campaign;

- to contribute ideas on the planning of the campaign;

- to ensure that all levels of the union organization are aware of the campaign;

- to ensure that every worker on site has access to campaigning activities.

With regard to the involvement of community organizations and individuals, the E-mail document entitled "Pledge of Solidarity" asks organizations and individuals

- to send one fax and E-mail a month with a solidarity message;
- to attend campaign activities;
- to help organize demonstrations.

Protest action against Rio has been global, intense, and sustained. The shareholders were one target. Union leaders from around the world attended Rio's Annual General Meeting in London on 10 May 2000, having formed the Coalition of Rio Tinto Shareholders. This was the first time that trade unions had organized a shareholder campaign that was global in scope. The coalition put forward two resolutions that called on the company to appoint a deputy chairperson to implement core ILO conventions. Union participants warned the company that in the new global economy, where cyberspace allows instantaneous communication across the globe, "Everything the company does is increasingly subject to public scrutiny—not just in the local community, but across the world. Rio Tinto's performance in Indonesia may well affect its right to operate in Canada or the USA."[10]

Although Rio's chairperson dismissed the resolutions as "irrelevant to corporate governance," skilful union organizing is likely to maintain the pressure on the board. The alliance of unions won support for its resolutions from some major institutional shareholders with over 65 billion pounds sterling in assets. Apart from this pressure, the alliance led by ICEM began to organize protest actions around the globe, in an effort to pressure Rio into signing a global agreement. These actions will probably continue until the company agrees to negotiate such an agreement.

SIGTUR is allied to ICEM through this global campaigning. This network organization is dedicated to mobilizing southern unions against Rio Tinto. For example, Pakistani workers marched through central Islamabad in an effort to reach the British Embassy to protest, but were blocked by military police. The All-Pakistan Federation of Trade Unions and the Working Women's Organization mobilized men and women workers from a range of sectors including telecommunications, water and power, the garment industry, nursing, teaching, and the railway, food, leather, and pharmaceutical industries. Leaders spoke of the global solidarity that the campaign expressed, and called on Rio to meet ICEM's demands. They called for an end to the violence against Brazilian workers. In California, chemical workers also demonstrated against Rio; in Indonesia, workers occupied the mine site, asserting their rights.

The civilizing potential of organizationally grounded cyberspace networking is apparent in this early phase of the global campaign. Consider, for example, the campaign in Brazil. Security guards at a Rio mine site in Brazil shot poor, landless people from the adjoining community when they entered at night in search of residues of gold in the tailings canals. As well, mine workers had high lead levels. RGUN put this violence under a global spotlight, which led to the company agreeing to end the violence against the landless and negotiate an agreement with the local union. Rio Tinto, it should be added, has also agreed to withdraw from its policy of forcing individual contracts in Australia.

The Rio campaign points towards the key vulnerabilities of capital in the era of globalization. Publicly listed companies are susceptible to campaigns focused on capital markets by unions because of union influence over certain major institutional investors through workers' pensions. Even small share price fluctuations pose a significant risk, in that corporate image is paramount in a world of globalized capital markets now dominated by large institutional investors. An effective global campaign can exploit this vulnerability. As a consequence, organizers are promoting the establishment of capital committees to explore and build strategies to exploit these possibilities.

Challenges Facing SIGTUR

Impediments to deepening the potential of a globalization-from-below remain. Despite the evidence presented in this chapter of a growing commitment to global action by SIGTUR unions, most still remain locked into the terrain of the national. In 2001, Korea's KCTU announced a prolonged general strike; South Africa's COSATU was mobilizing a general strike against the privatization of electricity; and Indian unions were campaigning ceaselessly against economic liberalization. Each of these actions is a significant contribution to the struggle against global restructuring. However, one can only imagine how much greater the impact would have been if such actions had been coordinated across nations, that is, if they had been globalized. This is a significant challenge that SIGTUR is currently addressing. In the coming years national unions will have to redirect resources to sustain new levels of global coordination, if global campaigns are to succeed.

SIGTUR has become a forum for Southern unions to address these critical questions. The severe impact of global change is uniting national unions in order to forge an effective global resistance as a prelude to building a genuine alternative to the neoliberal model. Civilizing globalization is a call to resist *and* a call to imagine alternatives. SIGTUR reveals that the labor movement has a contribution to make in both phases.

Notes

1. By network organization we mean a network that grows out of, and is grounded in, organization. This distinguishes SIGTUR from the networks that have

come to the fore following Seattle. These are pure networks that float free of organization. They are independent and not necessarily accountable to trade unions or other established civil society organizations.

2. SIGTUR grew out of The Indian Ocean Initiative, which had its founding conference in May 1991. Participating unions met regularly. Congresses were held in 1992, 1994, 1997, and 1999.

3. This orientation is defined in terms of ILO convention 87 on freedom of association, and 98 on collective bargaining rights. This is spelled out in the SIGTUR document *Principles of Participation,* July 1996.

4. This observation is drawn from a survey conducted at the Fifth SIGTUR Congress in Johannesburg in October 1999.

5. Here we are reminded of Bertolt Brecht's comment, "The insult that is added to the poor's injured lives is that their sufferings were deemed not worthy of even recording."

6. *Economist,* 3–9 August, 1996, 19–21, in an article entitled, "Indonesia, What Price Stability?" See also, World Bank 1995, which summarizes the claimed positive outcomes of export-oriented industrialization.

7. During Lambert's fieldwork in Indonesia during the 1990s, the issue of extreme working hours was *the* major grievance. A wide range of meetings with workers in their discussion groups revealed that the extreme situation experienced by Samina was common. One group of workers who worked for a South Korean toy company were set production targets each day and were only allowed to leave the factory when the targets were achieved. They started work at 7 A.M. and were often forced to work until 1 A.M. the following morning. Overwork is a feature of EOI.

8. The company focuses on large, long-term, low-cost mining and minerals processing in aluminium, copper, energy (coal, uranium), gold, industrial minerals, and iron ore.

9. Rio Tinto Global Campaign Fact Sheet, produced by the Rio Tinto Global Union Network, formed by ICEM with its coordinating center in California (E-mail address: tconrow@igc.org).

10. Speech by Tony Maher, President of CFMEU, Mining Division to Rio Shareholders Meeting, 10 May 2000. An ICEM communiqué, circulated through RGUN.

References

Burawoy, M., P. Krotov, and T. Lytkina. 2000. "Involution and Destitution: Russia's Gendered Transition to Capitalism." *Ethnography* 1(1).

Castells M. 1996. *The Rise of the Network Society.* Vol. 1 of *The Information Age: Economy, Society, and Culture.* Oxford: Blackwell Publishers.

———. 1997. *The Power of Identity*. Vol. 2 of *The Information Age: Economy, Society, and Culture*. Oxford: Blackwell Publishers.

———. 1998. *End of the Millennium*. Vol. 3 of *The Information Age: Economy, Society, and Culture*. Oxford: Blackwell Publishers.

Ferguson, J. 1999. *Expectations of Modernity: Myths and Meanings of Urban Life in Zambia's Copper Belt*. Berkeley: University of California Press.

Hobsbawm, E. 1964. *Laboring Men: Studies in the History of Labor*. London: Weidenfeld and Nicholson.

Lambert, R. 1997. *State and Labor in New Order Indonesia*. Perth: University of Western Australia Press.

O'Brien, R. 2000. "Workers and World Order: The Tentative Transformation of the International Labor Movement." *Review of International Studies* 26 (4): 533–55.

Sichone, O. 2000. "A Political Economy Perspective of the Prospect of SADC." *Conference on SADC Industrial Development through Regional Cooperation and Integration*. Windhoek, South Africa: Development Policy Research Unit, University of Cape Town.

Sitas, A. 2001. "The Livelihoods Sector: Opportunities for Unions." *South African Labor Bulletin* 25 (3).

World Bank. 1995. *World Development Report, 1995: Workers in an Integrating World*. New York: Oxford University Press.

Alternative Globalization

James H. Mittelman

As the indomitable Margaret Thatcher once remarked about neoliberal globalization: "There is no alternative."[1] Known as TINA, this slogan means that globalization is here to stay. Globalization is inevitable. Globalization is a juggernaut. Right?

Not at all. To understand why not, let's return to the globalization debate, as laid out in Richard Sandbrook's introduction to this book. In so doing, it is important to look beyond immediate events, however compelling they may be, and adopt a perspective that the French historian Fernand Braudel called the *longue durée*. The focus should be on a long-time horizon that extends to the future of globalization—alternatives to its current constitution.

Indeed, globalization can be politically disempowering if one regards it as a juggernaut, that is, a totalizing or inevitable force governing history. Two factors tend to sublimate the politics of globalization. First, there is the rush to implement a series of neoliberal policies—namely, liberalization, deregulation, and privatization—that promote market integration. Second, there is a preoccupation with market growth rather than balanced development or equity. What, then, are the possibilities for recapturing politics and the prospects for a shift in priorities?

In answering this question, I want to argue that globalization has opened spaces, expanding the boundaries associated with political life. Of course, one cannot predict the future from a set of structural disjunctures. History is fundamentally propelled by human will, albeit subject to evolving global forces; it is an open-ended process. But if globalization was made by humankind, then it can be unmade or remade by political agency. As with slavery, feudalism,

---

This chapter draws from, and extends, my previous work on alternative globalization in Mittelman 1999 and 2000.

and mercantile capitalism, there is no reason to believe that neoliberal globalization is eternal.

Neoliberal Globalization as Utopia

Sponsors of globalization seek to create a global market in which the
peoples of the world increasingly relate to each other only as individuals.
Putting it baldly, Margaret Thatcher declared, "There is no such thing as society, only individual men and women and their families." Neoliberalism undermines society, subordinating it to the market. From this perspective,
globalization is an attempt to achieve the utopia of freeing the market from social and political control. It is a utopia in the sense that this condition has
never existed.

Not only is the utopia of a free market comprised of individual actors ahis-
torical, but also, in Karl Polanyi's memorable phrase, "*Laissez-faire* was planned;
planning was not" (Polanyi 1957, 141). In an earlier century, concerted action by
a liberal state in Great Britain spawned a supposedly self-regulating economy, yet
the pressure for ensuing anti-laissez-faire legislation beginning in 1860 started in
a spontaneous manner and picked up gradually. Notwithstanding a variety of
such enactments, the opening of the so-called free market fomented an "economic earthquake": a socially disruptive and polarizing process amid periods of
apparent economic improvement. Polanyi traced the trajectory from social control over the market to a disembedding of market activities. The market gained
autonomy, leading to the subordination of society to market forces; in turn, this
subordination provoked a protectionist countermovement from social forces, particularly the English working class.

In his challenge to the myth of a self-running market, Polanyi not only un-
masked economic liberalism by providing an account of the dystopia of market
society, but also pointed to the need to *reembed* market forces in society. What
must be explicated, however, are the meaning of and strategies for this reem-
bedding, as will be discussed.

Globalization in Flux

Globalization calls into question the ability of the existing interstate system to cope with certain fundamental transnational problems. After all, the
Westphalian model of states is a relic of the seventeenth century, established in
the West and grafted on to other parts of the world. Strains on this system include the properties of new technologies—interconnectivity and lightning
speed—as well as massive concentrations of private economic power that dwarf
the resources of many national units and challenge state sovereignty.

Of course, the state does not remain idle. Those who hold the reins of power try to adjust by accommodating global flows and turning them to national and local advantage. Not all states suffer to the same extent from power deflation. So, too, it would be a mistake to portray global processes and the state as locked into a zero-sum relationship. With globalization, some elements within the state gain power while others lose. Among the winners are the economic portfolios and administrative agencies dealing with the external realm. Meanwhile, the offices charged with responsibility for social policy are reduced in scope. Nevertheless, to varying degrees, all states are losing autonomy in the emerging multilevel system. Quite clearly, they operate in a rapidly changing context. The interstate system is durable, but despite its persistence, when are states free to act independently of market constraints? Increasingly, market power disciplines the state, for example, via International Monetary Fund (IMF) conditionalities and currency speculation.

Against this backdrop, the state is reconstituting itself, attempting to be proactive in order to harness globalizing processes. However, the capacities of states to tame these processes differ markedly. The general pattern is the reduction of regulatory activity, the easing of borders, and the lowering of barriers. The restructuring of the state means that it is becoming more of a facilitator of globalizing activities, insofar as they are localized within the domain of a sovereign entity (Cox 1987, 253–65; and for an opposing point of view, see Weiss 1998).

To aggregate their power, states have established a highly institutionalized system. Not only has there been a proliferation of international organizations in recent decades, but also, when faced with new problems of globalization such as transnational cybercrime, the holders of state power seek a higher level of institutionalization and more effective coordination in the interstate system. Hence, there are many rounds of summitry in forums such as the Group of Eight for the most powerful countries, and the Group of Fifteen in the developing world. Another formula, increasingly evident, is informal attempts at policy coordination, for example, in the World Economic Forum (WEF), an annual gathering usually in Davos, Switzerland, which brings together CEOs of the one thousand largest corporations in the world, central bankers, presidents, prime ministers, journalists, and scholars. Another informal mode of governance is the Trilateral Commission, which consists of corporate, political, and intellectual leaders from the advanced capitalist countries. In addition, privatized forms of governance are becoming more prominent. The structural power wielded by legal and financial services firms (Sassen 1996) and credit-rating agencies, such as Moody's and Standard and Poor's, is based on evaluations of national economies that enable borrowers to raise money, or prevent them from doing so, and influences the terms of loans (Sinclair 1994a, 1994b). This power can make or break certain developing economies.

The nub of the problem is that the interstate system relies on national institutional forms at a level that does not correspond to an increasing portion of the world's political and economic activities. This incongruity between the cage of the nation-state and actual global flows is an invitation to use more fully the political imagination. Globalization, at bottom, involves a quest for an appropriate temporal and spatial scale for governance (Jessop 1997). But in this quest, what are the alternatives? The alternatives, I believe, are constituted not by well-meaning proposals that wish away the problems of power and conflict of interests, but by countervailing power, which, today, means a multiplicity of resistances to neoliberal globalization.

Resistances

Although Margaret Thatcher's argument about TINA is correct insofar as neoliberalism is predominant and may not have run its course, there are grounds for questioning the triumphalism reflected in her contention. This point is evident in South Africa, where, as the poet Dennis Brutus put it, there is a struggle between TINA and THEMBA, which in the Zulu language, stands for "There must be an alternative," or, in short, "hope" (Bond 1995, 3, 7). To be sure, it is important to ask whether the neoliberal way of ordering the world will stay or wane. Like prior forms of capitalism, neoliberalism has a history, and histories have their beginnings and ends. Certainly, neoliberalism will not simply peter out of its own accord. Rather, faced with myriad discontents and counterpressure, neoliberalism is being challenged by various forces that are incipient, but, arguably, mounting. Especially noteworthy is the drive, rapidly gaining momentum, toward *re-regulation*, particularly apparent in Latin America and evident elsewhere as well. Among the reasons for this trend were the detrimental ways in which the 1997–98 Asian economic crisis deeply affected other regions and the buildup of social problems linked to neoliberal policies.

In different contexts, resistance has emerged not only in the public sphere but also in the private, more personal, and even intimate realm. The resistance is not necessarily loudly voiced by the state or civil society; it may be quietly expressed in the life-ways of individuals. In other words, resistance to globalization may not be openly declared, but often blends with the latent, local, and uncongealed. Also, resistance is not merely against an imposing structure, but may contain positive and affirmative elements.

That said, the idiom "antiglobalization," which has become commonplace in the media and popular writing, warrants scrutiny, for it is vague and used promiscuously. By slotting a wide variety of stances on globalization in just two boxes—for and against—it obscures the varied complaints about globalizing trends that have emerged from different points on the political spectrum. Obscured are the diverse attempts to engage—not evade—globalization.

Applied to head-on confrontations—notably, the 1999 "Battle of Seattle" over World Trade Organization (WTO) policy, followed in 2000 by protests in Washington and Prague at the annual conference of the IMF and the World Bank, demonstrations in Melbourne at a gathering of the WEF, and clashes in Seoul surrounding the Asia-Europe Meeting, as well as the 2001 Quebec City Summit of the Americas and the Group of Eight meeting in Genoa—the label "antiglobalization" fails to capture crucial distinctions along the continuum between reformist and nonreformist positions. Some protesters advanced proposals for institutional adjustments, while others (not only on the left, but also proponents of free trade) advocated abolishing the institutions themselves. There were efforts to change the direction and content of policy, and intentions to transform the underlying structures. Indeed, it is important to distinguish along a spectrum between those against globalization but not capitalism, and those against capitalism itself, with globalization deemed to be the current phase.

My point is that the prevalent imagery of "antiglobalization" misses the important differentiation between what is openly manifest and declared, such as demonstrations and strikes, and the more subtle and undeclared forms, including films, novels, plays, cartoons, and popular music. Surely, "antiglobalization" is a problematic construct, since it defines a phenomenon solely as a negation. It impoverishes social criticism by watering down what may be learned from the debates over globalization. Marking social criticism as "antiglobalization" hinders the creation of alternatives. Many critics resist neoliberalism not because they are against globalization, but because, without indulging utopian dreams, they are for a more inclusive, participatory, and democratic globalization.

At the venues where public protests against globalization took place, collective action by varied social movements drew attention to the drawbacks to globalization, especially world inequality, a lack of transparency with regard to increasing market power relative to political authority, and, in some cases, the erosion of, or affronts to, cultural dignity. The "Battle of Seattle," whose significance is explored in chapter 16, has thus become a galvanizing metaphor signaling a new dynamic in globalization: a political intervention by a coalition of heterogeneous citizens groups in the global economy.

Yet, some countries, Japan being one of them, have not experienced such events in the streets dramatizing the harm of globalization. During the 1990s and into the new millennium, a period of heightened market integration when Japan's bubble burst, the steep decline of its economy has been accompanied by the buying up of many of its financial institutions and other assets by foreign capital, the breakdown of certain protectionist barriers, and increasing social dislocation of various sorts said to be unavoidable in the teeth of sharp global competition. While it is striking that public protests against market integration have not occurred in Japan, it would be shortsighted to overlook the points of resistance to market and state power that have emerged in the private and intimate realms of life.

Taking a close look, one may detect resistance to genetically modified foods by the Consumers Union of Japan and dairy farmers, not stridently sounded but softly spoken (elicited in interviews by student researchers at Ritsumeikan University in Kyoto). So, too, Japanese rice growers are tactfully challenging a key tenet of globalization—liberalization—because they do not want to face international competition. Opening to the global market is perceived as a threat to their identity, connections to nature, and cultural and spiritual heritage, of which rice is a principal part. Another palpable issue is global flows that directly affect women, including the transnational sex industry and child prostitution in locales such as Osaka Prefecture. Each of these matters surrounding food and gender pertains to the vital forces of the human body, the site where the philosopher Michel Foucault examined the capillaries of power and resistance.

Picking up on the Japanese case, there is considerable microresistance to globalization, a pattern freighted with macrosignificance. The challenge lies in the extension and blending of microresistance and macroresistance. The distinctive features of the Japanese illustration also suggest that there is no one best worldwide strategy for civilizing globalization. It would be facile to search for a single solution to a vast range of complex problems that manifest differently in various locales with distinctive histories, cultures, and resource endowments. There is no realizable alternative of a kind good for all times and places. But are there prototypes, diverse patterns from which alternatives can be derived?

Alternative Scenarios

The evidence points to a range of efforts to imagine alternatives and convert them into practice. They fall into three basic categories. The first involves modifications in neoliberal globalization without challenging its underlying structures, and the second and third call for the destruction of this paradigm and entail an attack on the ideas and type of policies that form the bedrock of neoliberalism.

The first category takes as axiomatic the proposition that within the globalization syndrome itself, there are real choices. Notwithstanding structural constraints, especially the rise of hypercompetition and the trend toward the "Washington consensus" (the wave of deregulation that began in the United States in the 1970s, accompanied by major reductions in social spending), the choice is essentially a political one. It is held that the market can benefit society while to some extent being kept at bay by innovative state policies.

In the vortex of enormous pressure to globalize more, France exemplifies a resistant state, one that maintains much regulation, generous welfare provi-

sions (in schooling, health care, vacations, retirement, and unemployment entitlements), and a large government-run infrastructure such as its reliable subways
and rail networks. Its critics point to a high unemployment rate far exceeding
that of the United States; a mounting government deficit; frequent strikes and
demonstrations impeding daily life, if not rendering it chaotic; and labyrinthine
labor legislation, banking codes, and an educational system that discourages innovation. Faced with the Anglo-American model of neoliberalism, and urged to
adopt "the American solution," President Jacques Chirac responded that his
country has a global sense of itself and will fight to maintain a way of life:
"France," he said, "intends to remain France" (as quoted in Truehart 1997). In
the face of unpopular changes to meet intensifying global economic pressures,
a nationalist backlash is thus emerging not only from the disadvantaged segments of society but also from some states themselves. France's resistance, of
course, is atypical, and far different from the courtesan role played by some
states in serving interests embodied in neoliberal globalization.

There are several modes of adaptation to globalization, and no dearth of
proposals for institutional reform. In the domestic arena, important adjustments
in administrative agencies and legal procedures—say, in the field of immigration—can alleviate some of the problems brought about by globalization. In the
realm of finance, proposed national reforms include tougher bank standards,
curbs on hedge funds, an "exit tax," which would penalize investors for quickly
withdrawing their money from a country, and other forms of re-regulation. Crucially, social policy may blunt the sharp edges of the market, especially the
global trend toward increased income inequality (Teeple 1995). Advocates of
safety nets and social clauses are pushing in this direction, but skeptics contend
that they may serve as public relations devices deflecting attention from more
fundamental issues. To be sure, there is debate about the proper role of the state
in the provision of public goods: specifically, in eliminating absolute poverty,
dispensing piped water as well as electricity and modern sanitation for all citizens, protecting the environment, supporting the family as a unit, alleviating
congested cities, curbing escalating crime, stopping corruption and cronyism,
and promoting the equality of women and the rights of children. If there is a political will for such measures, then the appropriate scale for these interventions
may be transnational as well.

Globally, calls for reform include some of the basic conditions on which
the IMF insists, notably transparency and greater accountability by government, aspects of structural adjustment that even the fund's critics find laudable.
(However, some of them add that the IMF practices double standards by maintaining secrecy in its operations and that the fund should take its own prescrip-
tion.) In practice, adopting the formula of transparency and accountability
requires that regimes confront the political economy of domination, often the
very basis of their political support. Hence, many leaders, as was the case in
Suharto's Indonesia, have found themselves in the dilemma of desperately

needing foreign capital and yet reluctant or unwilling to commit political suicide by dismantling the structures of dominance that sustain the state.

Another proposal for international reform is the Tobin tax, discussed in
chapter 9, which would place a small charge on cross-border capital flows in
order to discourage the rapid transfers by speculators that upset vulnerable
economies. Suggestions also include the creation of an "early warning system"
to alert the world to dangerous economic trends; a global central bank; and
semifixed exchange rates among leading currencies. There can be little doubt
about the need for institutional reform, but for the foreseeable future, it is difficult to conceive of heads of state galvanized to agree on and implement a new
architecture for global governance, let alone wield the wherewithal to rein in
corporate power, which, after all, is transnationally constituted and thus largely
escapes the jurisdiction of sovereign entities. More fundamentally, these alternatives cannot work if they fail to come to grips with the power relations in-
scribed in globalization. At bottom, a really "new international financial
architecture" would entail, or require, a new political architecture.

The second order of alternatives calls for structural change, and seeks to
rewrite the script of globalization. On the right of the political spectrum, activists
and intellectuals have sought to reassert identities based on membership in religious, racial, ethnic, or linguistic communities subject to globalizing forces, often
personified by the immigrant, a representation of the Other. Movements based
in religion have reacted sharply to the convulsive processes of globalization,
partly in recognition of the ways in which globalizing tendencies are undermining the values of community and ripping the social fabric. Inasmuch as neoliberal
globalization facilitates cross-boundary flows, challenges national culture, and
tolerates immigration, right-wing movements, especially in Europe and the
United States, have opposed major elements in this structure, though not market
society per se. Not only have xenophobic groups invoked a sense of nativism, but
also there has been opposition to regional schemes, such as the North American
Free Trade Agreement and the attempt to expand it beyond Mexico into Chile and
throughout South America, on the grounds that they weaken sovereignty and are
a precursor to world government. The right's political project embraces the principle of sovereignty, and would build a fortress around territorially bound notions
of the state, thereby implicitly calling for the downfall of globalization.

In the search for alternatives, there is a third, also structural, yet even more
embryonic project that similarly poses the question, Is globalization indefi-
nitely sustainable? The torchbearers involved in this effort represent a broad
constellation of social forces, generally the victims of globalization, elements
in civil society, some politicians, and organic intellectuals. They do not advocate a status quo ante; there is no going back to preglobalization conditions,
and the Keynesian welfare state of bygone decades is not the solution. Unlike
the right, this group would promote the relaxation of sovereignty in favor of

identities at other levels, which would involve redrawing the boundaries of political economy. This project affirms the importance of engaging yet localizing the global and the importance of bottom-up processes. If anything, the latter entails a greater diffusion of power. It includes new venues for experimentation and reinventing the relations between the market, state, and society. It is an effort to redefine politics, to expand the space for nonstate politics. It calls for participatory democratic control of market forces, which ultimately is a matter of political agency. It is also a matter of asserting, relative to globalizing structures, greater *autonomy*, a tenet discussed in chapter 11.

Autonomy is a political and moral precept that was used by ancient Greek writers, and in a somewhat different sense by social contract theorists and in Kantian ethics. The core of autonomy is self-determination—a tenet that resonates with contemporary liberalism, as illustrated by aspects of John Rawls's theory of justice (1993). The principle of autonomy implies that agents have the capacity for critical reflection and, notwithstanding structural pressures, the right to choose among options. Exercising this right requires some control over conditions and actions. The principle of autonomy thus means political and economic self-governance by the majority, and allows for freedom and equality in pursuit of the "common good" (Held 1995, 146–47; and on the coupling of globalization and democratic theory, Rosow 1999). Building autonomy from below should not be confused with fencing off and attempting to erect a fortress against the world, actions that could disable civil-society responses to globalization, which in fact often gain strength from their transnational elements. And an assertion of autonomy from below eventually requires topping up: initiatives within the arena of state politics to bring about greater accountability. After all, the netherworld below the state can be a perilous place, usually marked by fragmentation, and sometimes by intolerance and authoritarian forms of identity politics at odds with democratic life. In the face of the drive by neoliberalism to limit the scope of the state (both its activities and budget) and enforce market discipline, a strong state permitting broad access to power and a vibrant civil society pressing for democratic politics, as exemplified by the new environmental and feminist movements, stand to strengthen one another and possibly serve as a counterpoint to globalization-from-above (Walzer 1999). Although there is no reason to believe that the nation-state is eternal, at present the state and civil society, with their many joint members, seem to need each other in the quest for *democratic globalization*.

A Normative Way Forward?

One response to neoliberal globalization is to pose the question, Is it ethically sustainable? Morally and politically, is it possible to maintain a global system in which the world's 225 richest people have a combined wealth equal to the annual income of 2.5 billion people, the poorest 47 percent of the world's population? In which the three richest people have assets that exceed the combined gross domestic product of the forty-eight least-developed countries (United Nations Development Program 1998, 30)? Is it ethically defensible to claim that this is the price paid for the gains that accompany expanding market forces? Or would it be better to attempt to reduce the cost by searching for a democratic solution, which, is, above all, a normative preference? Surely this would not be a panacea; there are different versions of democratic theory, and normative preferences cannot be realized without counterpower. Knowing my own limitations, and given the scope of this chapter, I can offer only points for further consideration, not a full-blown analysis. These points are principles, not policies, for the latter must be devised to suit different conditions, which, as noted, is to say that the principles may not converge on one best answer for all times and places.

To clear the path for examining the nexus between globalization and democratization, it is important to assess the argument that economic globalization is an emancipatory political force. This thesis is "out there"—being discussed—in scholarly forums and now and again appears in the popular press (e.g., Friedman 1997, 1999). According to this contention, globalization emanates from neither above nor below, but from beyond. In this view, globalization—a lateral movement crossing state borders in the form of capital, technologies, tourism, information, and knowledge—spreads norms and values that penetrate the state. China and some other states have tried to block these forces, but have found that the values accompanying global flows are unstoppable. It is therefore argued that economic globalization brings democracy: "[G]lobal markets today are demanding, in return for their investments, the rule of law, transparency, predictability, cooperation and pluralism in financial affairs" (Friedman 1997).

True, neoliberalism is prevalent, but its correlation with liberal democracy is more varied and problematic than this interpretation suggests. While free market reforms and liberal democracy have taken root in some Latin American countries, such as Paraguay, there are also signs, overwhelmingly reflected in polls, that people are discontent with the impact of this combination: basic failings in the banking system and a major drop in the value of the currency, accompanied by large increases in unemployment, crime, poverty, and income inequality. Indeed, the argument that market liberalism fosters liberal democracy fails to allow for reverses and nondemocratic change: the erosion or downfall of democracy brought on, at least in good part, by economic reforms. For example, in 1997, a time of great economic tribulation, Bolivians returned their former dictator to the country's highest office. In Africa, there is wide variation:

diverse patterns of economic reform and very different types of democratization reflecting distinctive conjunctions of precolonial, colonial, and postcolonial systems as they encounter globalizing forces. Clearly, the conjecture that economic globalization is a source of democratic politics does not account for Africa's collapsed states, which, after incorporation into the Westphalian system and long contact with world markets, have taken a nondemocratic course.

More basically, the problem with the claim that economic globalization generates democracy is that it misses the point that economic markets themselves lack accountability. It also misspecifies the linkage between wealth and power. Markets exercise structural power, including the power to punish the state if it strays too far from the neoliberal path. This often entails coercion, as with the implementation of the structural adjustment programs that have triggered IMF riots in several countries. Adhering to the logic of a market system, the economically powerful, after all, seek to maximize profits and beat their competitors. Although liberal democracy may prove convenient or preferable to other methods of governance, the beneficiaries of globalization have no inherent interest in promoting democracy. The logics of markets and democracy clash over the issue of liberty versus equality, depending on the meaning attributed to these constructs.

Democracy in its several variations revolves around the notion of accountability. The Western liberal variant of democracy separates accountability in politics, economics, and society, each sphere subject to different forms of governance. Emphasis in the Western variant is accorded to institutional forms, especially electoral mechanisms. Equity among social strata—reducing inequality in the economic realm—is not the priority in a system whose cardinal feature is a rotation of political power among those who usually represent the interests of the privileged segments of society. Hence the tension between globalization and democratization.

How then can democracy be an antidote for a form of globalization that has spun out of control to the extent that its discontents are expressed by holders of state power, financiers, preeminent neoliberal economists, and the marginalized alike? In other words, how can the contents of globalization be revised so as to maintain its many important achievements and relieve the discontents?

To approach this compelling question, if only in a preliminary and schematic manner, one must grasp what democratic control in the context of globalization would mean. Chapter 11 deals with this question in some depth. Put briefly, democracy is a contested concept; different and competing forms are appropriate for varied social and historical structures, though accountability remains a central criterion of democratic rule. Additionally, democracy is not a final state of affairs but unfolds with changing dynamics. Democracy heretofore has been framed for territorially bounded states that purportedly can contain the movement of people, ideas, and technologies. However, many states, especially the ones with large concentrations of diasporic populations and citizens employed by firms based in other regions, are now subject to deterritorialization and denationalization. With globalization, democracy must be *reterritorialized* and strengthened both within and across state borders—as a method of governance for regions and, indeed, for solving global problems.

There are signs that in an intersubjective sense and in objective ways as well, the national state is becoming a *transnational state*. In a transnational state, citizens imagine their identities in terms of more than one state—as is the case with some diasporic populations—and actively participate in the politics of two or more countries, which is permitted by the laws and voting procedures in certain contexts (Glick Schiller 1999). The challenge then is to rethink the concept of national democracy and bring it in line with a form of politics in which boundaries are not eradicated but blurred or complicated by transborder arrangements, some of them authored by the state, and others rooted in economy and culture and either sanctioned by a reluctant state or not at all legitimated by the state.

A transition to democratic globalization is about both good governance and global governance. Good governance in the national realm is a key to reshaping globalization, even if the state is not the exclusive, or even an optimal, unit for managing this process. As Polanyi suggested, the task is to reembed political and economic power in society's rules and institutions. In both the countryside and the towns, this is a matter of civil-society empowerment, which includes the advancement of women. There is also the issue of establishing channels to power for the poor and most vulnerable strata, who have had little role in making decisions about the allocation of resources. Moreover, an appropriate legal framework includes not only the rule of law and the constitutional guarantee of human rights, but also free and vibrant media. These core values underpinning good governance are promoted by building viable linkages between civil society and the state, as well as to global governance.

In this transformation, a vital issue is the matter of access. How can global governance be recast so that civil society may participate meaningfully in the steering mechanisms and economic processes of a powerful structure, globalization, that has the potential to deliver to the many—not merely the few—aggregate economic gains (including a cornucopia of consumer goods), technological advances, greater information, new knowledge, and an escape from long-established forms of social control? There cannot be much assurance of the eventual outcome of an open-ended, historical process, but making clear the dynamics, knowing the constraints, and imagining the possibilities, if only a glimmer of the prospects, mark the direction likely to put humankind on a plausible path to a just and civilized future.

Globalization after September 11

Did the terrorist attacks on the Pentagon and World Trade Center, icons of U.S. power and global capitalism, change this direction? Have the September 11 terrorists killed hopes for making globalization work?

It would be a grave error to confuse the acute pain inflicted on September 11 and a chronic condition. The terrorist attacks did not demolish the entrenched structures of globalization. While homeland security tops the policy agenda in the United States and elsewhere, the basic trends marking globalization, especially global market integration and the expansion of regional processes, endure. Surely the underlying issues have not gone away.

Global terrorism and globalization are closely intertwined. Both are transborder phenomena that challenge the territorial basis of state sovereignty. Both rely on modern technologies and worldwide financial networks. And both feed on marginalization.

Some of the poor and disenfranchised, especially in countries with repressive and corrupt governments, have sought to escape their debilitating conditions, including unemployment rates of around 60 percent for young males. In societies in which fatalism—as in the expression *In sha Allah,* or "Whatever God wills"— is commonplace, and where *madrassas* (Muslim religious schools) have radicalized youth, it is not difficult to enlist marginalized men in suicide missions. These marginals believe that their deadly acts provide a ticket to paradise. Although their leaders are drawn from the middle classes and are bankrolled by Osama bin Laden's wealth, festering discontent fills a pool of on-the-spot losers in the globalization scenario, some of whom can be recruited into terrorist activities.

Global terrorists and globalizers alike propagate what they regard as universal truths. On the one side, terrorists and those who abet them use the idiom of religious values to control behavior—of women, children, and all those labeled "nonbelievers." On the other side, the beneficiaries of globalization also attempt to disseminate a value system—the freedom of markets, competition, efficiency, consumerism, and individualism—to promote a different vision of the way in which society should be ordered.

These competing visions are in no sense morally equivalent, but the rhetoric of the protagonists, Osama bin Laden and President George Bush, converges: a *jihad,* or holy war, pitting believers against "infidels" versus a "crusade" led by the U.S. government, also the torchbearer of globalization, against "evildoers."

Put in perspective, the globalization of terrorism is one in a series of crises in globalization. The first crisis was the defeat of the Multilateral Agreement on Investment, a treaty introduced by the United States in the Organization for Economic Cooperation and Development in1995. Far-reaching in scope, its objectives were to remove barriers on foreign trade and extend capital markets.

Ultimately, a coalition of citizens' groups pressured their governments to withdraw from the negotiations.

Second, the 1997–98 Asian financial crisis was not really Asian, but global, for it rippled to Brazil, South Africa, Russia, and elsewhere. It was about the risks of globalization. Directing his strident rhetoric at George Soros and other currency speculators, Malaysian prime minister Mahathir Mohamed, a leader in the mainstream Islamic world, found his country—indeed the entire region and beyond—in a dilemma: No one really governs globalization.

Third, the 1999 "Battle of Seattle" not only buffeted the WTO, but more generally signaled resistance to economic globalization. Plainly, the "Battle of Seattle" and subsequent street demonstrations in world cities on five continents represent rage over the underside of contemporary globalization.

Then, on September 11, 2001, the resistance perpetrated by a global network reached a crescendo that took the form of atrocities. The terrorism crisis is a globalization crisis. The root issue is the same set of heavily American values deemed loathsome by not only the terrorists but also by several global justice movements (which, nonetheless, do not endorse the grotesque September 11 tactics).

To come to grips with the implications of September 11 for globalization, it is worth recalling Adlai Stevenson's admonition. As U.S. ambassador to the United Nations, he quipped that the modern technology that Americans most need is a hearing aid. What must be heard today, above all, are messages about different value systems. This is not to suggest that all values are morally equivalent or right. Rather, making globalization work requires recognition that insistence on absolute values will not solve the chronic problem: a world order with unconscionable numbers of marginalized peoples living in sheer misery. It is well to remember that the Abrahamic faiths hold in common a belief in social justice.

Notes

1. Neoliberal globalization refers to the complex of ideas and policies centered on increasing integration in the world market.

References

Bond, Patrick. 1995. "Under the Microscope: The ANC in Power." *Southern Africa Report* (Toronto) 10 (3): 3–7.

Cox, Robert W. 1987. *Production, Power, and World Order: Social Forces in the Making of History*. New York: Columbia University Press.

Friedman, Thomas L. 1997. "Berlin Wall, Part 2: Asia's New Route to Democracy." *New York Times*, 6 May.

————. 1999. *The Lexus and the Olive Tree*. New York: Farrar, Straus and Giroux.

Glick Schiller, Nina. 1999. "Citizens in Transnational Nation-States: The Asian Experience." In *Globalization and the Asia Pacific: Contested Territories*, ed. Kris Olds, Peter Dicken, Philip Kelly, Lily Kong, and Henry Wai-chung Yeung. London: Routledge.

Held, David. 1995. *Democracy and the Global Order: From the Modern State to Cosmopolitan Governance*. Cambridge: Polity Press.

Jessop, Bob. 1997. Comments at workshop, The Logic(s) of Globalization, December, at the National University of Singapore, Singapore.

Mittelman, James H. 1999. *The Future of Globalization*. Bangi, Malaysia: Penerbit Universiti Kebangsaan Malaysia (National University of Malaysia Press).

————. 2000. *The Globalization Syndrome: Transformation and Resistance*. Princeton: Princeton University Press.

Polanyi, Karl. 1957. *The Great Transformation: The Political and Economic Origins of Our Times*. Boston: Beacon Press.

Rawls, John. 1993. *Political Liberalism*. New York: Columbia University Press.

Rosow, Stephen J. 1999. "Globalization/Democratic Theory: The Politics of Representation of Post-Cold War Political Space." Paper presented to the annual meeting of the International Studies Association, February, Washington, D.C.

Sassen, Saskia. 1996. *Losing Control? Sovereignty in an Age of Globalization*. New York: Columbia University Press.

Sinclair, Timothy J. 1994a. "Between State and Market: Hegemony and Institutions of Collective Action under Conditions of International Capital Mobility." *Policy Sciences* 27 (4): 447–66.

————. 1994b. "Passing Judgment: Credit Rating Processes as Regulatory Mechanisms of Governance in the Emerging World Order." *Review of International Political Economy* 1 (Spring): 133–59.

Teeple, Gary. 1995. *Globalization and the Decline of Social Reform*. Atlantic Highlands, N.J.: Humanities Press International.

Truehart, Charles. 1997. "French Hold Proudly Fast to Benevolent Central Rule." *Washington Post*, 14 July.

United Nations Development Program. 1998. *Human Development Report*. New York: Oxford University Press.

Walzer, Michael. 1999. "Rescuing Civil Society." *Dissent* (Winter): 62–67.

Weiss, Linda. 1998. *The Myth of the Powerless State*. Ithaca: Cornell University Press.

A New Urgency:
Civilizing Globalization in an Era of Terrorism

Richard Sandbrook

The liberalization of national and global markets is a far more disruptive and destabilizing process than its advocates imagine. President George W. Bush expressed the conventional wisdom when he reiterated, in the aftermath of the terrorist attacks of September 11, 2001, that free trade fights terrorism by promoting widespread prosperity. His administration pressed forward its neoliberal agenda, especially "fast-track" authority from Congress to negotiate trade agreements and a new round of trade and investment liberalization under the World Trade Organization. But this conventional wisdom that peace flows from unimpeded market exchange is almost certainly wrong. Rather, neoliberal globalization fosters political extremism and political violence worldwide by heightening socioeconomic and cultural insecurity. Thus, this book's strategies to civilize globalization have assumed greater urgency since the terrorist attacks.

One does not have to look far to see how globalization fosters extremism and violence. Terrorism is not a phenomenon that breeds only in far-off places in the Middle East, Africa, and Latin America. In the United States, too, one encounters right-wing extremism and periodic political violence inspired by bizarre conspiracy theories. If even the principal architect and beneficiary of globalization suffers such disintegrative tendencies, one can expect these tendencies to be even more pronounced in countries in a less privileged position within the global system.

In the United States, socioeconomic insecurity and cultural change, provoked by market liberalization and technological revolution, have fomented despair, anger, and frustration, especially among working-class and middle-class white males. In the absence of a left discourse of class struggle that might have channeled this rage, far-right populists have, instead, capitalized on the malaise. Manipulating such dominant symbols, myths, and attitudes as individualism, distrust of Big Government, and Christian values, they frame issues so that far-fetched conspiracy theories seem to make sense of complex economic, social, and cultural forces. The alleged right of citizens to oppose, by force of arms, tyrannical government has legitimated citizen militias and, for some few individuals, violent acts against an allegedly overweening state and complicit civilians. Globalization thus acts as an underlying or remote cause of terrorism even in the United States.

The Patriot Movement, formed in the 1980s, loosely unites far-right groups who command the support of as many as 5 million Americans (Junus 1995, 228). The nonviolent and more moderate wing of this movement includes the waning John Birch Society and the Christian Coalition, led by Pat Robertson until early 2002. They adhere to a conspiracy theory in which wealthy global elites, in league with the U.S. government, aim to establish a tyrannical world government to undermine Christianity. A more militant and more extremist wing holds an anti-Semitic and white supremacist view of this global conspiracy and the racial struggle required to reclaim individual liberty and Christian civilization. However, the latter's recruitment campaigns now astutely eschew racist rhetoric to broaden the movement's popular appeal; they now refer to an "international banking conspiracy" (rather than an "international Jewish conspiracy"), linked to a repressive U.S. government (Gallagher 2000, 668).

Citizen militias, dedicated to confronting what they see as an incipient police state, emerged from the Patriots. Those who track right-wing extremists claim that, by 1996, at least 441 citizen militias operated in the United States (Dees 1996, 199). The hard-core membership of these militias numbered between ten thousand and thirty thousand men (Junas 1995, 227). Police officers and soldiers from elite units on American bases (especially Fort Bragg, Fort Carson, and Fort Louis) are a particular focus for recruitment by far-right militias, as well as by neo-Nazis and skinheads (Mozzochi 1995; *Newsweek,* 25 March 1996, 34–35). These recruits, like former soldier Timothy McVeigh, who was convicted of bombing the Murrah Federal Building in Oklahoma City in 1995, are highly trained in weapons and munitions. Militia units are well armed and, in some cases, dangerous.

The militias' most popular operations manual, besides the racist *Turner Diaries*, is Louis Beam's *Leaderless Resistance.* This manual outlines a cell system akin to that of the al-Qaeda terrorist network. It rejects a pyramidal organization to resist state tyranny, as this sort of organization is too easily infiltrated. Instead, the manual advocates (see Dees 1996, 210) a secret cell system, in which each cell chooses its own mode of resistance—creating a "thousand points of resistance"—to the United States government and its allies. The existence of such secret cells was confirmed in February 2002 when a defector from a cell code-named Project 7 revealed a bizarre plot to assassinate local officials in Northwestern Montana. The apparent objective of the plot was to draw first the

National Guard and then federal troops into an armed confrontation that would radicalize the citizenry. The FBI and Bureau of Alcohol, Tobacco, and Firearms had to take the plot seriously, because the cell had stockpiled a cache of automatic weapons, ammunition, explosives, and booby traps extensive enough to do considerable damage (*New York Times,* 3 March 2002, 18).

Domestic terrorist plots have proliferated during the past decade. In 1993, the authorities foiled plots to blow up a federal courthouse in Spokane, Washington; an Internal Revenue Service building in Austin, Texas; and offices of the Southern Poverty Law Center and the Anti-Defamation League, both of which publicize the activities of racist groups. Militia members have been apprehended with deadly bubonic plague virus and an even deadlier poison, ricin. The heaviest death toll from domestic terrorism was perpetrated in Oklahoma City in 1995 by McVeigh and his associate(s). Although the extent of the latter conspiracy is unclear, McVeigh had links to a couple of citizen militias, to the neo-Nazi National Alliance, and to the far-right Christian Identity compound on the Oklahoma-Arkansas border (Dees 1996). In 1997, the FBI reported that they had thwarted ten terrorist attacks on U.S. targets, including the planned bombing of a Texas natural gas refinery by the Ku Klux Klan and a planned raid on a military base in Fort Worth, Texas (*U.S. News & World Report,* 28 September 1998, 6). Bridges and telephone relay centers were also targeted in the 1990s, together with efforts to stockpile arms, including hand-held missile launchers.

Whereas the notion of an international communist conspiracy united far-right elements during the Cold War, the collapse of the Soviet bloc refocused their attention on global plots by large corporations, bankers, and Big Government. This shift in orientation stems partly from global economic restructuring since the early 1980s. "Economic uncertainty, job insecurity, corporate downsizing, declining real wages, changing technology, and competition from cheap foreign labor are scaring people to death. Corporations report higher earnings, executives earn huge salaries, stock markets hit new highs, but the average worker feels abandoned and betrayed" (Dees 1996,116; see also Gallagher 2000; Junus 1995, 228). The United States has indeed registered a dramatic growth in inequality since the mid-seventies. In the quarter-century following 1947, the median earnings of U.S. workers more than doubled, and the bottom 20 percent achieved the biggest gains. In marked contrast, the median earnings of workers fell by about 15 percent between 1974 and 1998, with the bottom 20 percent experiencing the greatest drop. Meanwhile, more than 40 percent of all gains in earnings have accrued to the richest 1 percent of the population (United States Census Bureau 2001). What this means, according to one authoritative analysis, is that "the richest one percent accumulated 53 percent of the total gain in marketable wealth," with the next 19 percent of the top accumulators accounting for another 39 percent of the wealth (*New*

York Times, 28 October 2001). Moreover, by 1999, the average compensation package of a top chief executive officer, inclusive of bonuses and stock options, was 475 times that of the average blue-collar worker, according to *Business Week.* Hence, the fruits of economic growth under globalization were concentrated in a small share of the population, while others suffered severe dislocation and diminishing rewards.

The economic pain was felt not only by blue- and white-collar workers but also by farmers, as the family farm came under severe pressure. Dispossessed and heavily indebted farmers have formed a pool of recruits for the rural-based militias since the 1980s. A crisis in the Midwest saw the restructuring of U.S. agriculture from "a system dominated by small and medium-sized family farms to one dominated by agribusiness" (Gallagher 2000, 676). In the 1970s, the government sought to promote efficiency by encouraging farmers to adopt new technologies and augment the size of the average farm. A federal authority made loans available for these purposes at a floating rate. A dramatic increase in interest rates in 1979 forced a million farms into bankruptcy between 1980 and 1995, as land prices collapsed (Gallagher 2000, 676). In addition, farmers in various localities chafed under legal restrictions imposed by the federal government to achieve conservationist and other goals: for example, restrictions on the growing of industrial hemp in Kentucky, and on the use of Bureau of Land Management lands in Nevada. Organizers for the Patriot Movement and militias directed this rural anger against the federal government. A sophisticated media campaign yielded many new recruits for right-wing extremism, especially the burgeoning militias.

In addition, white males, already under stress from rapid economic change, have seen their "traditional privileges and status challenged" by new social movements that now operate globally (Junus 1995, 228). These movements champion equal rights for women, minority rights and affirmative action, gay rights, and environmentalism, especially restrictions on hunting, fishing, and land use. The media megacorporations, mainly U.S.-based, are seen as propagating these "liberal" values throughout the world. Angry white males demand explanations for their cultural, as well as socioeconomic, plight. Some of them have found answers in the antigovernment, antiglobalization rhetoric of the far right.

The antisystemic alternative to the conspiracy theories propagated by the extreme right is a leftist, class-based discourse. A class analysis might have achieved some resonance in a context of growing inequality and social dislocation, a situation that is aggravated by an increasingly freewheeling capitalism. Yet the U.S. left is fragmented and ineffectual, and almost nonexistent outside of university campuses. Neoliberalism triumphed in its clash with socialism and social democracy. Ironically, that victory has allowed right-wing populists and neofascists to exploit antisystemic sentiment.

These elements have framed issues in a manner that broadens their appeal beyond their initial racist leanings. They repackaged their message in the 1980s to de-emphasize racism and appeal to such patriotic virtues as individual liberty, opposition to tyranny, and defense of Christian purity. In this way, they exploit the antigovernment sentiment and religious traditions that thrive within America. A grand conspiracy, or web of conspiracies, is used to explain trends that have negatively affected the livelihoods of working-class and middle-class supporters alike. In essence,

> patriots from across the United States . . . believe that their locally specific problems result from a globalized economy and the power structures that support it. In particular, patriots believe that members of the US government are conspiring with international elites, the leaders of transnational corporations, and multilateral organizations such as the United Nations and the International Monetary Fund to create a "New World Order." Once in place, patriots believe this New World Order will deny US citizens their rights as guaranteed in the US constitution, and will secure a system to control all of the world's land, labor, and wealth. (Gallagher 2000, 668)

This simplistic worldview thus explains impersonal global economic forces by reference to the machinations of identifiable national and international conspirators.

Organizers, many of whom were originally leaders of white supremacist groups including the Ku Klux Klan, interpret a series of events to reinforce these conspiracy theories centering on the role of Big Government (Dees 1996). They see the hand of a tyrannical government in the FBI's armed standoff with white-supremacist Randy Weaver at Ruby Ridge, Idaho, in 1992, which resulted in the killing of Weaver's son and wife. The dead are deemed martyrs in the cause of individual liberty. The assault by the Bureau of Alcohol, Tobacco, and Firearms on the Branch Davidian compound in Waco, Texas, in 1993 produced more martyrs in the same cause, according to the far right's interpretation. And the periodic governmental tightening of restrictions on the purchase of hand guns and assault rifles since 1993 is taken as further evidence of the federal government's intention to disarm citizens in order to impose a New World Order (Junus 1995, 229).

This far-right worldview has been "mainstreamed" by radio talk shows with hosts such as C. Gordon Liddy and Chuck Baker. Local and widely syndicated shows encourage racist, antifeminist, and homophobic guests to air their views before large audiences. Inflammatory comments about "lynching a few liberals," doing away with "traitors," and "shoot[ing] illegal immigrants" have become standard fare (Cohen and Solomon 1995, 241–43). The far right has effectively exploited hot-button issues and dominant myths to popularize their paranoid views.

The American case suggests a link between globalization, extremism, and terrorism, but it also suggests this link is neither direct nor simple. Although domestic and external liberalization fosters a potentially explosive situation of frustration and rage, domestic factors shape whether an explosion actually occurs. Socioeconomic and cultural insecurities, arising from conditions associated with global capitalism, exist in many societies. However, only in some of them, at certain times, do these objective conditions lead to violence. What is important is how objective reality comes to be subjectively perceived. Central to molding popular orientations are contingent domestic factors, especially (a) the skill of radical movements in manipulating "cultural tool-kits" (Swidler 1986) and specific grievances to win supporters, and (b) the capacity of state institutions to tame or repress public anger. While the first factor received attention in the U.S. case study, the latter deserves further mention. Democracy in America, however diluted, provides legitimate channels for right-wing militants to assert themselves politically and, indeed, win many concessions. Although far-right extremists are mean-spirited and angry, these dangerous sentiments are mainly contained within conventional politics. If the United States actually constituted the police state its radical dissidents depict, violence and repression would feature more centrally in the U.S. story of market supremacy. The perception that the system remains open—to individual upward mobility and to the redress of grievances—holds the disintegrative tendencies of global capitalism in check.

So, a plausible theory of globalization and political violence must avoid reductionism. Deregulated markets unleash seismic forces that affected groups struggle to understand and defend against. But simply to ascribe political extremism and violence to a drastically fluctuating and destabilizing market system is wholly unpersuasive. For one thing, there are other, independent causes of radicalization—economic mismanagement and geopolitical grievances, for example. For another, the effectiveness of the governmental apparatus and dissident movements mediate global processes and shape political behavior. The analytical task is to understand how the stresses and strains of neoliberal globalization work themselves out, sometimes disastrously, in specific national contexts.

What, more specifically, are these stresses and strains? Contemporary globalization marks a dramatic transformation in the human impact of market forces. Three trends accentuate the disruptive potential of contemporary economic liberalism, as compared to its earlier dominance from 1850 until 1929. First, the market today fluctuates with lightning speed. During the first globalization era, events moved at a slower pace: transport was unhurried; telegraph remained a crude instrument of communications by today's standards; and record-keeping was cumbersome. The recent revolutions in transport, telecommunications, and information-processing have not only linked the destinies of people worldwide but also accelerated the pace of change. Even a mighty megacorporation such as Enron can evaporate into thin air. An economic success-story like South Korea or Argentina can self-destruct in a few months. Economic turbulence is an ever-present threat.

Secondly, few people today, anywhere in the world, are insulated from market fluctuations, though many were in the earlier epoch. A century ago, much of the world's population lived in self-provisioning peasant societies in colonies and semicolonies, or on family farms in industrializing countries. A degree of self-sufficiency shielded such people from the devastation of economic downturns. However, the decline of the family farm in industrial countries, the deepening commercialization of agriculture in poor countries, and high rates of rural-urban migration have rendered a growing proportion of the world's population vulnerable to market conditions. Furthermore, the collapse of communism and the Soviet Union in 1991 further extended the sway of the market system, as formerly socialist countries undertook transitions to capitalism. China alone has added more than a billion potential market actors as it has gradually liberalized its economy since 1980. The market reigns supreme, so everyone is now vulnerable to its fluctuations.

Thirdly, not only is the vast majority now affected by market relations, but young men—the potential shock troops of extremist politics—form a growing proportion of burgeoning populations. In many developing countries, half or more of the population is under twenty-five years of age. In Pakistan and Afghanistan, for example, over half of the people fall into this category. High population growth, when combined with such conditions as sporadic growth, limited employment prospects, and marked inequalities, creates instability in the cities. Young men are disproportionately represented among those adversely affected by market conditions.

So these three trends—the rapidity of economic change, the enhanced vulnerability of populations to market forces, and the predominance of young men among the disadvantaged—magnify the impact of market liberalization.

In this historical context, four processes associated with globalization, by augmenting economic and cultural insecurity, belie the promise that market freedom will usher in peace and prosperity. As these processes feature in earlier chapters, they need only be briefly mentioned.

Consider, first, the impact of trade liberalization and its attendant policies. In agriculture, neoliberals typically prescribe a reduction or elimination of price controls and subsidies to producers, in addition to export orientation and low tariffs, as the best way to improve economic conditions. Such a program, however, can wreak havoc in the livelihoods of smallholders, as the case of India shows. Cheap imports may undermine local production. For example, India liberalized the import of soybean and soy oil imports in August 1999. The result was that subsidized imports from Western countries rose by 60 percent in the first year. "[P]rices crashed by more than two-thirds, and millions of oilseed-producing farmers had lost their market, unable even to recover what they had spent on cultivation. The entire edible oil production and processing industry was also destroyed. Millions of small mills have closed down" (Mittal 2001). The phasing out of fertilizer subsidies—often required under IMF conditionality—raises production costs, and helps drive many small farmers into insolvency. As these policies drive many smallholders to the wall, export-oriented large companies buy them out. Former farmers head for the burgeoning urban slums. Export receipts may increase and subsidized wheat and rice imports from the European Union and the United States may lower food prices, but at the expense of declining food self-sufficiency, growing insecurity and inequality, and much bitterness.

Trade liberalization in industry also produces many losers, along with winners. Even if the freer trade maintains or increases overall output and labor productivity, it will lead to the failure of some firms, to widespread retrenchment of workers, and to unemployment in some sectors. Chronic insecurity grows, especially in industrialized countries like the United States where unions are weak, as industries rapidly wax and wane, better-paid permanent jobs vanish, and unskilled and even skilled workers see their real wages fall (see Luttwak 1999 for a thorough review). If this insecurity fosters anger, intolerance, and extremism, that should not be surprising.

Secondly, financial liberalization breeds periodic currency crises that undercut living standards and employment. Liberalization of domestic banking, followed by international financial deregulation, have opened up transborder capital movements throughout the world since the 1980s. IMF conditionality presses developing countries in the direction of removing capital controls. Today, at least $1.5 trillion passes through currency markets each day in a world of instantaneous trading where markets never close. The result is a high volatility of financial flows leading to "turbulence": a rise in the frequency and severity of financial crises. Mexico in 1994, East Asia and Russia in 1997–98, and Argentina in 2001–2 are just the best-known instances of devastating financial crises resulting in a collapse in the local currency, in economic activity, and in employment. Financial liberalization is a major contributor to the chronic insecurity of the market system (Kaplinsky 2001).

Thirdly, domestic and external liberalization has fueled economic insecurity by fostering inequality within societies, both vertically among social groups and horizontally among regions of countries. Since the early 1980s, "inequality has risen in most countries, and in many cases sharply" (Cornia and Court 2001, 1). Other recent reviews confirm this general trend (Berry and Serieux 2001, 8, 13–14; Kaplinsky 2001, 19). Countries with the most rigorous neoliberal programs, such as the United States, Britain, and New Zealand, have registered the most striking increases in inequality. Although data is limited, they also point to growing regional inequality. China, India, and Thailand manifest growing regional gaps and high rates of rural-urban migration. Market conditions also favor some regions of the world, while marginalizing others.

This worsening income distribution is directly related to neoliberal policies. Economic stabilization programs induce deep recessions while cutting programs that benefit the poor (food subsidies, public employment, accessible education and health care). Financial liberalization, besides inducing periodic recessions, shifts income to lenders and rentiers at the expense of wages and borrowers. Privatization often concentrates the ownership of public assets in the hands of wealthy political insiders, further exacerbating inequality. Tax systems tend to become less progressive and more reliant on value-added taxes, less redistributive, and more reliant on user payments, all of which promotes inequality. And the quest for more "flexible" labor markets generally translates into reduced employment protection, lower minimum wages, curtailed union rights, and falling public employment. In all these ways, liberalization and globalization hammer the living standards and prospects of middle-class sectors and workers in many countries, while benefiting the owners of capital—physical, financial, and intellectual (Cornia and Court 2001, 14–18).

Growing inequality breeds insecurity in two ways. In the first place, high inequality reduces the contribution that growth makes to reducing poverty. Defined as those who survive on less than $1 per day (1985 purchasing power parity), the poor remained constant at about 1.2 billion people between 1987 and 1998 (World Bank 2000). By the latter date, nearly half the world's population still lived below a poverty line of $2 per day. Expectations that free markets would transform the living standards of the poor have been dashed in many countries. In the second place, inequalities shape expectations. "People feel insecure in relation to what they have come to expect as 'normality'; the distance between social groups is also part of this 'normality', so when it increases, people feel more insecure" (Kaplinsky 2001, 20). Hence, growing inequality can profoundly shape political orientations, as the disadvantaged search for explanations, and ultimately political solutions. Conspiracy theories and extremist politics are common reactions to this search for understanding and redress—the complex, impersonal forces unleashed by neoliberal globalization are not easily grasped.

Fourthly, neoliberal globalization is not just a matter of economics; it also threatens entire ways of life. The global penetration of the mass media and the values, images, and tastes they purvey have a devastating impact upon non-Western cultures. Television, films, popular music, and advertising, "industries" dominated by U.S. megacorporations, pervade the world. These industries

- transmit a possessive individualism that fragments tightly knit communities;

- propagate consumer tastes that influence the dress, language, food, and attitudes of young people;

- popularize notions of sexual, gender, and authority relations that clash with local notions of virtuous behavior;

- reflect a secular, narcissistic outlook in conflict with sacred worldviews defended by local elites.

Media conglomerates are driven by a quest for profits, not hegemony; yet "the seemingly innocuous market quest for fun, creativity, and profits puts whole cultures in harm's way and undermines autonomy in individuals and nations alike" (Barber 1996, 81).

The dialectical reaction to "McWorld"—the homogenizing, consumer-oriented, and secular popular culture—is often "Jihad," a reversion to a world defined by religion, hierarchy, and tradition. Benjamin Barber (1996, 215) graphically depicts the latter,

> Jihad in its most elemental negative form is a kind of animal fear propelled by anxiety in the face of uncertainty and relieved by self-sacrificing zealotry—an escape out of history. . . . Moral preservationists, whether in America, Israel, Iran, or India, have no choice but to make war on the present to secure a future more like the past: depluralized, monocultured, unskepticized, reenchanted.

This fundamentalist holy war against the global forces of hypermodernity takes diverse forms: Christian, Jewish, Hindu, as well as Islamic.

These four processes—trade liberalization, financial liberalization, growing inequalities, and cultural globalization—together comprise our drastically fluctuating and inadvertently destructive global capitalism. People, especially young men who are heavily exposed to this whirlwind, are left feeling alienated, frustrated, and angry. They seek an explanation of the seemingly inexplicable forces to which they are subjected, and a means of dealing with these forces.

In some cases, this quest leads to political extremism and political violence; in other cases, not. The different responses depend on the two domestic factors mentioned earlier.

The first is the strength of mediatory institutions. Strong institutions include political rules and organizations—political parties, legislatures, elections, and courts—able to manage conflict; safety nets capable of buffering groups who lose out in market liberalization; and state bureaucracies with the capacity to implement programs. This point is obvious and, indeed, risks collapsing into a tautology. What are the indicators of institutional strength, other than the effect of conflict management that this strength is supposed to explain? Although we recognize an effective state when we see one—for example, Chile is a strong state and Haiti a weak one—measures of "stateness," other than political order, are difficult to devise.

"Governance" theorists have optimistically tended to equate efficacy in conflict management with democratic institutions. Paradoxically, established or consolidated democracies are effective in peacefully resolving conflict, but transitions to democracy are risky (Sandbrook 2000, chap. 3; Snyder 2000). "Democratization . . . is a highly disruptive process in itself; it encourages the conflicts that exist in a collapsing state to manifest themselves freely, but without the restraint of the checks and balances, and of agreement on the basic rules, that regulate conflict . . . in a well-established democratic system. Democracy as a stable state is highly desirable, but democratization, or the process of getting to such stable democracy, can trigger highly undesirable side effects" (Ottaway 1995, 235–36). Democratization in developing countries, therefore, offers no panacea for extremist politics and violent conflict.

Although we cannot simply equate institutional strength with democracy, the methodological problem of establishing independent indicators of state capacity is not insurmountable. States with long-established institutionalized orders, with a high extractive capacity, with institutions that command generalized support, with bureaucracies that get things done, with judicial systems that are not corrupt, and with safety nets that buffer potentially disruptive losers are much better placed to handle the strains of a fluctuating global capitalism.

But, to add a further complication, the strength of national political systems is not independent of the global processes that we have identified. Neoliberal globalization promotes, in dialectical fashion, both *transnational integration* and *national disintegration*. Transnational integration occurs as governing national elites buy into the global neoliberal doctrine (the Washington or Post-Washington Consensus). This transnational elite integration, achieved on the basis of a secular worldview of economic and usually political liberalism, risks driving a wedge between these elites and national classes and groups who clamor for protection from unleashed market forces. The political turbulence, in turn, motivates threatened political leaders to move toward more centralized and authoritarian governance, despite democratic constitutions. National disintegration is then manifest in growing regional, communal, or class challenges to state authority. Revolts arise as people, especially young men, perceive the government as a mere puppet of external forces.

This dynamic operates in even such a stable Third World democracy as India, according to one of its leading political scientists. "Large sections of the people will be left with no option but to join a growing culture of revolt and rebellion, strikes and [demonstrations], most of them peaceful but a number of them being forced to become part of a growing culture of violence adopting ever more angry and defiant modes of rebellion, revulsion and 'revolution'" (Kothari 1995, 1596). This dynamic suggests it is foolhardy to rely wholly on national state structures as a bulwark against the political stresses of neoliberal doctrine.

A second domestic factor shapes how people perceive objective conditions: the strategies of radical movements to mobilize support. "Moral entrepreneurs" manipulate cultural tool-kits—dominant symbols, myths, historical memories, and attitudes—to interpret events, attribute blame, and legitimate action, including political violence (Zald 1996, 269). Leaders compete to "frame" issues in a way that will gain support among their target groups.

Al-Qaeda has been particularly effective in exploiting an Islamist tool-kit to recruit militants and build popular support. Whether al-Qaeda's terrorism is motivated by injustices, poverty, insecurity, or "root causes" in general is a controversial question. Poverty and perceived injustices, certain analysts rightly note, can exist without terrorism, and terrorists are not necessarily poor or unjustly treated. Instead, they claim, terrorists such as those who crashed jetliners into the World Trade Center and the Pentagon are driven by religious zealotry and hatred of Western values (Hitchens 2001; Rothstein 2001). Although the motivations of such fanatics cannot be neatly traced to the insecurities of unbound markets, this obvious point does not obviate the importance of socioeconomic and cultural conditions as underlying causes. Al-Qaeda does resemble a millenarian cult, as the "civilizational clash" analysts suggest—albeit a cult that is unusual in operating transnationally. However, revolutionary movements exhibiting extreme religious passions have historically arisen from conditions of socioeconomic and cultural insecurity (Hobsbawm 1971; Talmon 1962). Religious fanaticism and "root causes" are, therefore, not separate or alternative explanations; despair and dislocation spawn millenarian movements.

Whatever their mix of motives, Islamists such as al-Qaeda have filled the ideological vacuum left by the failure of state-led modernization in the Middle East. Modernizing regimes, epitomized by Gamal Abdel Nasser's government in Egypt (1954–70), aimed to be nonaligned, to develop secular societies, and to substitute nationalism for Islamic traditionalism. This radical alternative has declined over the past three decades, partly due to the contradictions of state-centered development and partly due to the strategic alliances formed during the Cold War. Distrustful of "socialist" regimes, Western governments allied themselves with conservative and autocratic ruling elites who professed a pro-West orientation and safeguarded crucial oil supplies (Benhabib 2001; Mehio 2001). The United States even recruited the fundamentalist Mujahadeen as allies against the Soviet Union in Afghanistan in the 1980s. The Soviet Union's decline in the late 1980s deprived the Nasserite alternative to political Islam of its powerful patron. That, together with the embrace of fundamentalism by conservative ruling elites eager to enhance their legitimacy (especially the Saudi regime), allowed the Islamists to flourish.

The cultural tool-kit on which Islamic radicals draw features themes of religious piety, resistance to foreign incursions, and rejection of Western-style political liberalism. These themes resonate with this audience's historical memories and current geopolitical realities. Radical Islamic movements draw on a long history of conflict between Muslims and Christians, beginning with the Crusades in the Middle Ages and Saladin's victory in 1187. Lengthy struggles later ensued between Muslim and Christian empires in Europe, both in the east and the west, lasting until the breakup of the Ottomon Empire in World War I. In the twentieth century, many Arab countries experienced a humiliating colonial rule, followed in certain cases by violent wars of national liberation. American support of Israel in its armed struggles with the Palestinians and their Arab supporters currently reinforces a perception of Western hostility to Arab interests. This historical background, taken in conjunction with economic and social despair, cultural challenge, and despotic politics, provides fertile ground for radical movements (Kuran 2001).

Islamic radicals have been adept at framing issues (see Rushdie 2001, 11). Osama bin Laden and other radicals portray Islam as under attack by "the Jews" and "infidels." The infidels, in particular the United States, are said not only to support Israel against the Palestinian cause but also to buttress corrupt governing elites in the Middle East and elsewhere. The infidels, in league with their decadent Muslim allies, are blamed for the ills of Muslim societies. This analysis leads to a call for the "Muslim nation" to unite to eliminate Western influences and undertake a radical spiritual renewal. This renewal requires the imposition of a theocracy, not a liberal, representative government. In the struggle against the enemies of Islam, violence is a just tactic. The ultimate duty of all Muslims is to serve Allah and the Islamic community. These themes feature centrally in the curriculum of the *madrassas*, or private Koranic schools for males from poor backgrounds, which serve as recruitment centers for radical Islamic movements.

In short, cultural framing "enables violent groups to justify their destructiveness as essential to rid the world of evil and build an Islamic utopia" (Kuran 2001, 3).

If this theory captures the urgent dilemma of neoliberal globalization—a dilemma that afflicts North America as well as distant lands—its policy implications are clear. They return us to the theme of civilizing globalization. Terrorism breeds in conditions of injustice, despair, and resentment. Therefore, there cannot be any purely military solution to terrorism, though an armed response is certainly part of any solution. Bin Laden can be killed, for example, but more bin Ladens will take his place (Ignatieff 2001, 13). Fanatics will always be present—even in the United States. We can, however, tackle the conditions that breed fanaticism and terrorism in order to limit their appeal. For the

United States and other progenitors of neoliberal globalization, the best approach is summed up in the aphorism "Physician, heal thyself." Taming market forces and enhancing equity will reduce the malignant insecurity so rife in our societies. For Western countries, an antiterrorism politics will also involve an international dimension: prodding corrupt and autocratic allies toward political reform, resolving festering regional conflicts, and reforming the global economic order along the lines proposed in this book. Although there is no antidote for terrorism, a stable, redistributive, and culturally sensitive global economy will be an important element in building a peaceful world.

References

Barber, Benjamin. 1996. *Jihad vs. McWorld: How Globalization and Tribalism are Reshaping the World.* New York: Ballantine Books.

Benhabib, Sayla. 2001. "Unholy Politics." Social Science Research Council Essays, New York. Access at <www.ssrc.org/sept11/essays/benhabib.htm>.

Berry, Albert, and John Serieux. 2001. "Convergence, Divergence, or Confusion? Recent Trends in World Income Distribution." Unpublished paper, North-South Institute, Ottawa.

Cohen, J., and N. Solomon. 1995. "Guns, Ammo, and Talk Radio." In *Eyes Right! Challenging the Right-Wing Backlash*, ed. C. Bartlet, 241–43. Boston: South End Press.

Cornia, G. A., and John Court. 2001. *Inequality, Growth, and Poverty in the Era of Liberalization and Globalization.* Policy Brief No. 4, World Institute for Development Economics Research, Helsinki.

Dees, Morris. 1996. *Gathering Storm: America's Militia Threat.* New York: HarperCollins.

Gallagher, Carolyn. 2000. "Global Change, Local Angst: Class and the American Patriot Movement." *Environment and Planning D* 18:667–91.

Hitchens, Christopher. 2001. "Against Rationalization." *The Nation,* 8 October, 8.

Hobsbawm, Eric. 1971. *Primitive Rebels: Studies in Archaic Forms of Social Movements in the Nineteenth and Twentieth Centuries.* 3d ed. Manchester: Manchester University Press.

Ignatieff, Michael. 2001. "Plans for the Peace to Come." *Guardian Weekly,* 23–31 October, 13.

Junas, D. 1995. "The Rise of Citizen Militias." In *Eyes Right! Challenging the Right-Wing Backlash*, ed. C. Bartlet, 226–35. Boston: South End Press.

Kaplinsky, Raphael. 2001. "Globalisation and Economic Insecurity." *Institute for Development Studies Bulletin* 32(2): 13–24.

Kothari, Rajni. 1995. "Under Globalization, Will Nation State Hold?" *Economic and Political Weekly*, 1 July, 1593–1603.

Kuran, Timur. 2001. "The Religious Undercurrents of Muslim Economic Grievances." Social Science Research Council Papers, New York. Access at <www.ssrc.org/sept11/essays/kuran.htm>.

Luttwak, Edward. 1999. *Turbo-Capitalism: Winners and Losers in the Global Economy.* New York: HarperCollins.

Mehio, Saad. 2001. "How Islam and Politics Mix." *New York Times*, 2 December 2, 15.

Mittal, Anuradha. 2001. "Land Loss, Poverty, and Hunger." In *Does Globalization Help the Poor?* ed. International Forum on Globalization. San Francisco: International Forum on Globalization.

Mozzochi, J. 1995. "America under the Gun." In *Eyes Right! Challenging the Right-Wing Backlash*, ed. C. Bartlett, 236–40. Boston: South End Press.

Ottaway, Marina. 1995. "Democratization in Collapsed States." In *Collapsed States: The Disintegration and Restoration of Legitimate Authority*, ed. I. W. Zartman, 235–49. Boulder, Colo.: Lynne Rienner.

Rothstein, E. 2001. "Exploring the Flaws in the Notion of the 'Root Causes' of Terror." *New York Times,* 17 November.

Rushdie, Salman. 2001. "Islam's Battle with the Islamists." *Guardian Weekly*, 8–14 November, 11.

Sandbrook, Richard. 2000. *Closing the Circle: Democratization and Development in Africa.* London: Zed Books.

Snyder, Jack. 2000. *From Voting to Violence: Democratization and Nationalist Conflict.* New York: W. W. Norton.

Swidler, Ann. 1986. "Culture in Action: Symbols and Strategies." *American Sociological Review* 51(2): 273–86.

Talmon, Yonina. 1962. "The Pursuit of the Millennium: The Relationship between Religious and Social Change." *Archives Européenes de Sociologie* 3(1): 125–48.

United States Census Bureau. 2001. *Supplemental: Income Inequality.* Washington, D.C.: Government Printing Office.

World Bank. 2000. *World Development Report, 2000/2001: Attacking Poverty.* New York: Oxford University Press.

Zald, Mayer. 1996. "Culture, Ideology, and Strategic Framing." In *Comparative Perspectives on Social Movements*, ed. D. McAdam, J. D. McCarthy, and M. Zald, 261–74. Cambridge: Cambridge University Press.

Contributors

Albert Berry is professor of economics at the University of Toronto and research director of the Programme on Latin America and the Caribbean at the university's Centre for International Studies. His main research areas, with focus on Latin America, are labor markets and income distribution, the economics of small and medium enterprise, agrarian structure and policy, and the impacts of the recent economic reforms in Latin America. He has worked with the Ford Foundation, the Colombian Planning Commission, and the World Bank, and has served as consultant for a number of international and other agencies.

David Coburn is a sociologist in the Department of Public Health Sciences, University of Toronto, whose recent interests lie in the political economy of health and health care. He has written extensively on the rise and fall of medicine and on the health effects of globalization.

Frank Cunningham is professor of philosophy and political science at the University of Toronto and Principal of its Innis College. His works that relate to the topic of this book include *Democratic Theory and Socialism* (1987) and *Theories of Democracy: A Critical Introduction* (2001).

Hans Edstrand, a recent graduate from Queen's University, Canada, has been working with humanitarian relief in Central America since February 1998.

Richard Falk retired in 2001 from Princeton University after being on the faculty for forty years. There he was Albert G. Milbank Professor of International Law and Practice. His recent books include *Human Rights Horizons* (2000) and *Religion and Humane Global Governance* (2001).

Heather Gibb is a senior researcher at the North-South Institute, a policy-oriented research institute based in Ottawa, Canada. Her current research interests include linkages between labor standards and poverty reduction,

269

gender and trade, and informal sector workers. Her recent publications include *Time for Work: Linkages between Paid and Unpaid Work in Human Resource Policy (*1999*), Gender Front and Centre: An APEC Primer* (1997*), Canadian Perspectives on Labour Mobility in APEC* (editor, 1997), and *What's in a Job? Human Resource Development in Asia-Pacific Economies* (coeditor, 1995).

Joy Kennedy is a consultant to ecumenical justice coalitions in Canada and the World Council of Churches.

Rob Lambert is currently chair of the Department of Organisational and Labour Studies at the University of Western Australia. He is also the Coordinator of SIGTUR, a new democratic union formation in the South, dedicated to challenging the logic of neoliberal globalization. He is currently researching the impact of globalization on the manufacture of white goods.

James H. Mittelman is professor in the School of International Service at American University, Washington, D.C. From 1997 to 1999, he served as the Pok Rafeah Chair in International Studies and Distinguished Visiting Professor, National University of Malaysia. His recent publications include, as editor and contributor, *Globalization: Critical Reflections* (1996) and *The Globalization Syndrome: Transformation and Resistance* (2000); and, as coeditor and contributor, *Capturing Globalization* (2001).

Jens L. Mortensen received his Ph.D. from the European University Institute, Florence, Italy, and is an assistant professor at the Center of Social Science Research on the Environment (CeSam), Aarhus University, Denmark. He is currently working on a research project regarding the role of the World Trade Organization in global environmental policy-making.

Garry Neil, president of Neil Craig Associates, is a consultant on the management of cultural policy issues for a variety of clients in Canada and abroad. Previously the General Secretary of the Alliance of Canadian Cinema, Television, and Radio Artists and the Executive Director of the Association of Canadian Publishers, Mr. Neil works for producers, broadcasters, trade associations, unions, and others with an interest in public policy, the cultural industries, and the arts. He is a frequent media commentator and author.

Robert O'Brien is an associate of the Institute on Globalization and the Human Condition and associate professor of political science at McMaster University in Canada. He is coauthor of *Contesting Global Governance: Multilateral Economic Institutions and Global Social Movements* (2000).

Louis W. Pauly is a professor of political science and director of the Centre for International Studies at the University of Toronto. His publications include *Democracy beyond the State? The European Dilemma and the Emerging Global Order* (coeditor and coauthor, 2000), *The Myth of the Global Corporation* (coauthor, 1998/1999), *Who Elected the Bankers? Surveillance and Control in the World Economy* (1997), *Choosing to Cooperate: How States Avoid Loss* (coeditor and coauthor, 1993), *Opening Financial Markets: Banking Politics on the Pacific Rim* (1988), and numerous articles in scholarly journals.

Cranford Pratt is a professor emeritus at the University of Toronto. He has published extensively on development issues, including *Internationalism under Strain: The North-South Policies of Canada, Denmark, the Netherlands, Norway, and Sweden* (1989) and *Canadian International Development Assistance: An Appraisal* (1994, 2d ed., 1996).

Richard Sandbrook is a professor of political science at the University of Toronto. He has written and edited eight books in the areas of the political economy of Africa and development studies. His most recent book is *Closing the Circle: Democratization and Development in Africa* (2000).

Michelle Swenarchuk is director of International Programmes of the Canadian Environmental Law Association in Toronto and a senior practitioner of law in the fields of environmental protection, trade, aboriginal rights, labor, and administrative law.

Judith Teichman is a professor of political science at the University of Toronto. She is the author of various articles on Mexico and Argentina, and of *Policymaking in Mexico: From Boom to Crisis* (1988), *Privatization and Political Change in Mexico* (1995), and *The Politics of Freeing Markets in Latin America: Chile, Argentina, and Mexico* (2001).

Anil Mathew Varughese is a research scholar and activist from Jawaharlal Nehru University in New Delhi, India.

Eddie Webster is a professor of sociology and the director of the Sociology of Work Unit at the University of Witwatersrand, South Africa. His current research activities include an exploration of the response of labor movements to globalization.

Robert Weissman is the editor of *Multinational Monitor*, a magazine founded by Ralph Nader in Washington, D.C. He has reported on several of the major globalization protests.

Rodney R. White is a geographer and infrastructure planner with experience in Africa and China. He is currently director of the Institute for Environmental Studies at the University of Toronto. His most recent book is *Building the Ecological City* (2001).

Index